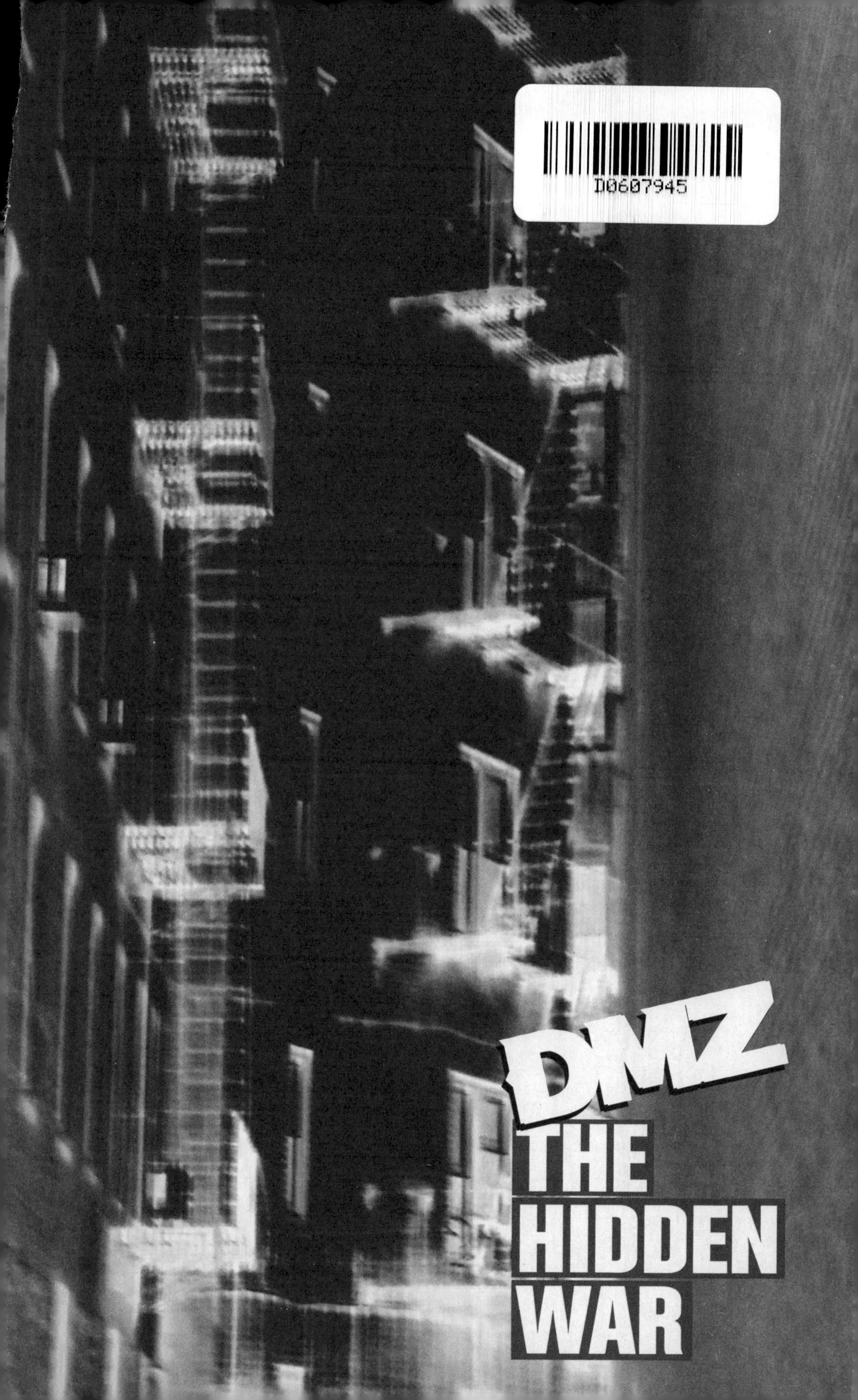

DMZ
THE HIDDEN WAR

Cover illustration and logo design by Brian Wood
Publication design and additional photography by Amelia Grohman

DMZ: THE HIDDEN WAR

Published by DC Comics. Cover and compilation Copyright © 2008 DC Comics. All Rights Reserved.
Originally published in single magazine form as DMZ 23-28. Copyright © 2007, 2008 Brian Wood and Riccardo Burchielli.
All Rights Reserved. VERTIGO and all characters, their distinctive likenesses and related elements featured in this publication
are trademarks of DC Comics. The stories, characters and incidents featured in this publication are entirely fictional.
DC Comics does not read or accept unsolicited submissions of ideas, stories or artwork.

DC Comics
1700 Broadway, New York, NY 10019 | A Warner Bros. Entertainment Company
Printed in Canada. First Printing. ISBN 13: 978-1-4012-1833-1

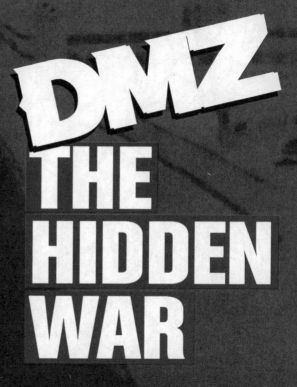

BRIAN WOOD
WRITER

DECADE LATER AMINA KELLY SOAMES
RICCARDO BURCHIELLI
ARTIST

WILSON
DANIJEL ZEZELJ
ARTIST

RANDOM FIRE
NATHAN FOX
ARTIST

JEROMY COX
COLORIST

JARED K. FLETCHER
LETTERER

BRIAN WOOD
ORIGINAL SERIES COVERS

DMZ CREATED BY
BRIAN WOOD AND
RICCARDO BURCHIELLI

DMZ
THE
HIDDEN
WAR

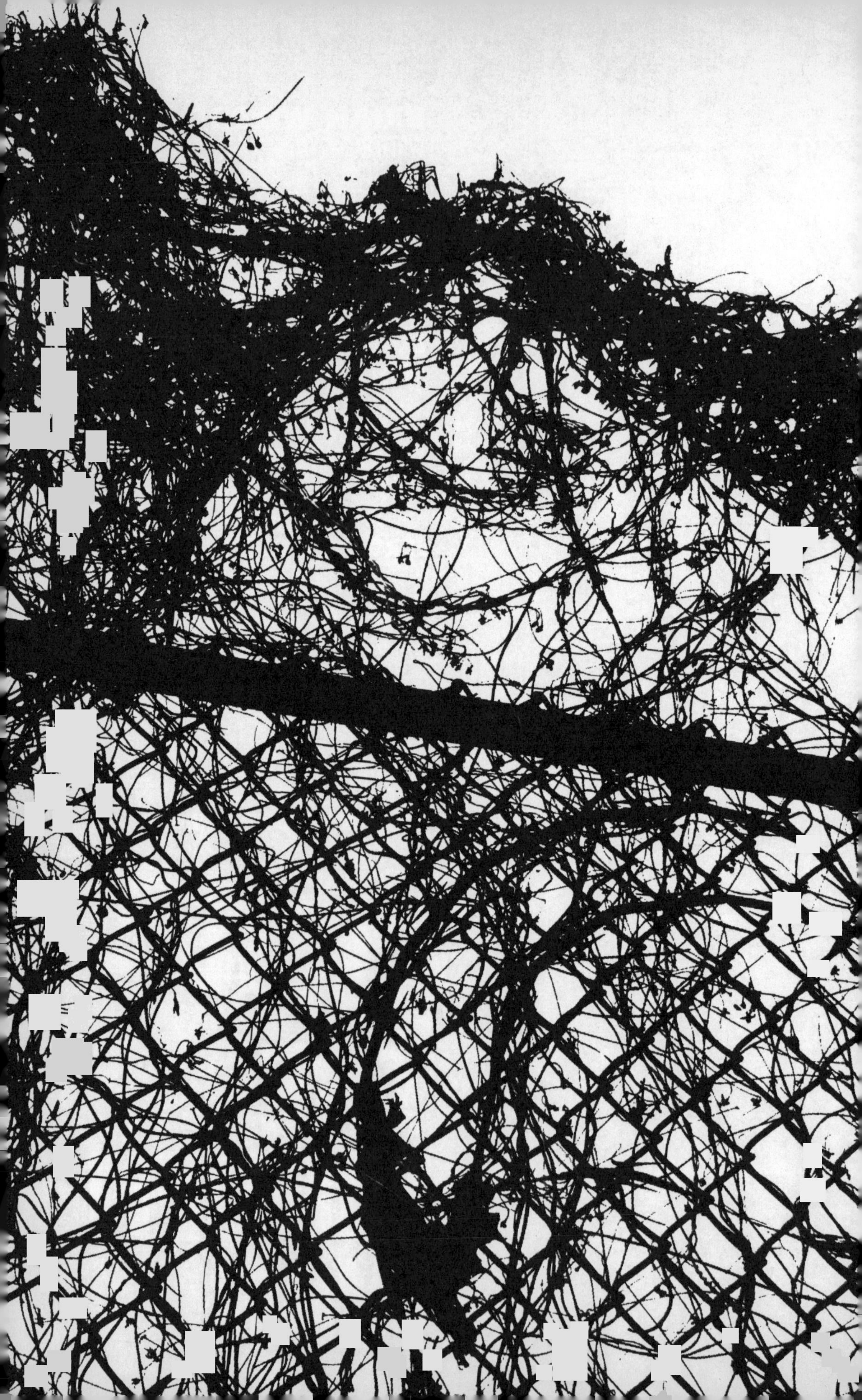

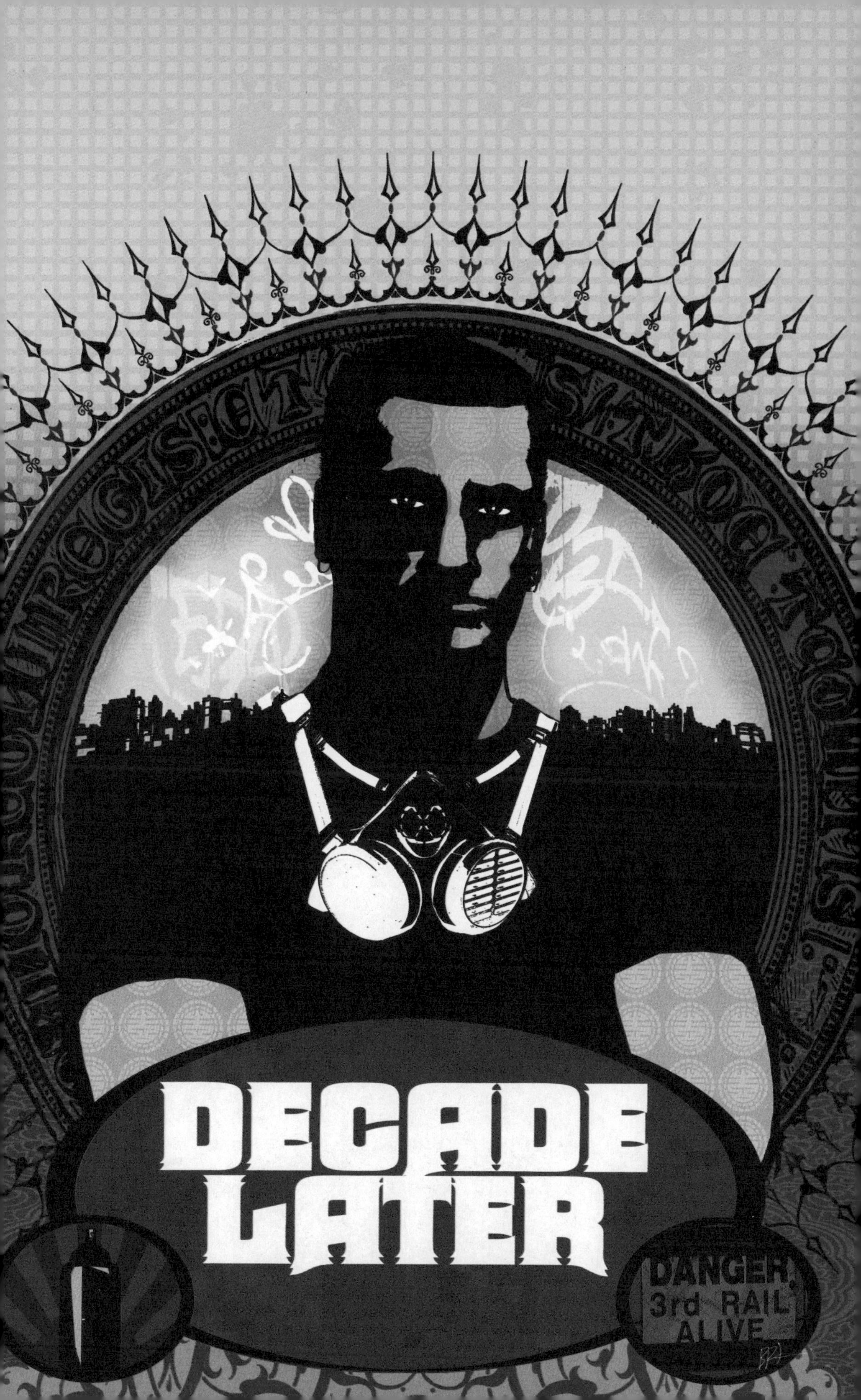
DECADE
LATER
DANGER
3rd RAIL
ALIVE

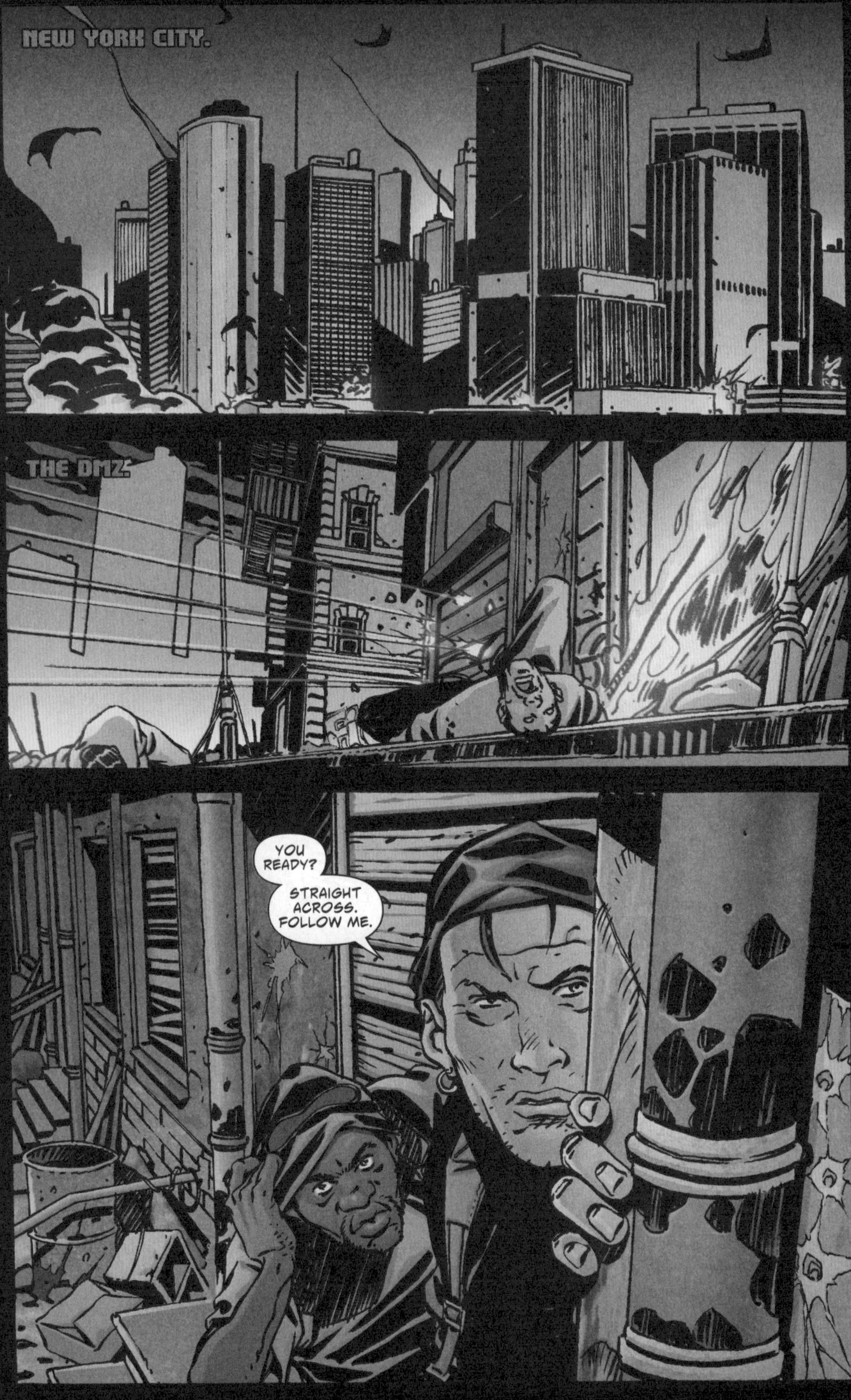
NEW YORK CITY.
THE DMZ.
YOU READY?
STRAIGHT ACROSS. FOLLOW ME.

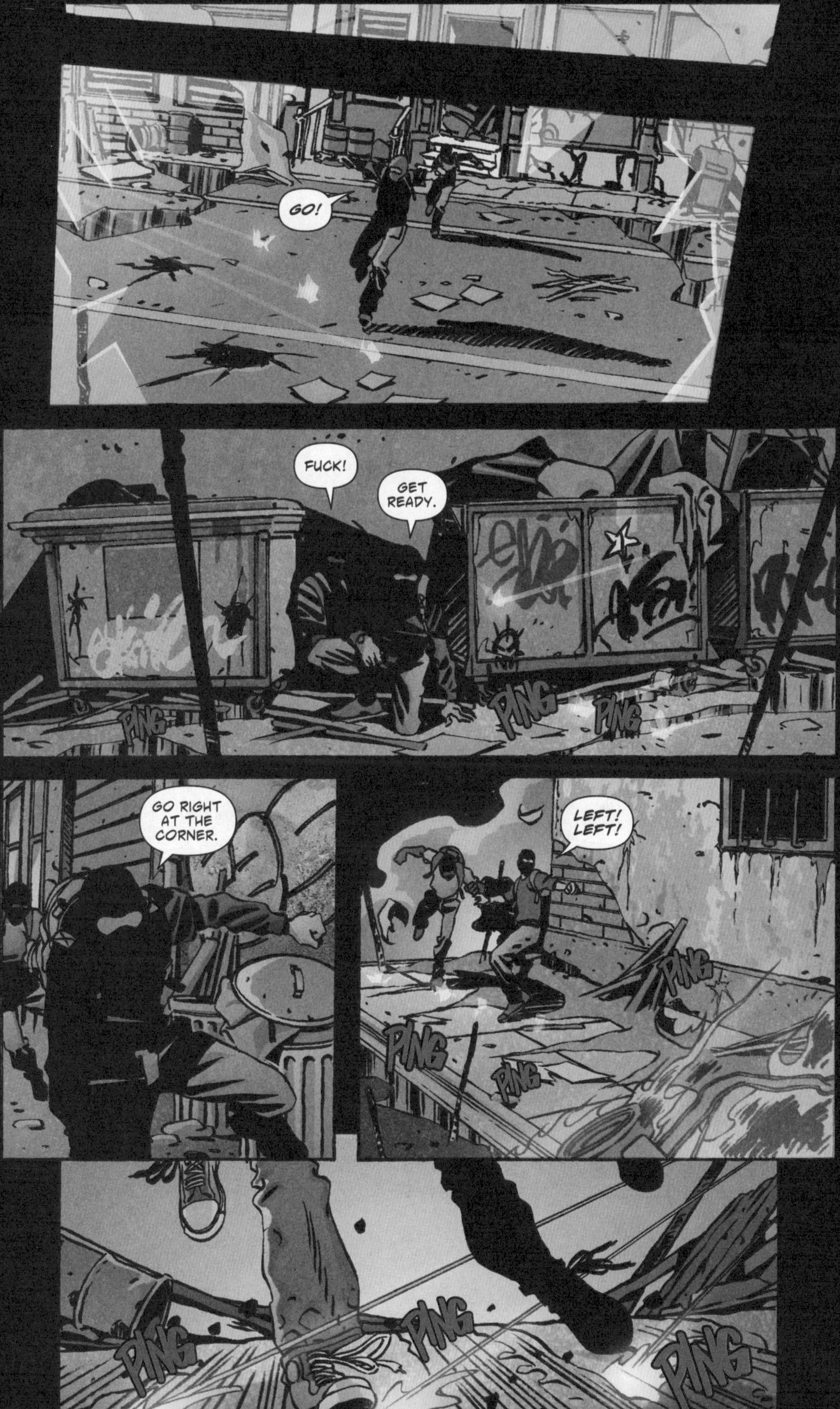
GO!
FUCK!
GET READY.
PING
PING
PING
GO RIGHT AT THE CORNER.
LEFT! LEFT!
PING
PING
PING
PING
PING
PING

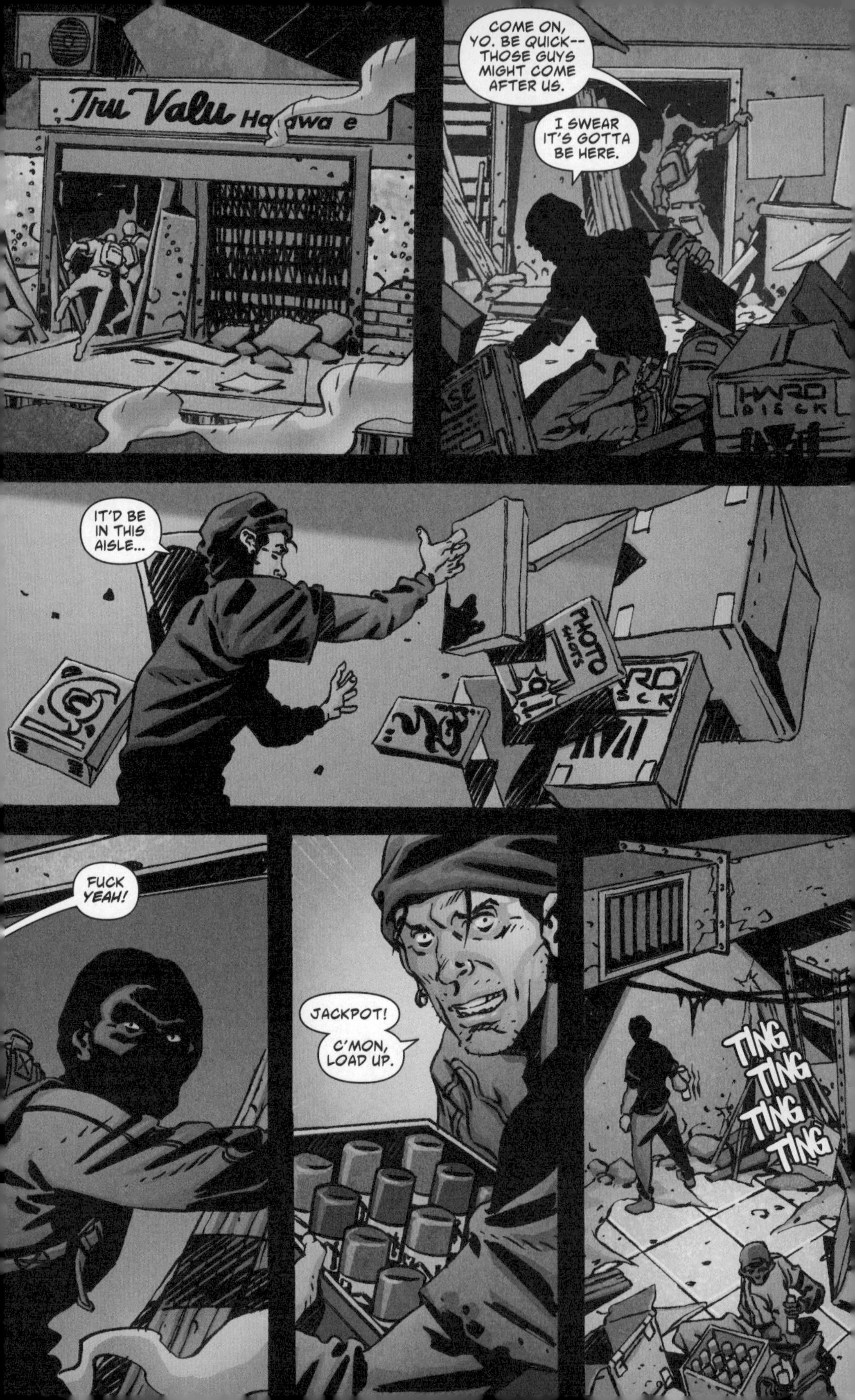
Tru Valu Ha dwa e
COME ON, YO. BE QUICK-- THOSE GUYS MIGHT COME AFTER US.
I SWEAR IT'S GOTTA BE HERE.
IT'D BE IN THIS AISLE...
PHOTO
FUCK YEAH!
JACKPOT!
C'MON, LOAD UP.
TING TING TING TING

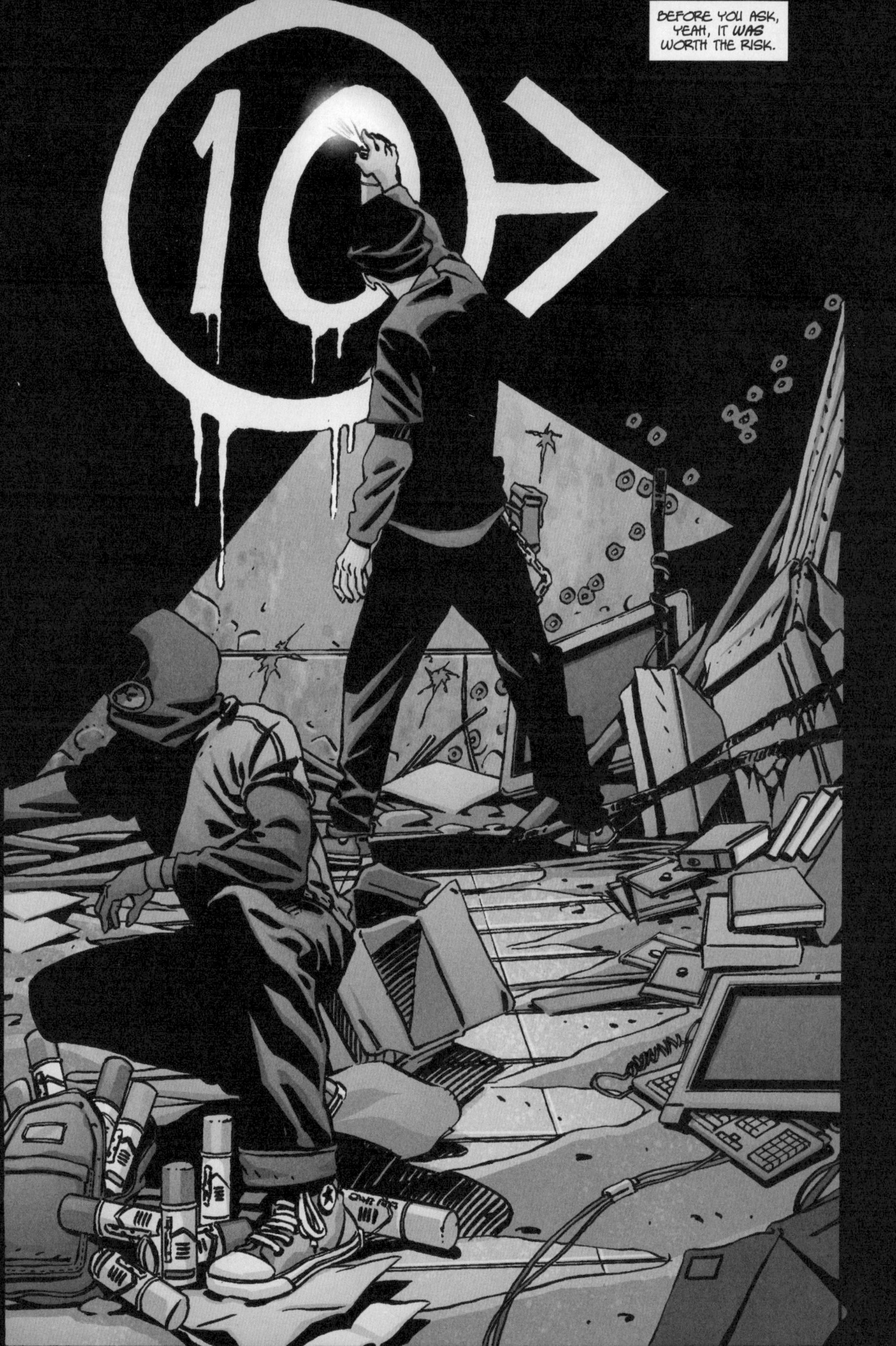
BEFORE YOU ASK,
YEAH, IT WAS
WORTH THE RISK.

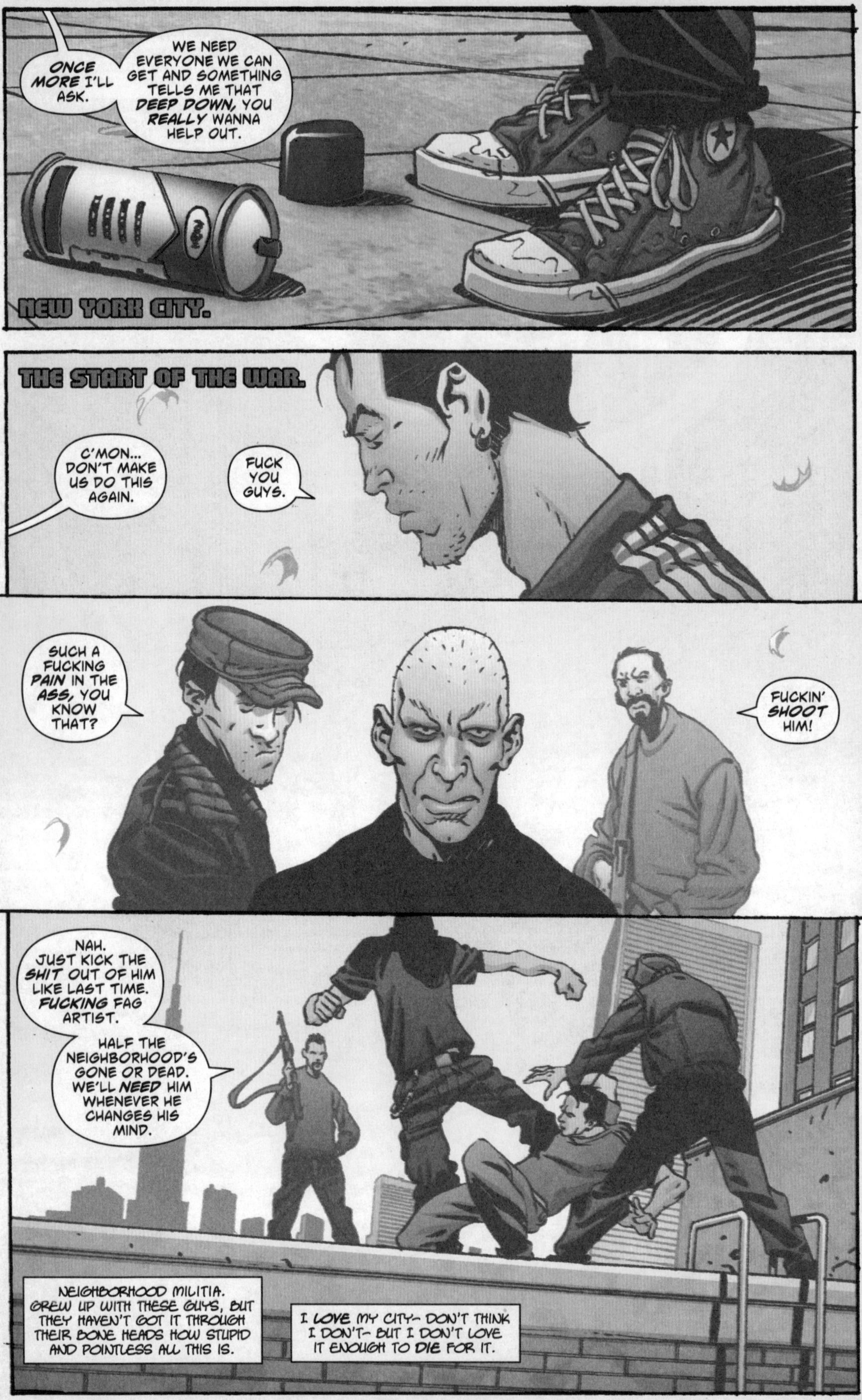

ONCE MORE I'LL ASK.
WE NEED EVERYONE WE CAN GET AND SOMETHING TELLS ME THAT DEEP DOWN, YOU REALLY WANNA HELP OUT.
NEW YORK CITY.
THE START OF THE WAR.
C'MON... DON'T MAKE US DO THIS AGAIN.
FUCK YOU GUYS.
SUCH A FUCKING PAIN IN THE ASS, YOU KNOW THAT?
FUCKIN' SHOOT HIM!
NAH. JUST KICK THE SHIT OUT OF HIM LIKE LAST TIME. FUCKING FAG ARTIST.
HALF THE NEIGHBORHOOD'S GONE OR DEAD. WE'LL NEED HIM WHENEVER HE CHANGES HIS MIND.
NEIGHBORHOOD MILITIA. GREW UP WITH THESE GUYS, BUT THEY HAVEN'T GOT IT THROUGH THEIR BONE HEADS HOW STUPID AND POINTLESS ALL THIS IS.
I LOVE MY CITY- DON'T THINK I DON'T- BUT I DON'T LOVE IT ENOUGH TO DIE FOR IT.

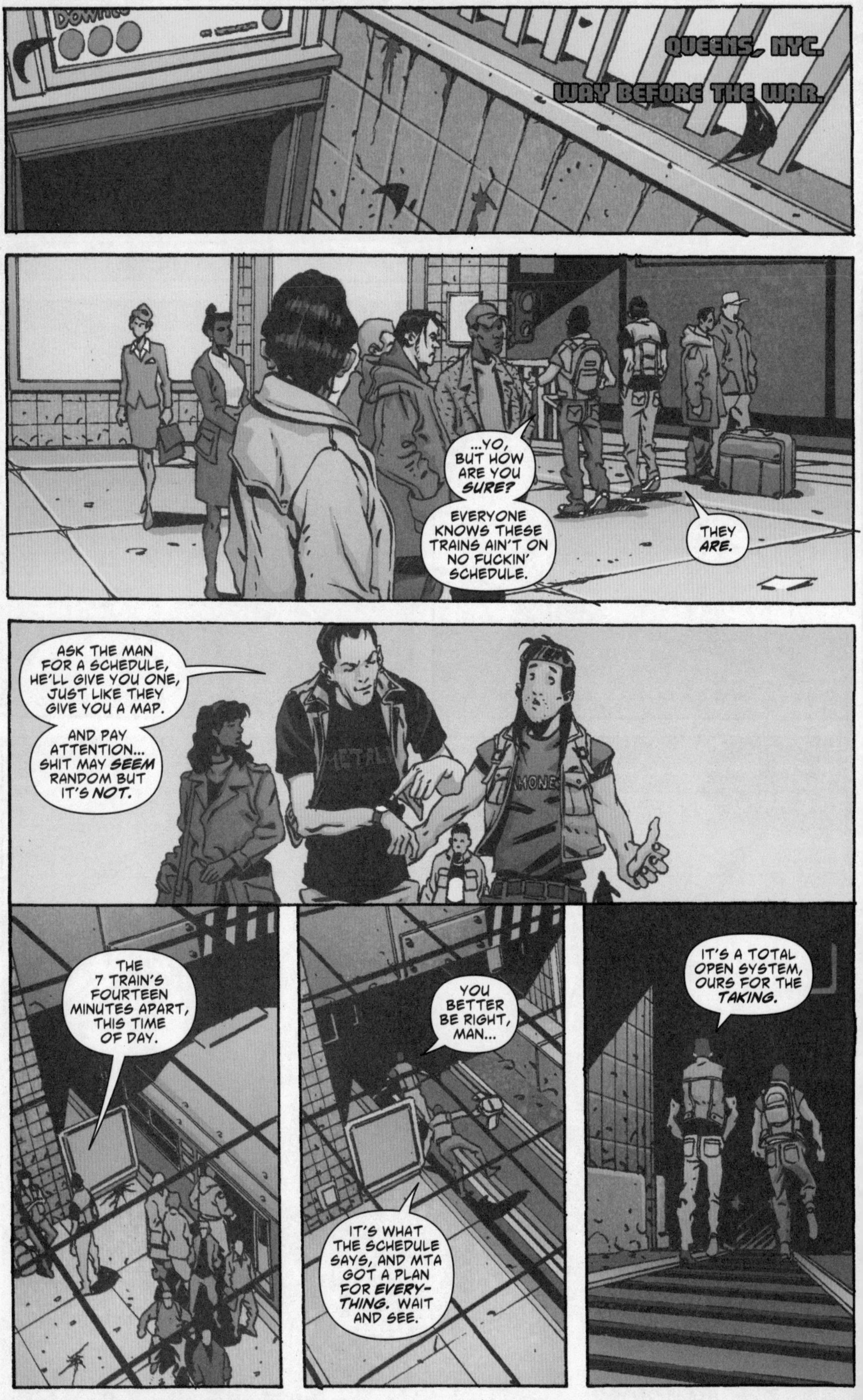
QUEENS, NYC.
WAY BEFORE THE WAR.
...YO, BUT HOW ARE YOU SURE?
EVERYONE KNOWS THESE TRAINS AIN'T ON NO FUCKIN' SCHEDULE.
THEY ARE.
ASK THE MAN FOR A SCHEDULE, HE'LL GIVE YOU ONE, JUST LIKE THEY GIVE YOU A MAP.
AND PAY ATTENTION... SHIT MAY SEEM RANDOM BUT IT'S NOT.
THE 7 TRAIN'S FOURTEEN MINUTES APART, THIS TIME OF DAY.
YOU BETTER BE RIGHT, MAN...
IT'S WHAT THE SCHEDULE SAYS, AND MTA GOT A PLAN FOR EVERY-THING. WAIT AND SEE.
IT'S A TOTAL OPEN SYSTEM, OURS FOR THE TAKING.

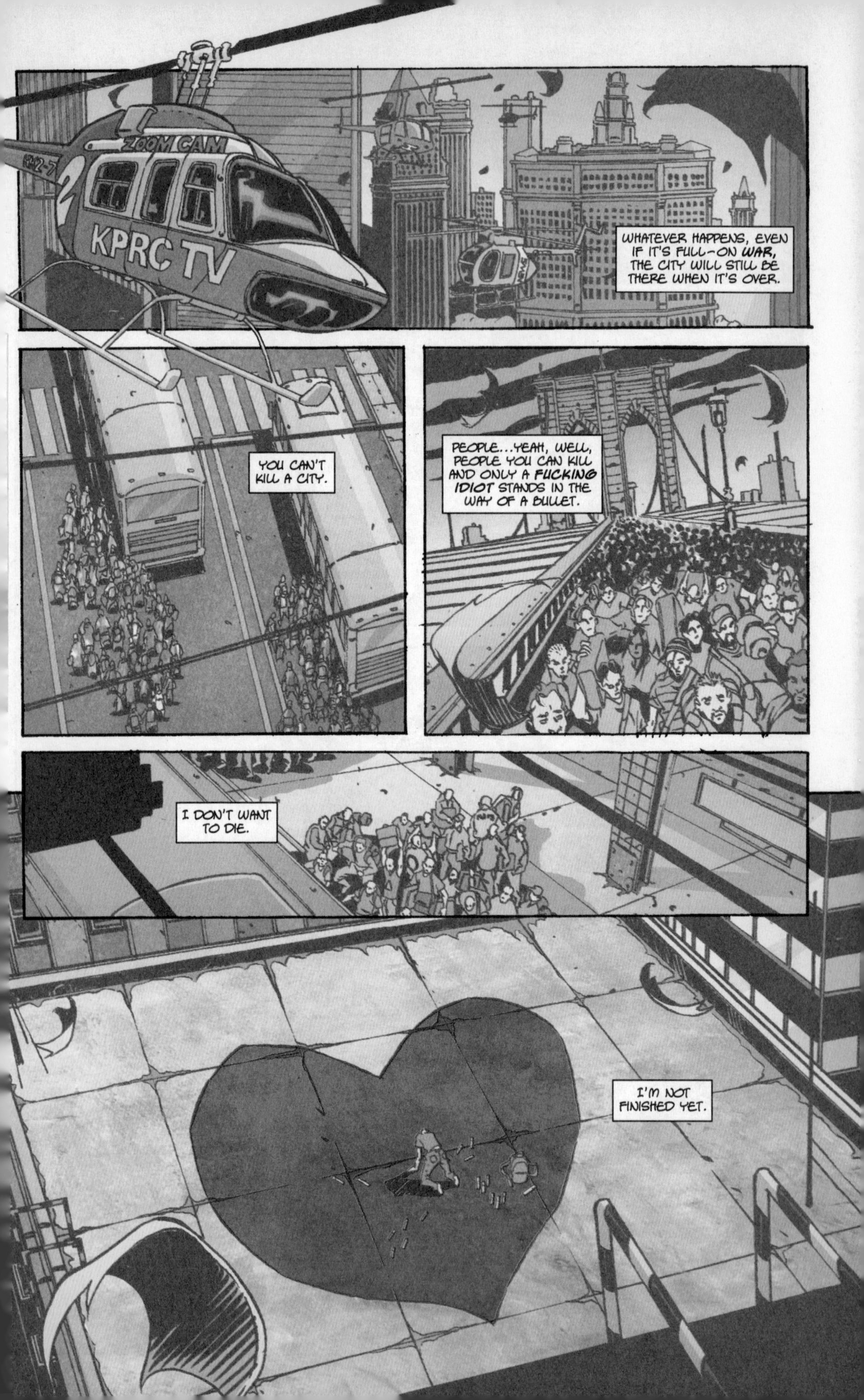
ZOOM CAM
KPRC TV
WHATEVER HAPPENS, EVEN IF IT'S FULL-ON WAR, THE CITY WILL STILL BE THERE WHEN IT'S OVER.
YOU CAN'T KILL A CITY.
PEOPLE...YEAH, WELL, PEOPLE YOU CAN KILL AND ONLY A FUCKING IDIOT STANDS IN THE WAY OF A BULLET.
I DON'T WANT TO DIE.
I'M NOT FINISHED YET.

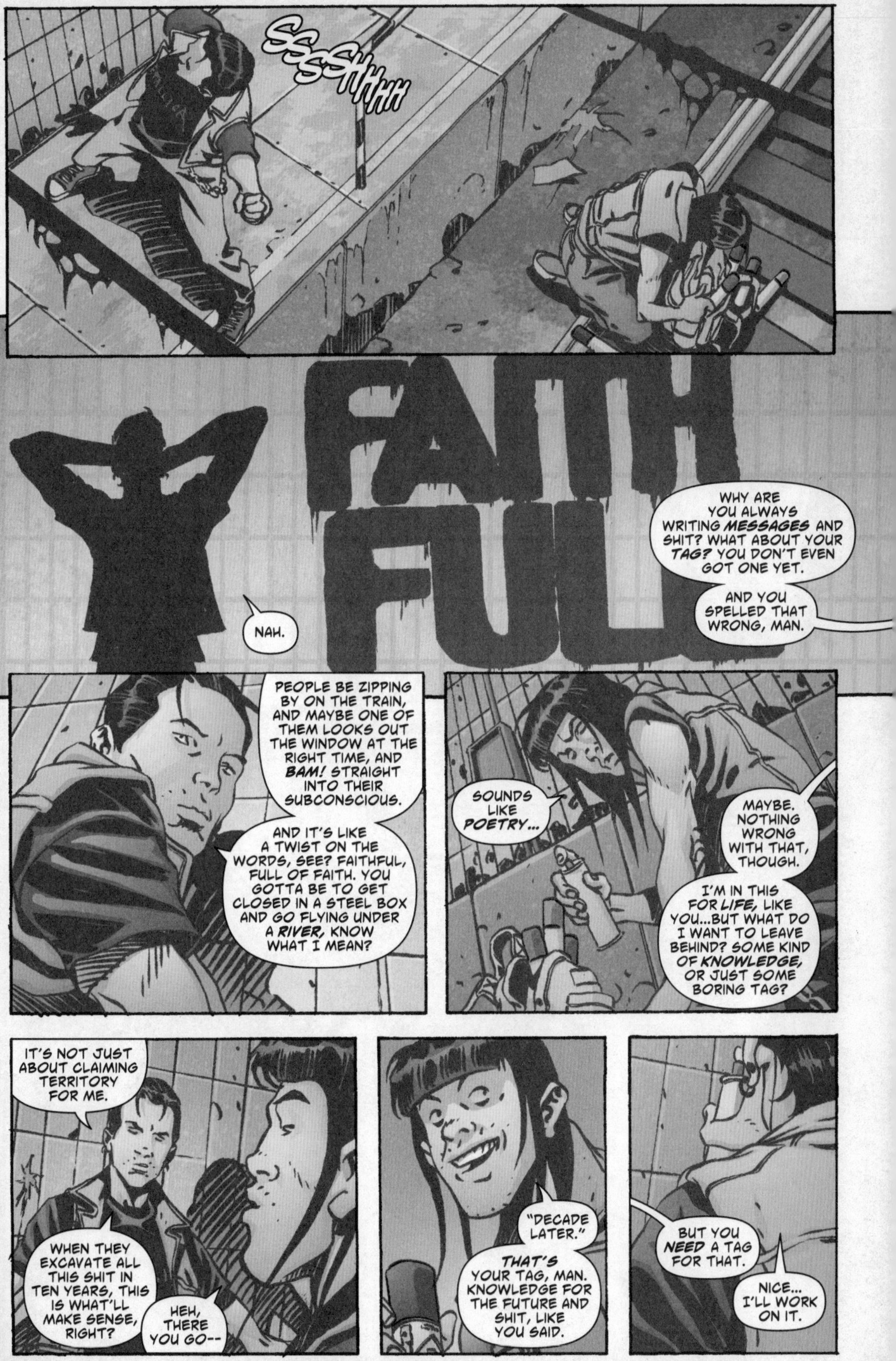
SSSSHHHHH
FAITH FULL
NAH.
WHY ARE YOU ALWAYS WRITING MESSAGES AND SHIT? WHAT ABOUT YOUR TAG? YOU DON'T EVEN GOT ONE YET.
AND YOU SPELLED THAT WRONG, MAN.
PEOPLE BE ZIPPING BY ON THE TRAIN, AND MAYBE ONE OF THEM LOOKS OUT THE WINDOW AT THE RIGHT TIME, AND BAM! STRAIGHT INTO THEIR SUBCONSCIOUS.
AND IT'S LIKE A TWIST ON THE WORDS, SEE? FAITHFUL, FULL OF FAITH. YOU GOTTA BE TO GET CLOSED IN A STEEL BOX AND GO FLYING UNDER A RIVER, KNOW WHAT I MEAN?
SOUNDS LIKE POETRY...
MAYBE. NOTHING WRONG WITH THAT, THOUGH.
I'M IN THIS FOR LIFE, LIKE YOU...BUT WHAT DO I WANT TO LEAVE BEHIND? SOME KIND OF KNOWLEDGE, OR JUST SOME BORING TAG?
IT'S NOT JUST ABOUT CLAIMING TERRITORY FOR ME.
WHEN THEY EXCAVATE ALL THIS SHIT IN TEN YEARS, THIS IS WHAT'LL MAKE SENSE, RIGHT?
HEH, THERE YOU GO--
"DECADE LATER."
THAT'S YOUR TAG, MAN. KNOWLEDGE FOR THE FUTURE AND SHIT, LIKE YOU SAID.
BUT YOU NEED A TAG FOR THAT.
NICE... I'LL WORK ON IT.

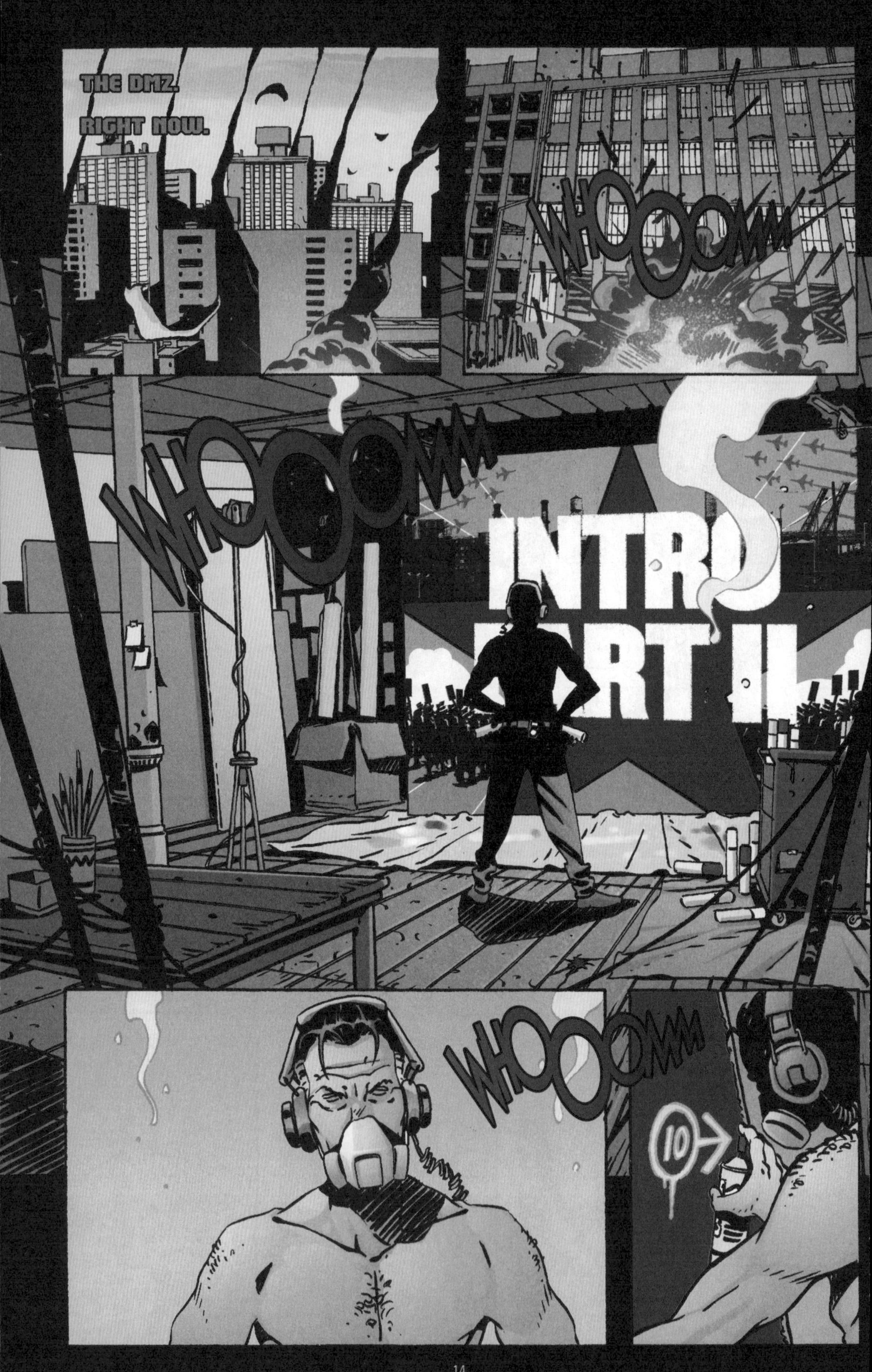
THE DMZ.
RIGHT NOW.
WHOOOMM
WHOOOMM
INTRO PART II
WHOOOMM
10

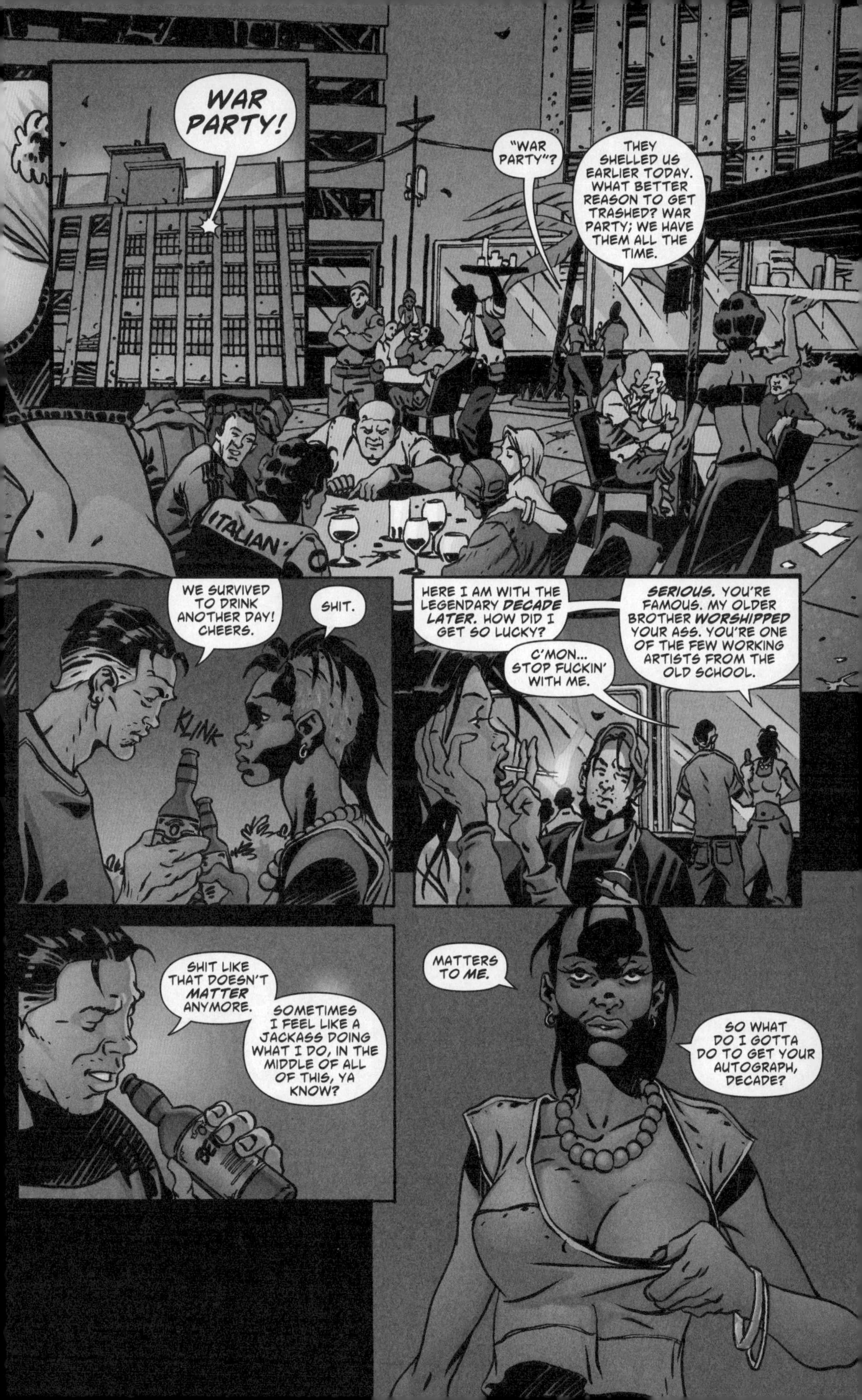
WAR PARTY!
"WAR PARTY"?
THEY SHELLED US EARLIER TODAY. WHAT BETTER REASON TO GET TRASHED? WAR PARTY; WE HAVE THEM ALL THE TIME.
ITALIAN
WE SURVIVED TO DRINK ANOTHER DAY! CHEERS.
SHIT.
KLINK
HERE I AM WITH THE LEGENDARY *DECADE LATER*. HOW DID I GET SO LUCKY?
C'MON... STOP FUCKIN' WITH ME.
SERIOUS. YOU'RE FAMOUS. MY OLDER BROTHER ***WORSHIPPED*** YOUR ASS. YOU'RE ONE OF THE FEW WORKING ARTISTS FROM THE OLD SCHOOL.
SHIT LIKE THAT DOESN'T *MATTER* ANYMORE.
SOMETIMES I FEEL LIKE A JACKASS DOING WHAT I DO, IN THE MIDDLE OF ALL OF THIS, YA KNOW?
MATTERS TO *ME*.
SO WHAT DO I GOTTA DO TO GET YOUR AUTOGRAPH, DECADE?

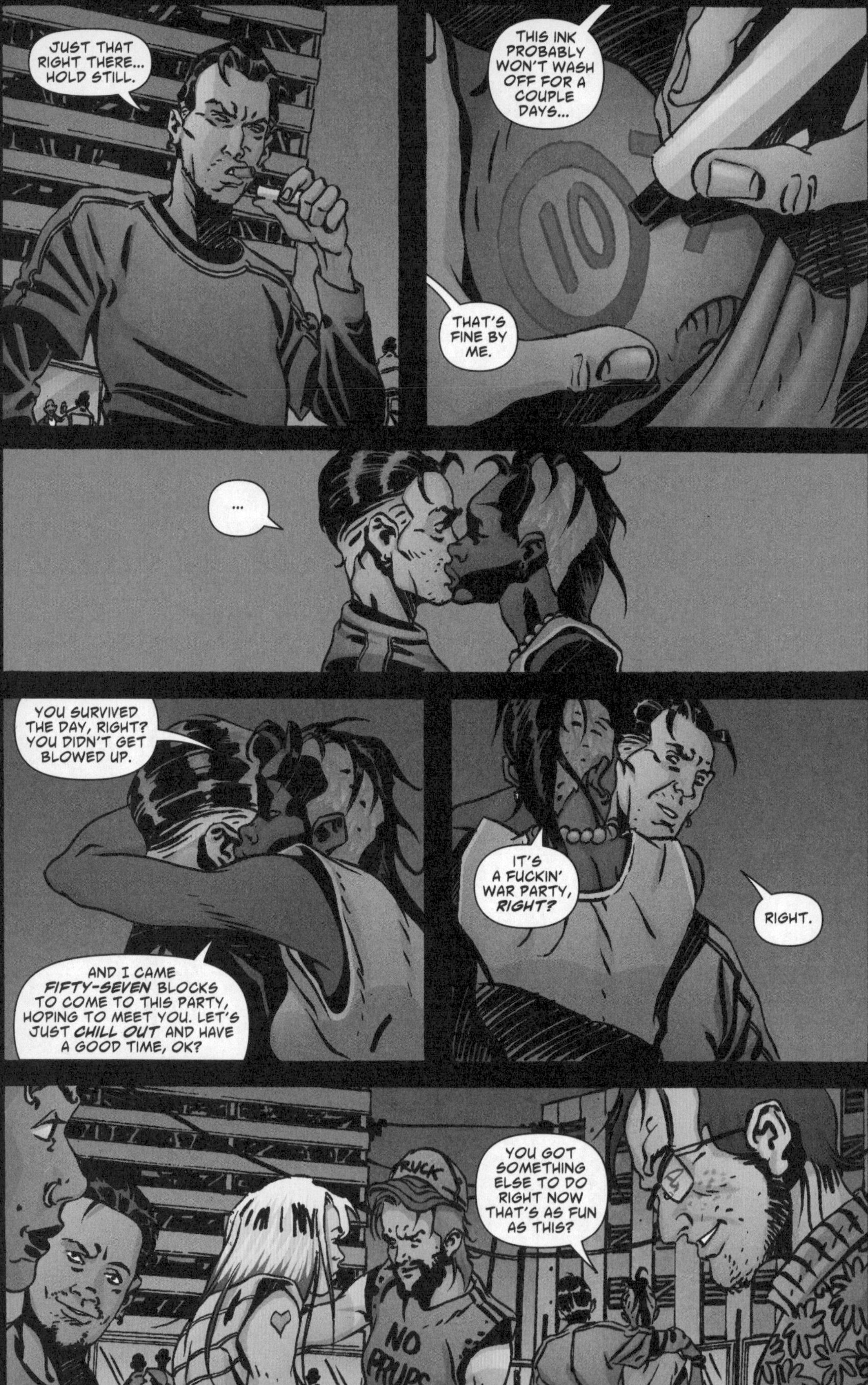
JUST THAT RIGHT THERE... HOLD STILL.
THIS INK PROBABLY WON'T WASH OFF FOR A COUPLE DAYS...
THAT'S FINE BY ME.
10
...
YOU SURVIVED THE DAY, RIGHT? YOU DIDN'T GET BLOWED UP.
AND I CAME FIFTY-SEVEN BLOCKS TO COME TO THIS PARTY, HOPING TO MEET YOU. LET'S JUST CHILL OUT AND HAVE A GOOD TIME, OK?
IT'S A FUCKIN' WAR PARTY, RIGHT?
RIGHT.
YOU GOT SOMETHING ELSE TO DO RIGHT NOW THAT'S AS FUN AS THIS?
NO PRUPS

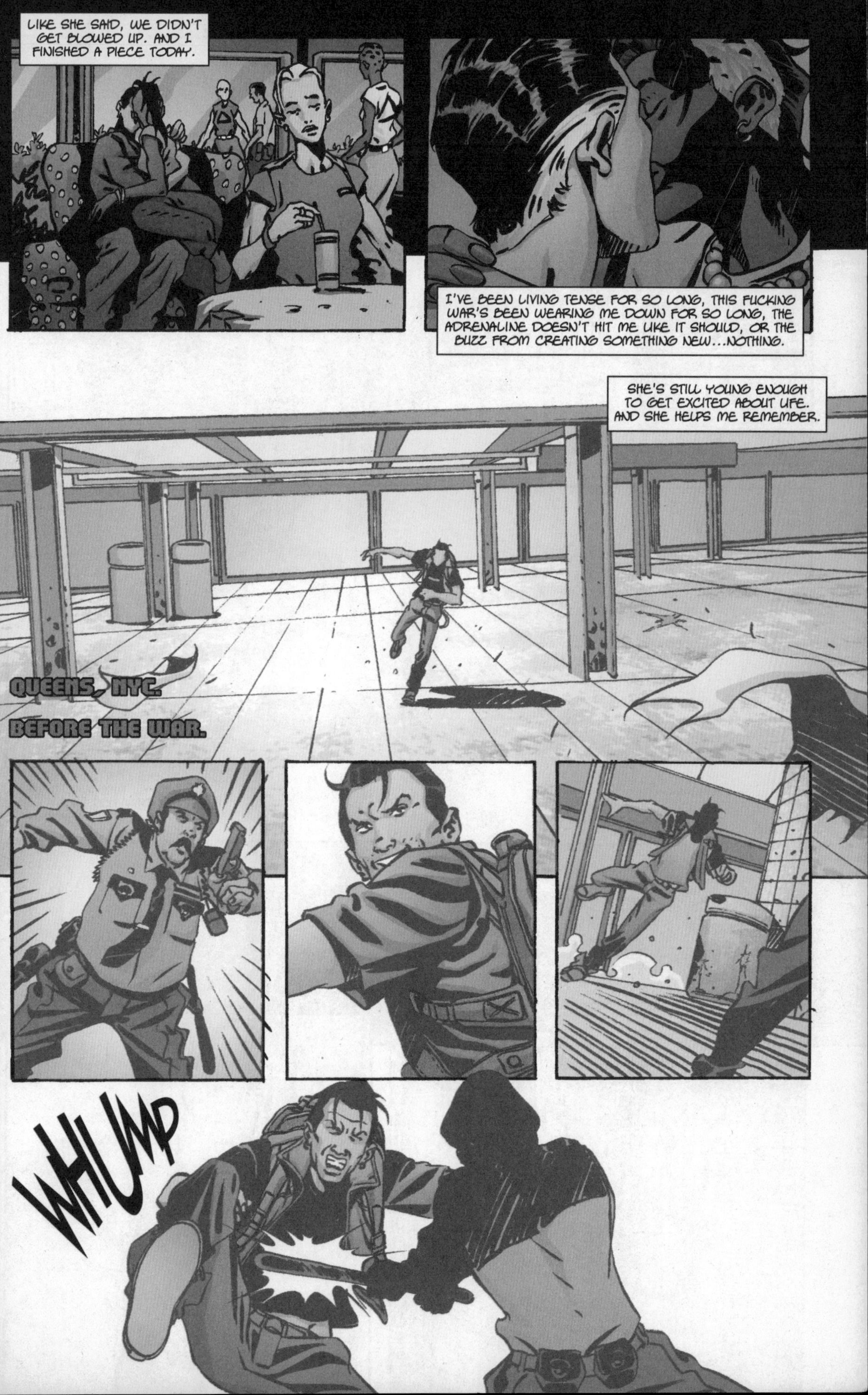
LIKE SHE SAID, WE DIDN'T GET BLOWED UP. AND I FINISHED A PIECE TODAY.
I'VE BEEN LIVING TENSE FOR SO LONG, THIS FUCKING WAR'S BEEN WEARING ME DOWN FOR SO LONG, THE ADRENALINE DOESN'T HIT ME LIKE IT SHOULD, OR THE BUZZ FROM CREATING SOMETHING NEW...NOTHING.
SHE'S STILL YOUNG ENOUGH TO GET EXCITED ABOUT LIFE. AND SHE HELPS ME REMEMBER.
QUEENS, NYC.
BEFORE THE WAR.
WHUMP

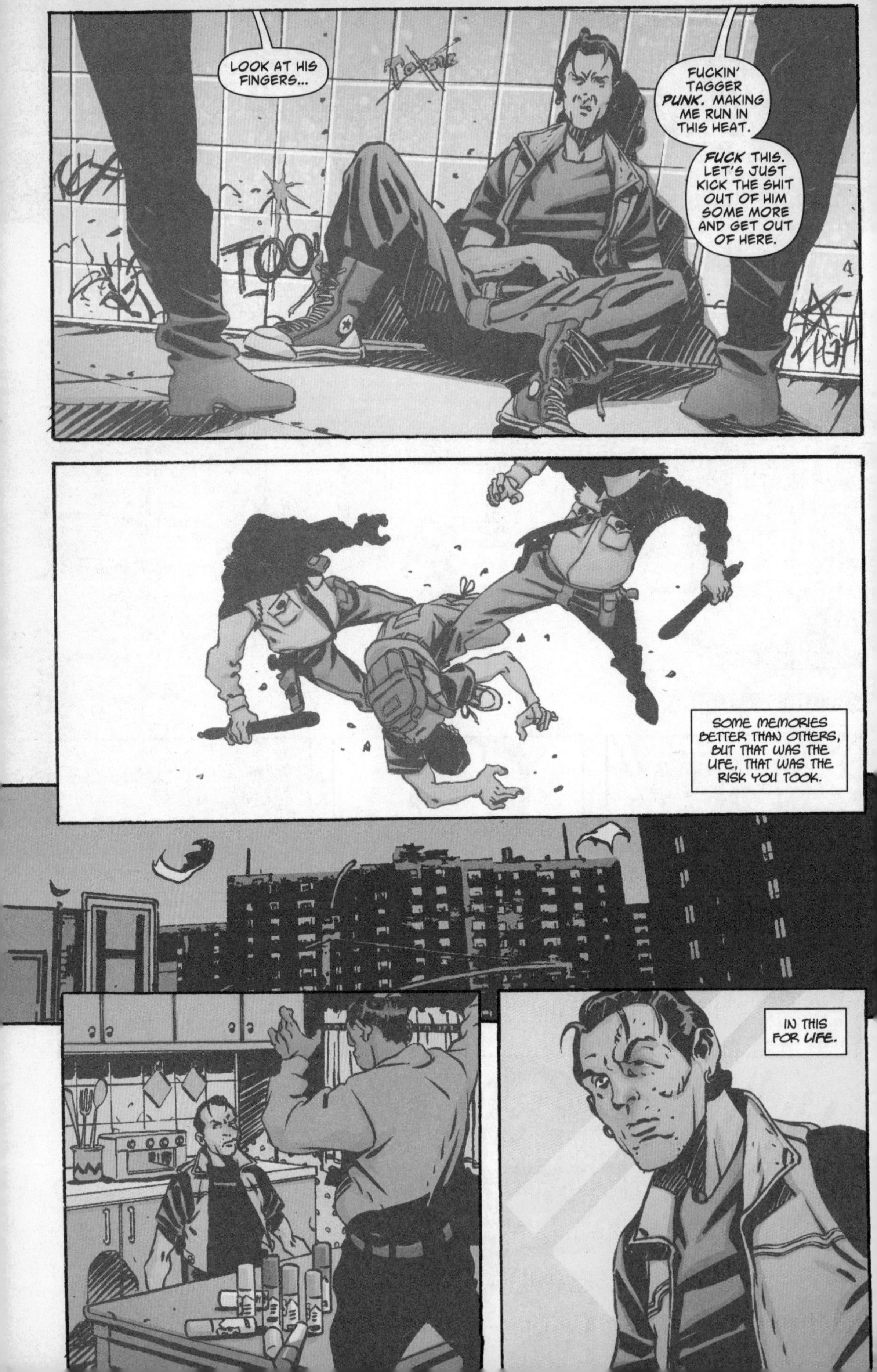
LOOK AT HIS FINGERS...
FUCKIN' TAGGER PUNK. MAKING ME RUN IN THIS HEAT.
FUCK THIS. LET'S JUST KICK THE SHIT OUT OF HIM SOME MORE AND GET OUT OF HERE.
SOME MEMORIES BETTER THAN OTHERS, BUT THAT WAS THE LIFE, THAT WAS THE RISK YOU TOOK.
IN THIS FOR LIFE.

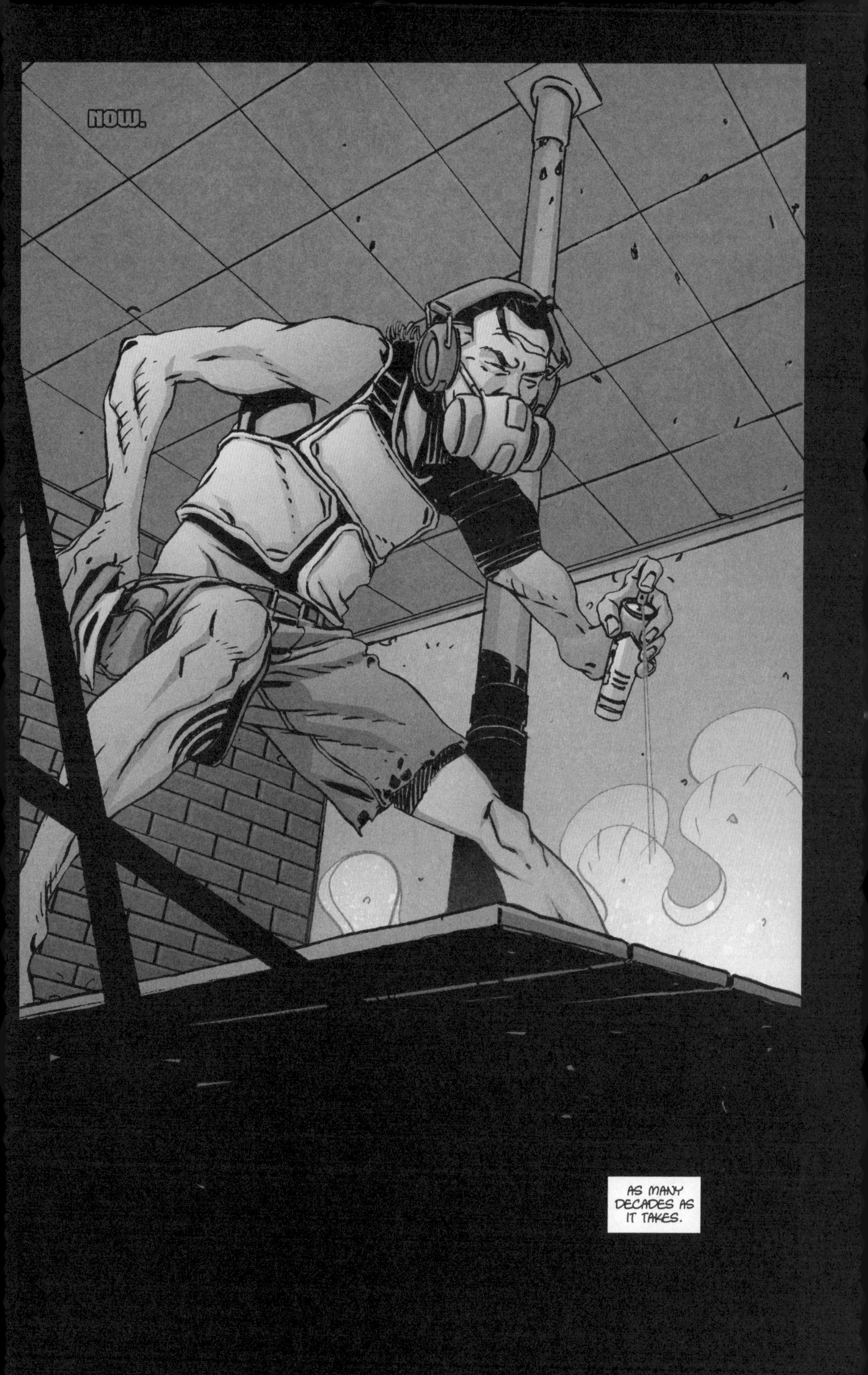
NOW.
AS MANY DECADES AS IT TAKES.

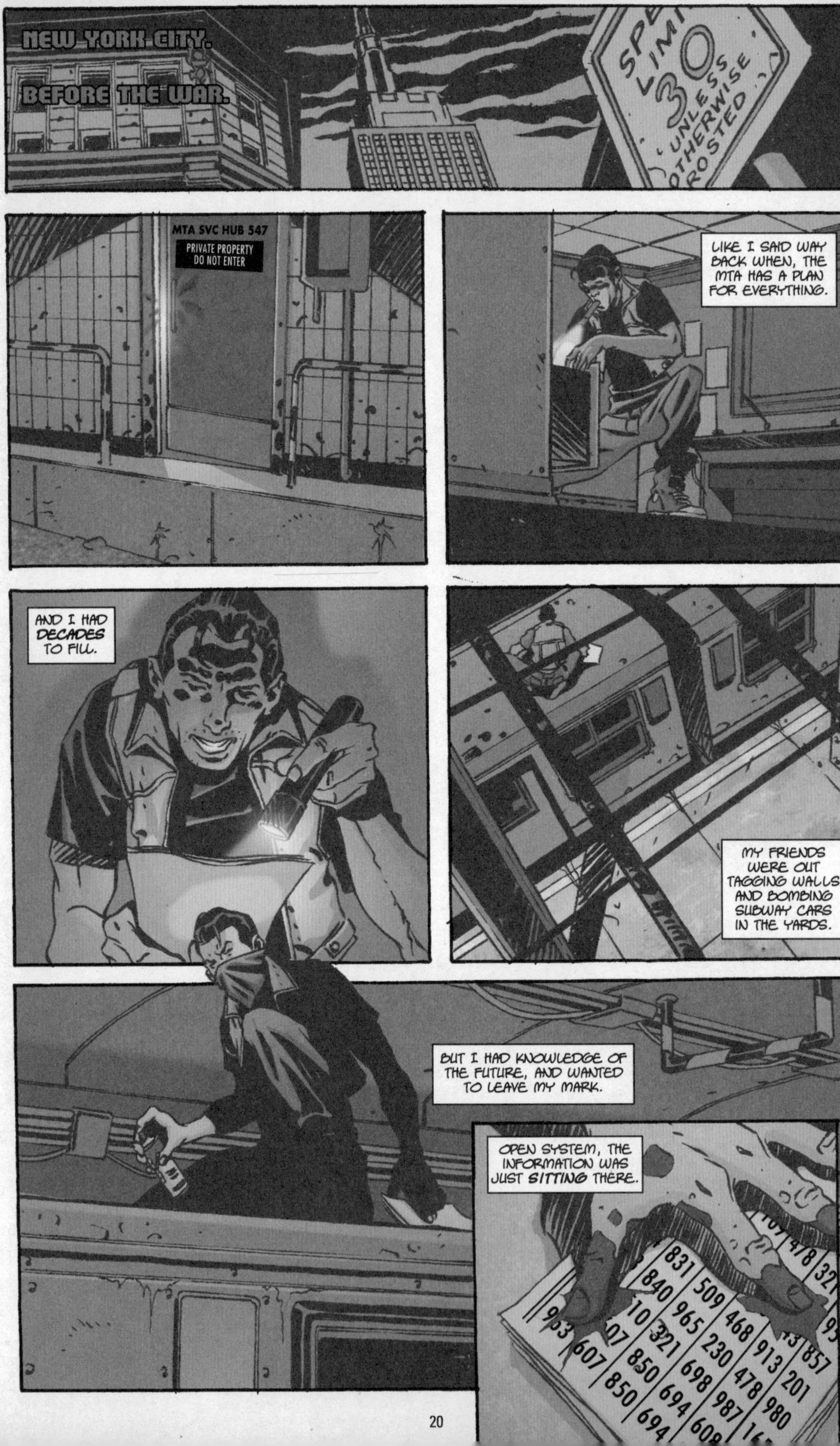
NEW YORK CITY.
BEFORE THE WAR.
SPEED LIMIT 30 UNLESS OTHERWISE POSTED
MTA SVC HUB 547
PRIVATE PROPERTY DO NOT ENTER
LIKE I SAID WAY BACK WHEN, THE MTA HAS A PLAN FOR EVERYTHING.
AND I HAD DECADES TO FILL.
MY FRIENDS WERE OUT TAGGING WALLS AND BOMBING SUBWAY CARS IN THE YARDS.
BUT I HAD KNOWLEDGE OF THE FUTURE, AND WANTED TO LEAVE MY MARK.
OPEN SYSTEM, THE INFORMATION WAS JUST SITTING THERE.

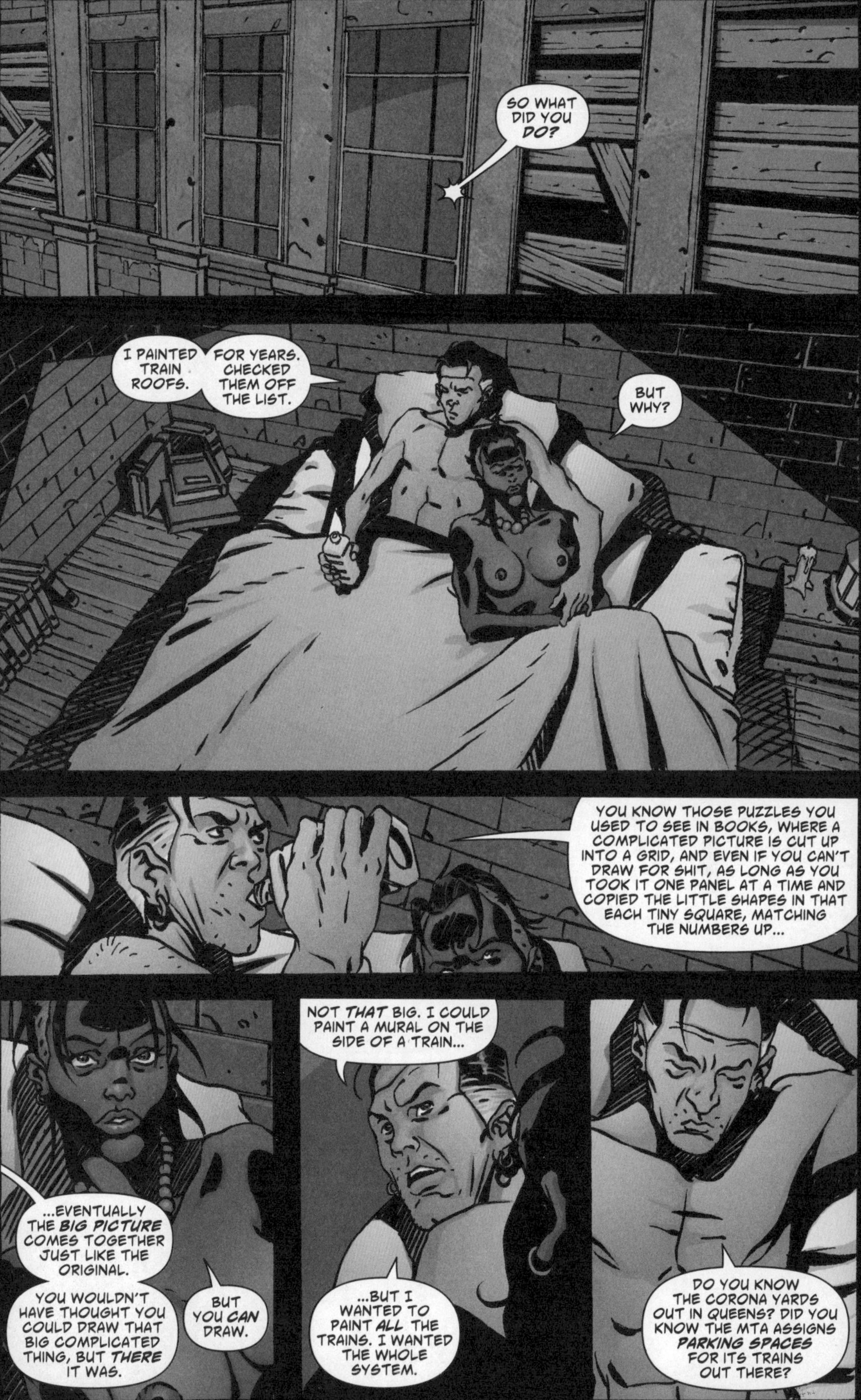
SO WHAT DID YOU *DO*?
I PAINTED TRAIN ROOFS.
FOR YEARS. CHECKED THEM OFF THE LIST.
BUT WHY?
YOU KNOW THOSE PUZZLES YOU USED TO SEE IN BOOKS, WHERE A COMPLICATED PICTURE IS CUT UP INTO A GRID, AND EVEN IF YOU CAN'T DRAW FOR SHIT, AS LONG AS YOU TOOK IT ONE PANEL AT A TIME AND COPIED THE LITTLE SHAPES IN THAT EACH TINY SQUARE, MATCHING THE NUMBERS UP...
...EVENTUALLY THE *BIG PICTURE* COMES TOGETHER JUST LIKE THE ORIGINAL.
YOU WOULDN'T HAVE THOUGHT YOU COULD DRAW THAT BIG COMPLICATED THING, BUT *THERE* IT WAS.
BUT YOU *CAN* DRAW.
NOT *THAT* BIG. I COULD PAINT A MURAL ON THE SIDE OF A TRAIN...
...BUT I WANTED TO PAINT *ALL* THE TRAINS. I WANTED THE WHOLE SYSTEM.
DO YOU KNOW THE CORONA YARDS OUT IN QUEENS? DID YOU KNOW THE MTA ASSIGNS *PARKING SPACES* FOR ITS TRAINS OUT THERE?

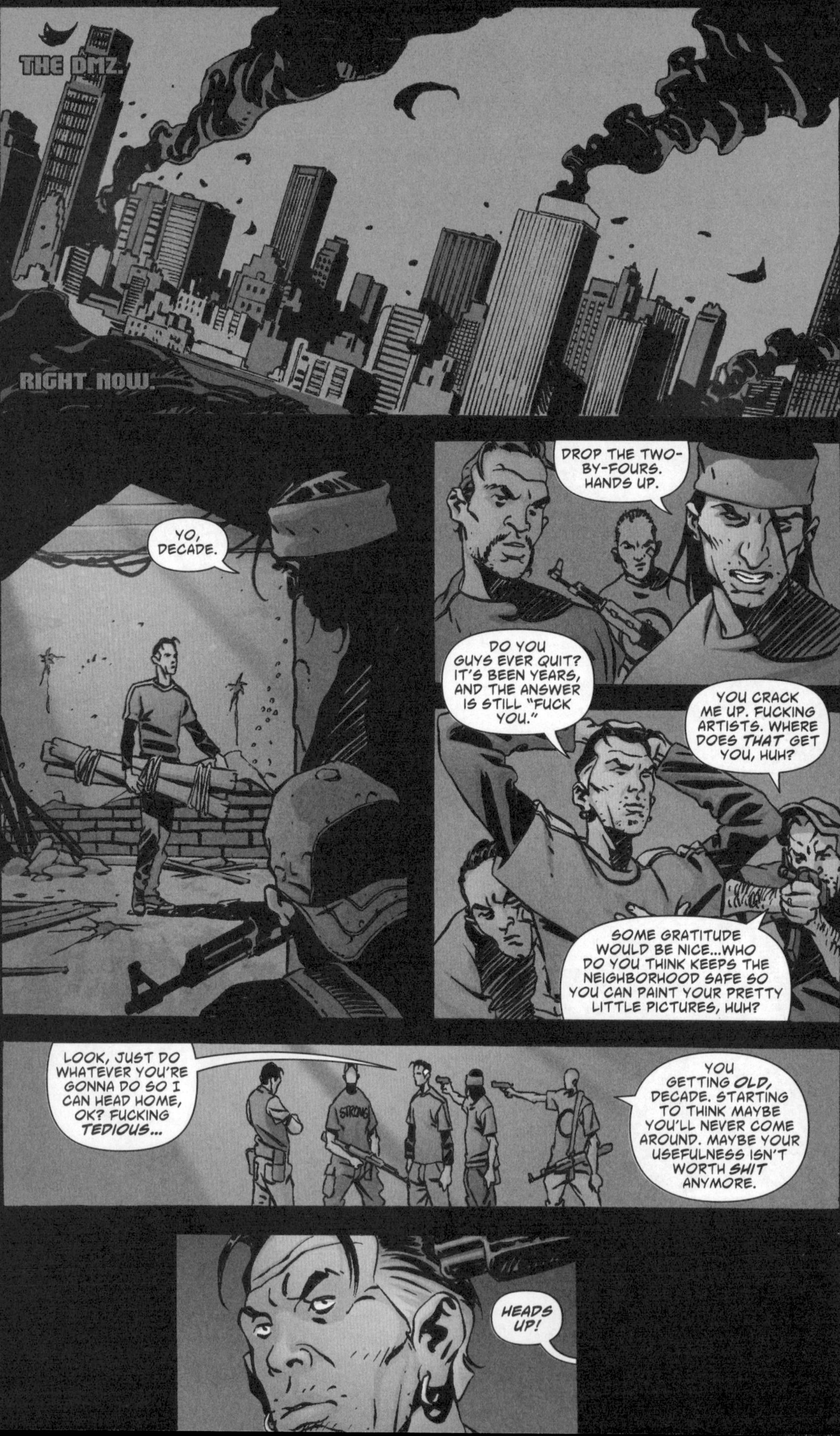
THE DMZ.
RIGHT NOW.
YO, DECADE.
DROP THE TWO-BY-FOURS. HANDS UP.
DO YOU GUYS EVER QUIT? IT'S BEEN YEARS, AND THE ANSWER IS STILL "FUCK YOU."
YOU CRACK ME UP. FUCKING ARTISTS. WHERE DOES *THAT* GET YOU, HUH?
SOME GRATITUDE WOULD BE NICE...WHO DO YOU THINK KEEPS THE NEIGHBORHOOD SAFE SO YOU CAN PAINT YOUR PRETTY LITTLE PICTURES, HUH?
LOOK, JUST DO WHATEVER YOU'RE GONNA DO SO I CAN HEAD HOME, OK? FUCKING *TEDIOUS*...
YOU GETTING *OLD*, DECADE. STARTING TO THINK MAYBE YOU'LL NEVER COME AROUND. MAYBE YOUR USEFULNESS ISN'T WORTH *SHIT* ANYMORE.
HEADS UP!

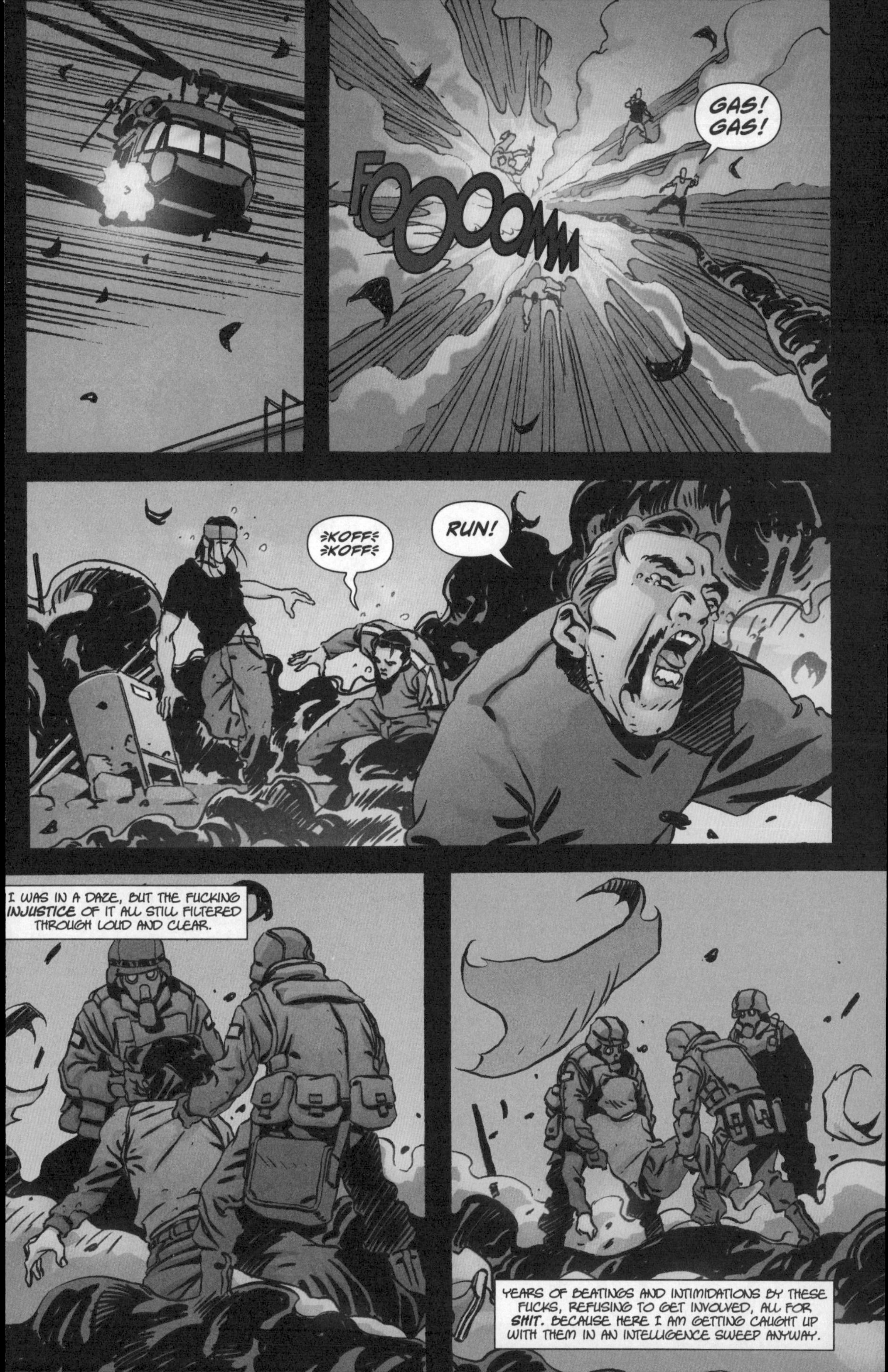
FOOOOOMM
GAS! GAS!
KOFF KOFF
RUN!
I WAS IN A DAZE, BUT THE FUCKING INJUSTICE OF IT ALL STILL FILTERED THROUGH LOUD AND CLEAR.
YEARS OF BEATINGS AND INTIMIDATIONS BY THESE FUCKS, REFUSING TO GET INVOLVED, ALL FOR SHIT. BECAUSE HERE I AM GETTING CAUGHT UP WITH THEM IN AN INTELLIGENCE SWEEP ANYWAY.

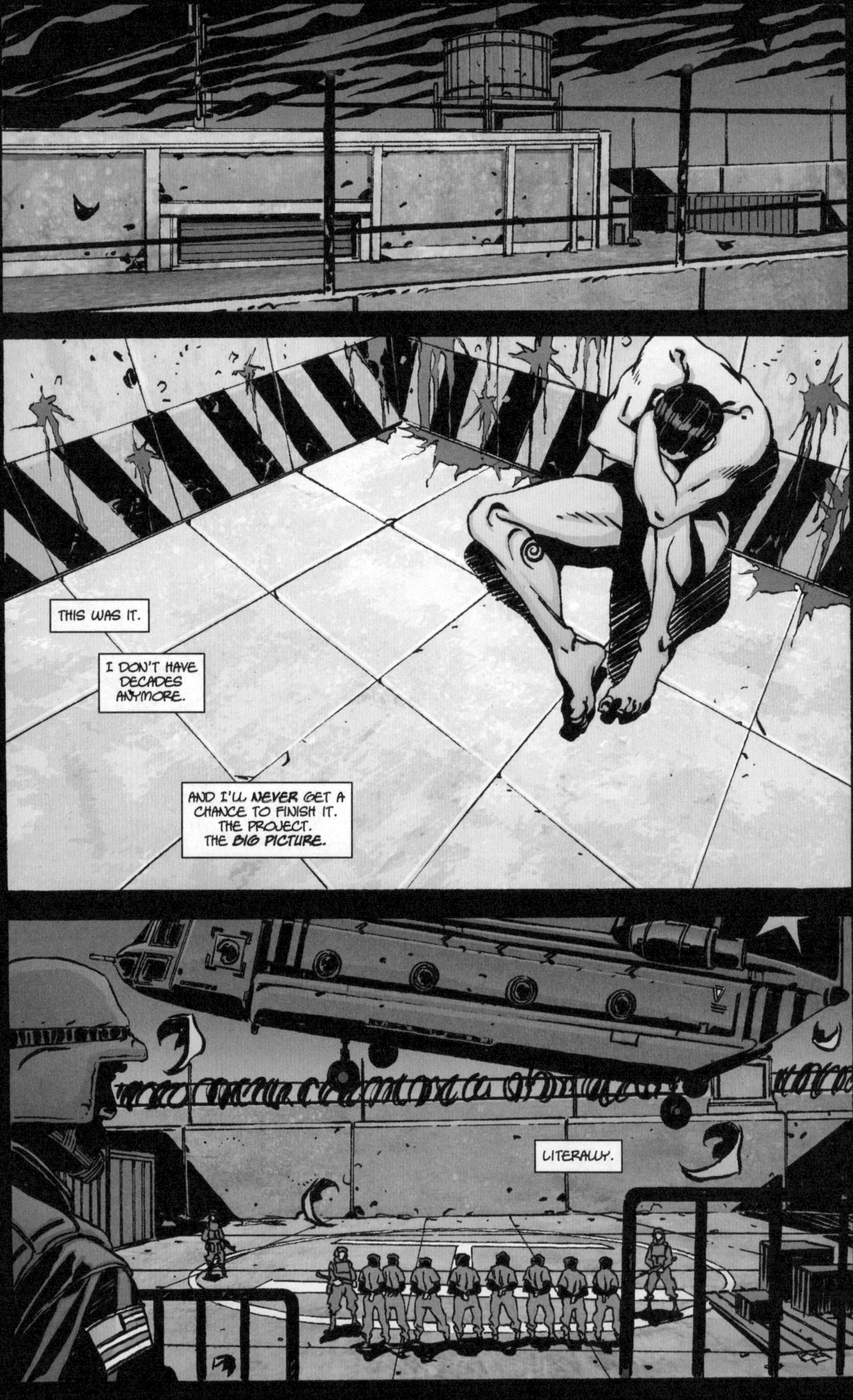
THIS WAS IT.
I DON'T HAVE DECADES ANYMORE.
AND I'LL NEVER GET A CHANCE TO FINISH IT. THE PROJECT. THE BIG PICTURE.
LITERALLY.

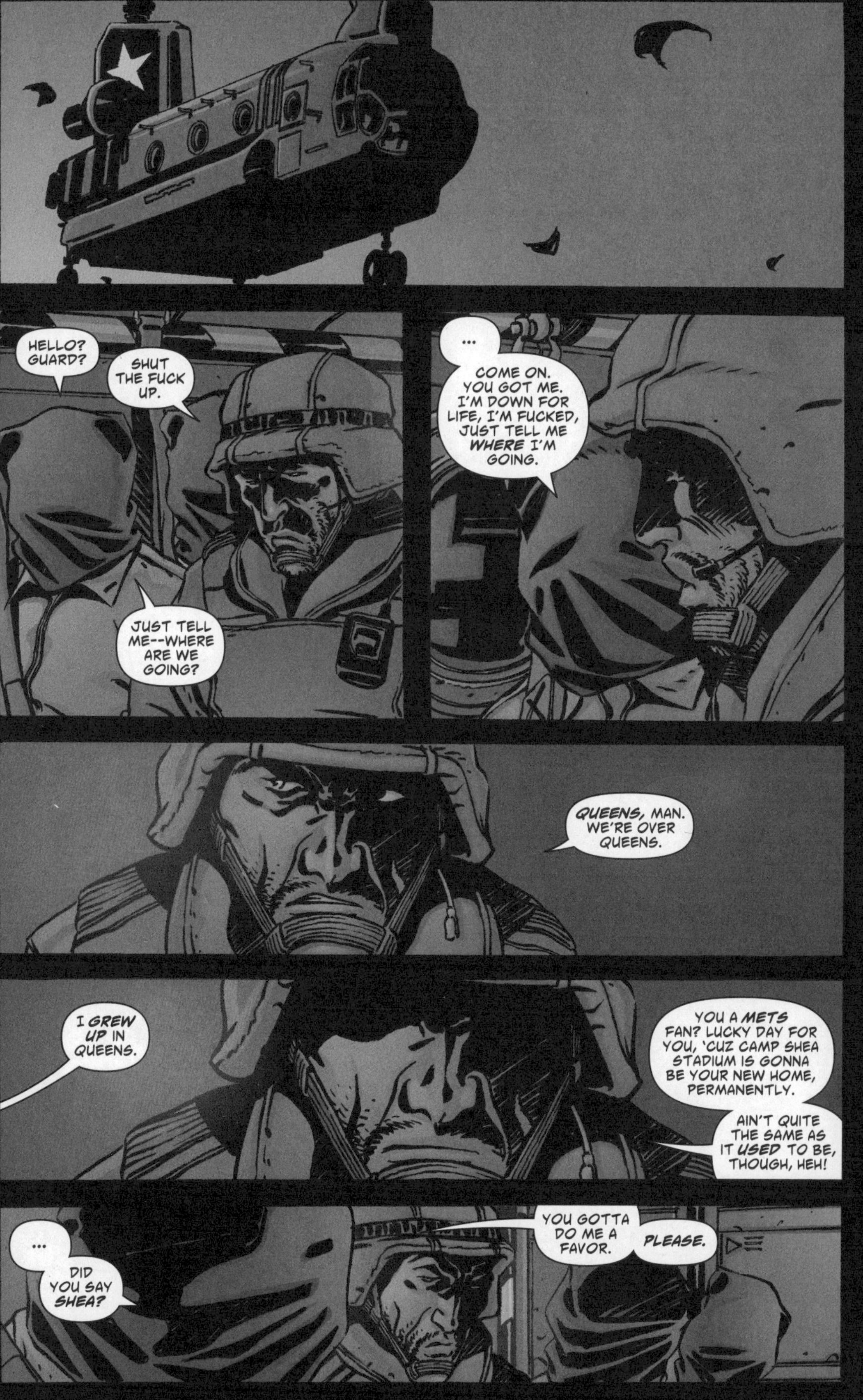
HELLO? GUARD?
SHUT THE FUCK UP.
JUST TELL ME--WHERE ARE WE GOING?
...
COME ON. YOU GOT ME. I'M DOWN FOR LIFE, I'M FUCKED, JUST TELL ME WHERE I'M GOING.
QUEENS, MAN. WE'RE OVER QUEENS.
I GREW UP IN QUEENS.
YOU A METS FAN? LUCKY DAY FOR YOU, 'CUZ CAMP SHEA STADIUM IS GONNA BE YOUR NEW HOME, PERMANENTLY.
AIN'T QUITE THE SAME AS IT USED TO BE, THOUGH, HEH!
...
DID YOU SAY SHEA?
YOU GOTTA DO ME A FAVOR.
PLEASE.

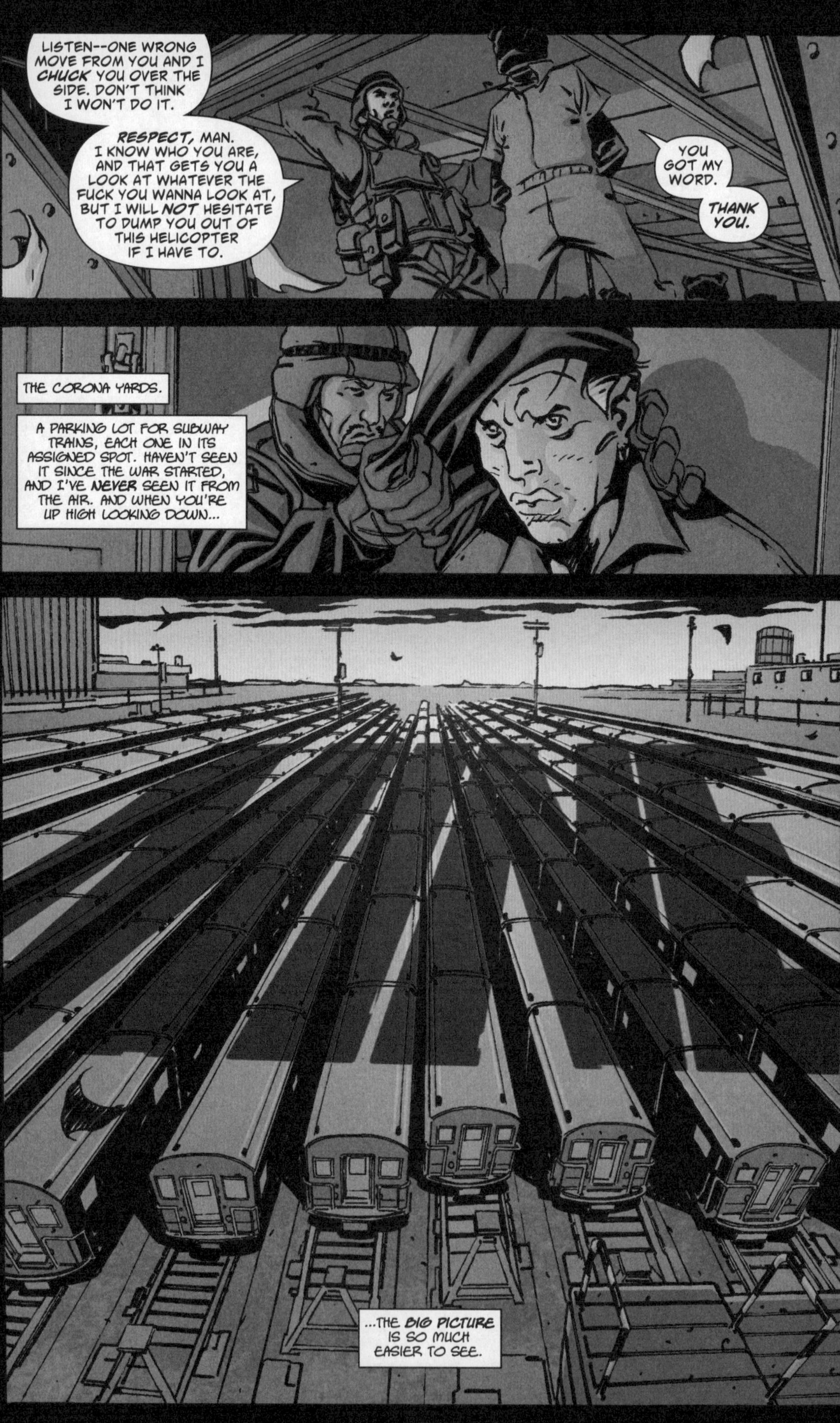
LISTEN--ONE WRONG MOVE FROM YOU AND I CHUCK YOU OVER THE SIDE. DON'T THINK I WON'T DO IT.
RESPECT, MAN. I KNOW WHO YOU ARE, AND THAT GETS YOU A LOOK AT WHATEVER THE FUCK YOU WANNA LOOK AT, BUT I WILL NOT HESITATE TO DUMP YOU OUT OF THIS HELICOPTER IF I HAVE TO.
YOU GOT MY WORD.
THANK YOU.
THE CORONA YARDS.
A PARKING LOT FOR SUBWAY TRAINS, EACH ONE IN ITS ASSIGNED SPOT. HAVEN'T SEEN IT SINCE THE WAR STARTED, AND I'VE NEVER SEEN IT FROM THE AIR. AND WHEN YOU'RE UP HIGH LOOKING DOWN...
...THE BIG PICTURE IS SO MUCH EASIER TO SEE.

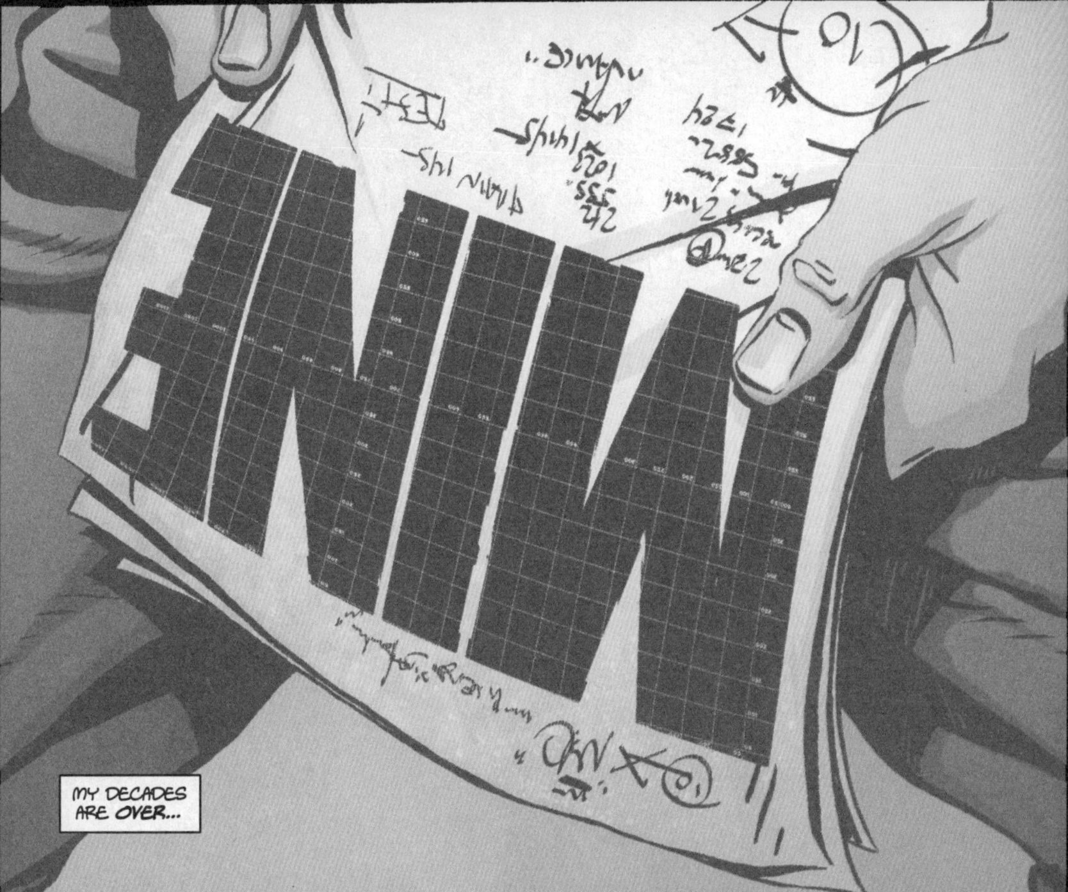
MY DECADES ARE OVER...

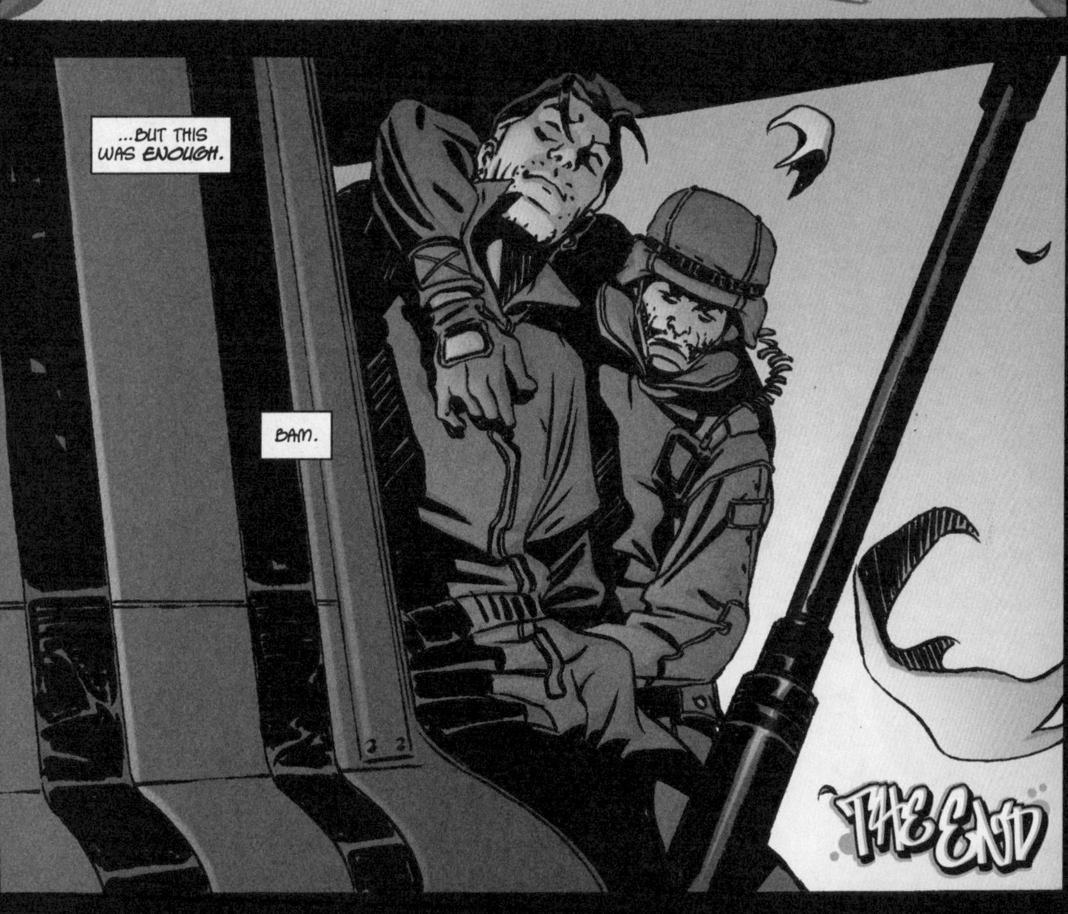
...BUT THIS WAS ENOUGH.
BAM.
THE END

شدهئش
AMINA

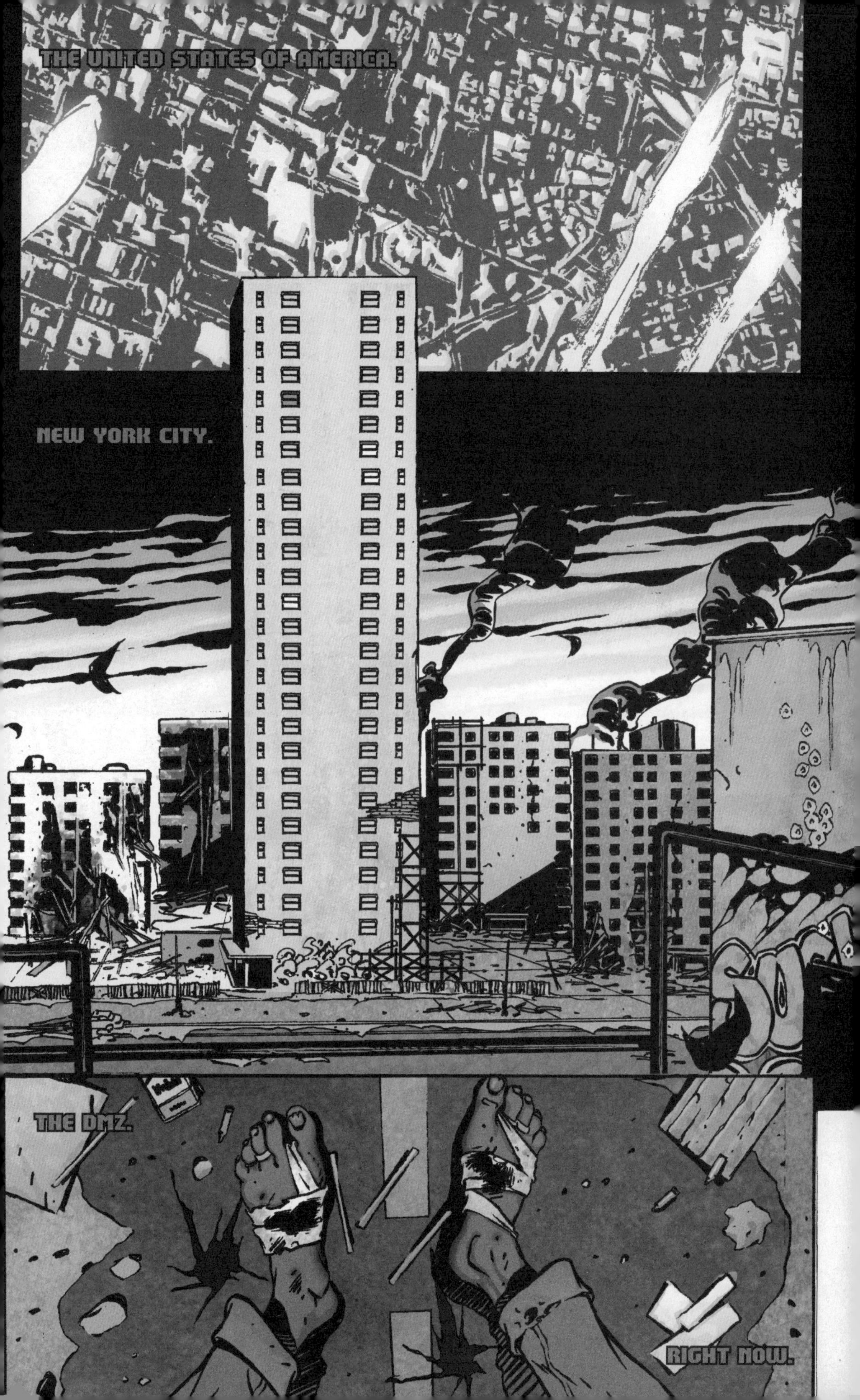
THE UNITED STATES OF AMERICA.
NEW YORK CITY.
THE DMZ.
RIGHT NOW.

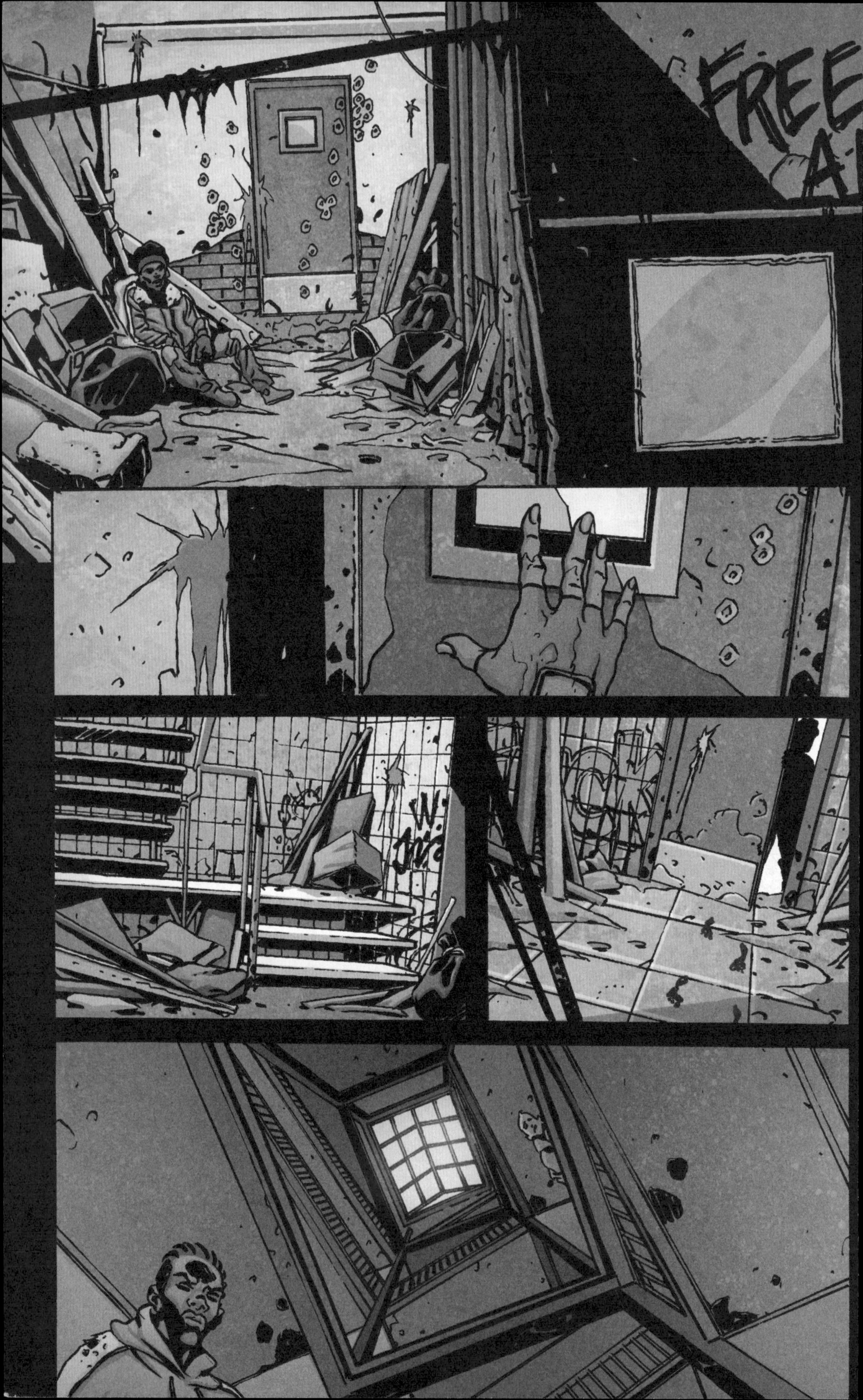

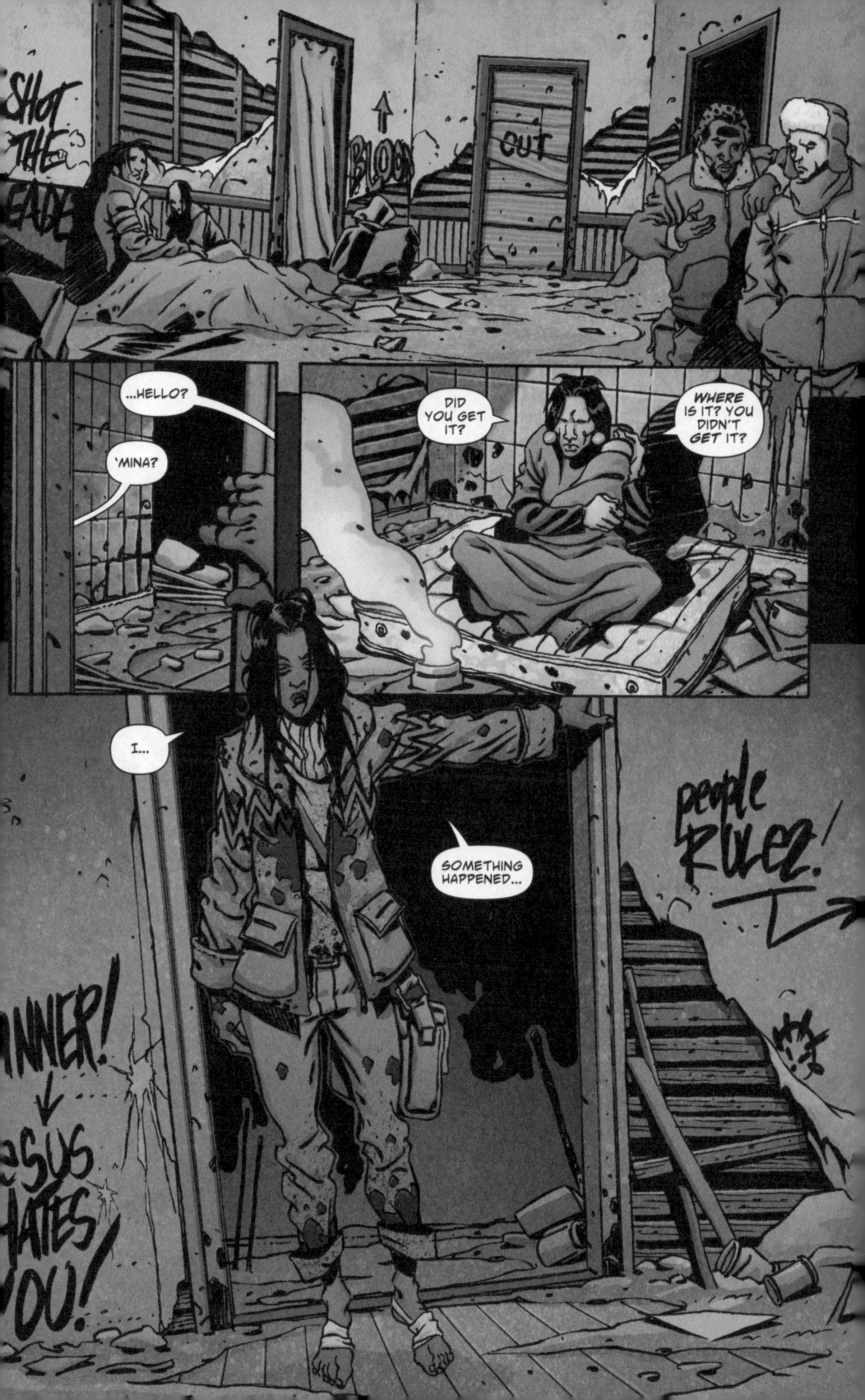
SHOT THE
OUT
...HELLO?
'MINA?
DID YOU GET IT?
WHERE IS IT? YOU DIDN'T GET IT?
I...
SOMETHING HAPPENED...
people RULEZ.

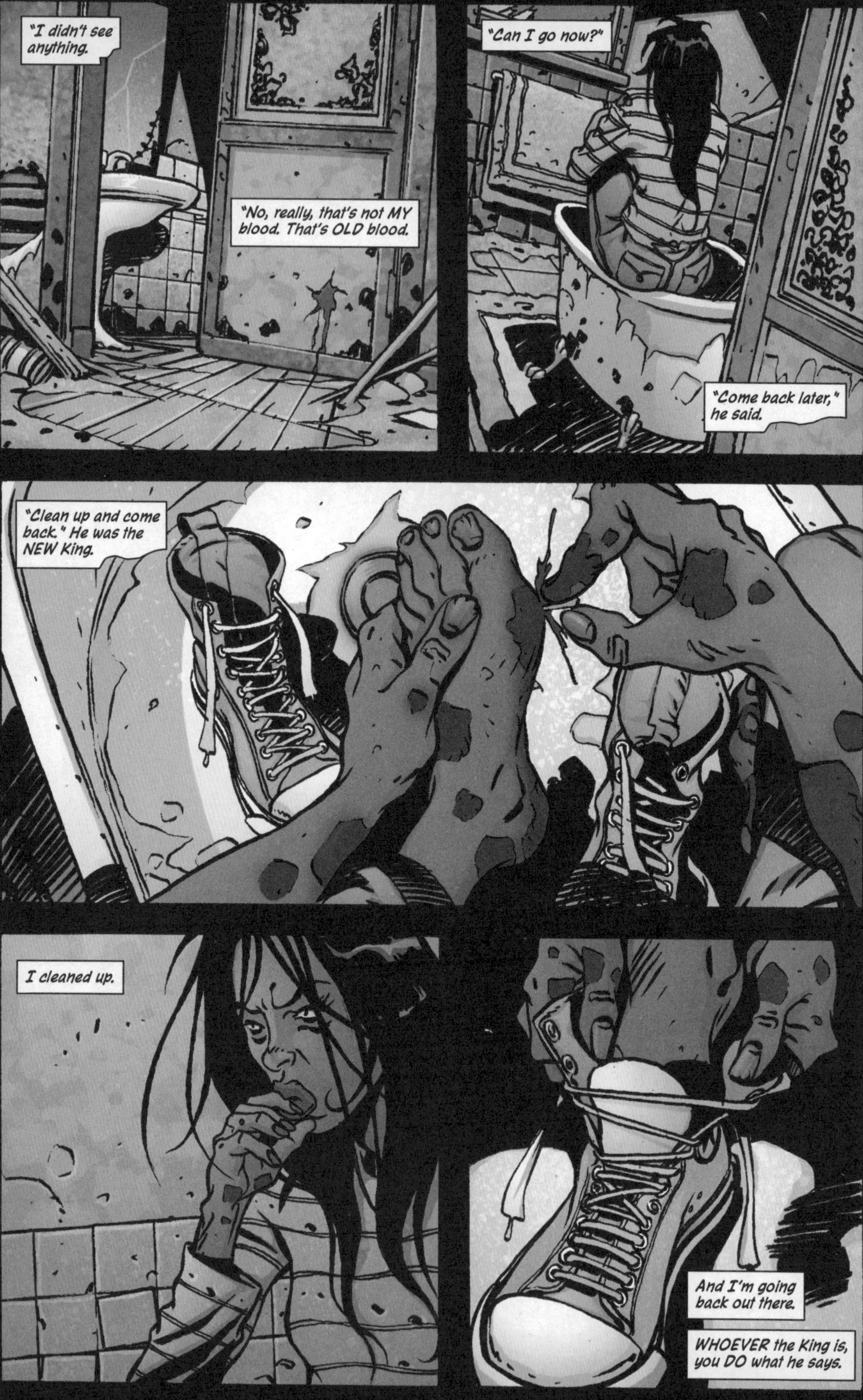
"I didn't see anything.
"No, really, that's not MY blood. That's OLD blood.
"Can I go now?"
"Come back later," he said.
"Clean up and come back." He was the NEW King.
I cleaned up.
And I'm going back out there.
WHOEVER the King is, you DO what he says.

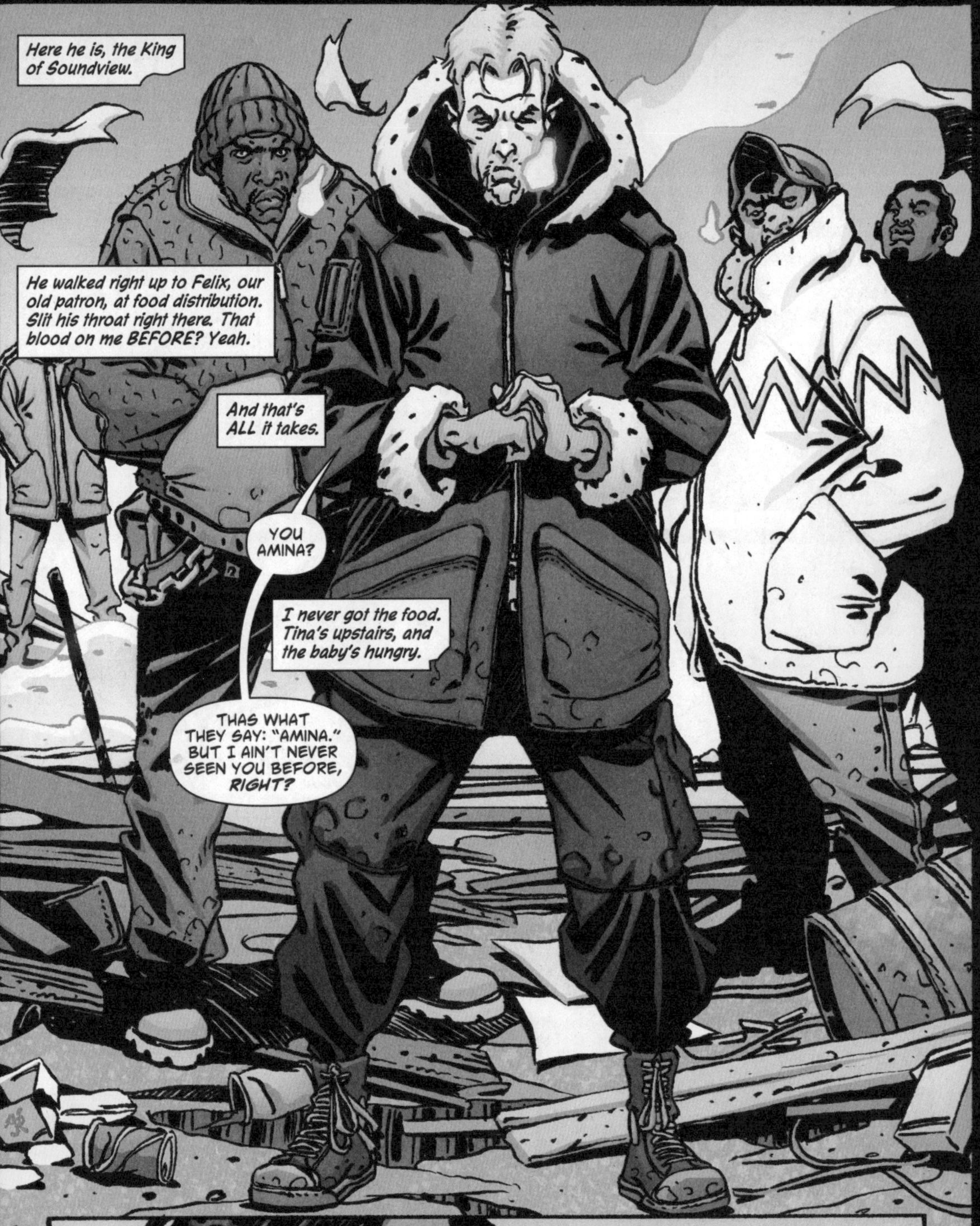
Here he is, the King of Soundview.
He walked right up to Felix, our old patron, at food distribution. Slit his throat right there. That blood on me BEFORE? Yeah.
And that's ALL it takes.
YOU AMINA?
I never got the food. Tina's upstairs, and the baby's hungry.
THAS WHAT THEY SAY: "AMINA." BUT I AIN'T NEVER SEEN YOU BEFORE, RIGHT?

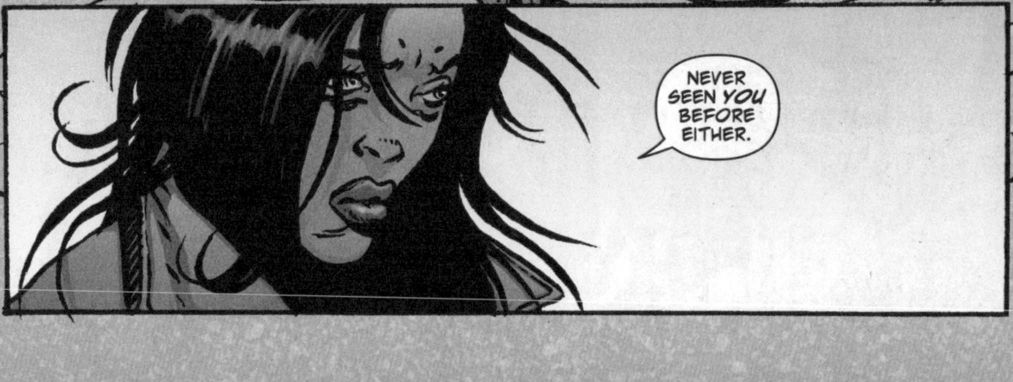
NEVER SEEN YOU BEFORE EITHER.

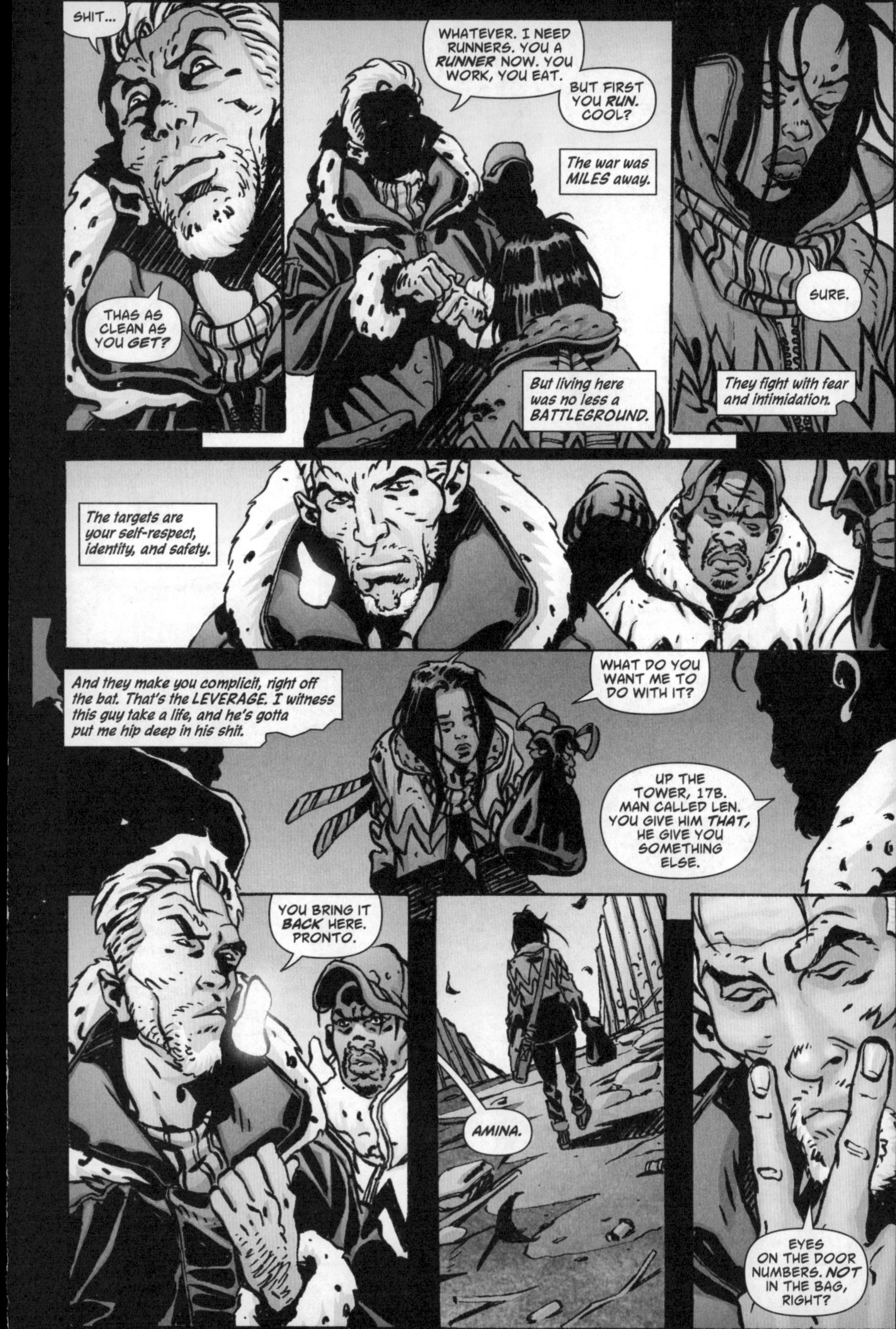
SHIT...
THAS AS CLEAN AS YOU GET?
WHATEVER. I NEED RUNNERS. YOU A RUNNER NOW. YOU WORK, YOU EAT.
BUT FIRST YOU RUN. COOL?
The war was MILES away.
But living here was no less a BATTLEGROUND.
SURE.
They fight with fear and intimidation.
The targets are your self-respect, identity, and safety.
And they make you complicit, right off the bat. That's the LEVERAGE. I witness this guy take a life, and he's gotta put me hip deep in his shit.
WHAT DO YOU WANT ME TO DO WITH IT?
UP THE TOWER, 17B. MAN CALLED LEN. YOU GIVE HIM THAT, HE GIVE YOU SOMETHING ELSE.
YOU BRING IT BACK HERE. PRONTO.
AMINA.
EYES ON THE DOOR NUMBERS. NOT IN THE BAG, RIGHT?

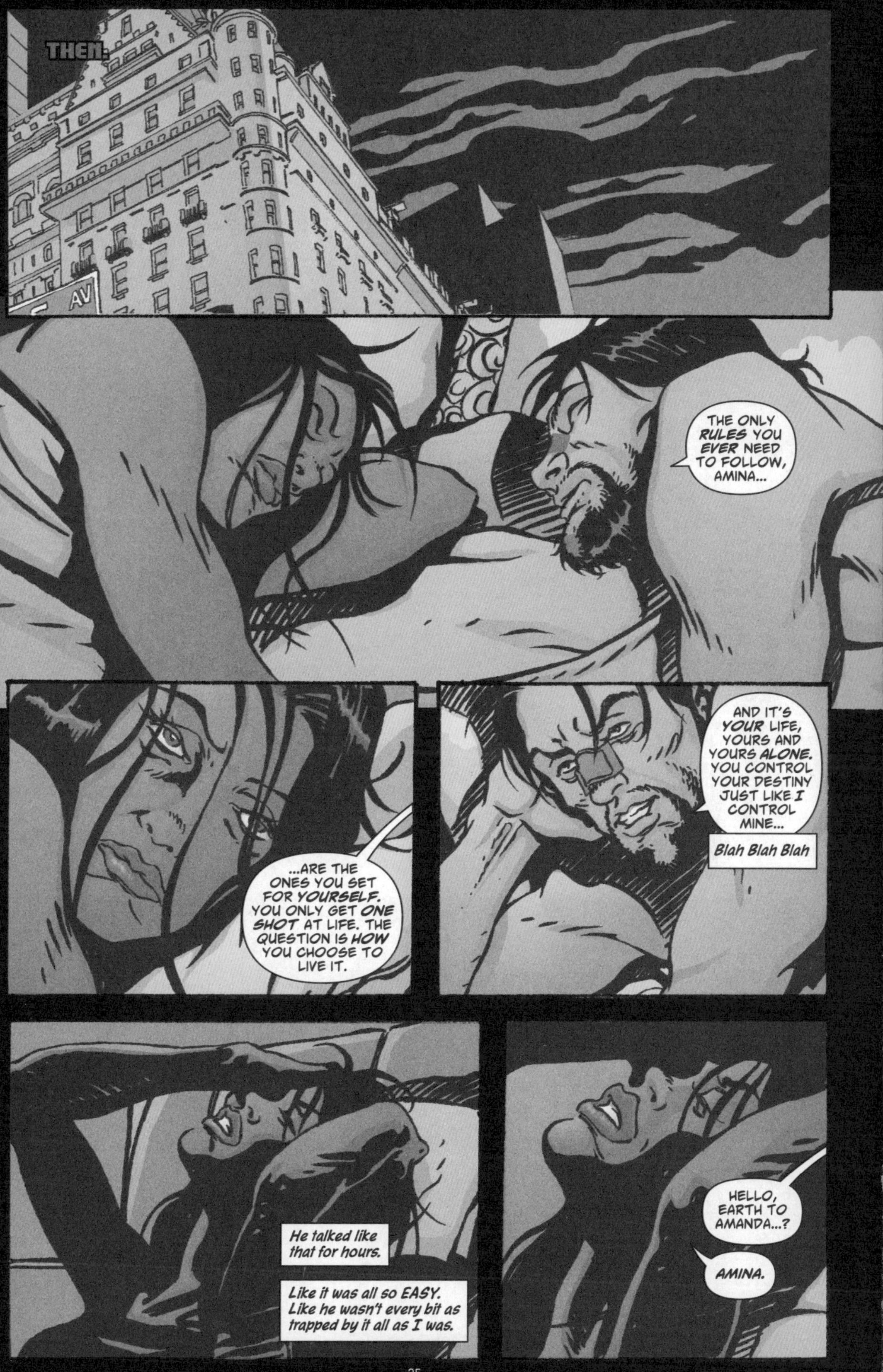
THEN.
THE ONLY RULES YOU EVER NEED TO FOLLOW, AMINA...
...ARE THE ONES YOU SET FOR YOURSELF. YOU ONLY GET ONE SHOT AT LIFE. THE QUESTION IS HOW YOU CHOOSE TO LIVE IT.
AND IT'S YOUR LIFE, YOURS AND YOURS ALONE. YOU CONTROL YOUR DESTINY JUST LIKE I CONTROL MINE...
Blah Blah Blah
He talked like that for hours.
Like it was all so EASY. Like he wasn't every bit as trapped by it all as I was.
HELLO, EARTH TO AMANDA...?
AMINA.

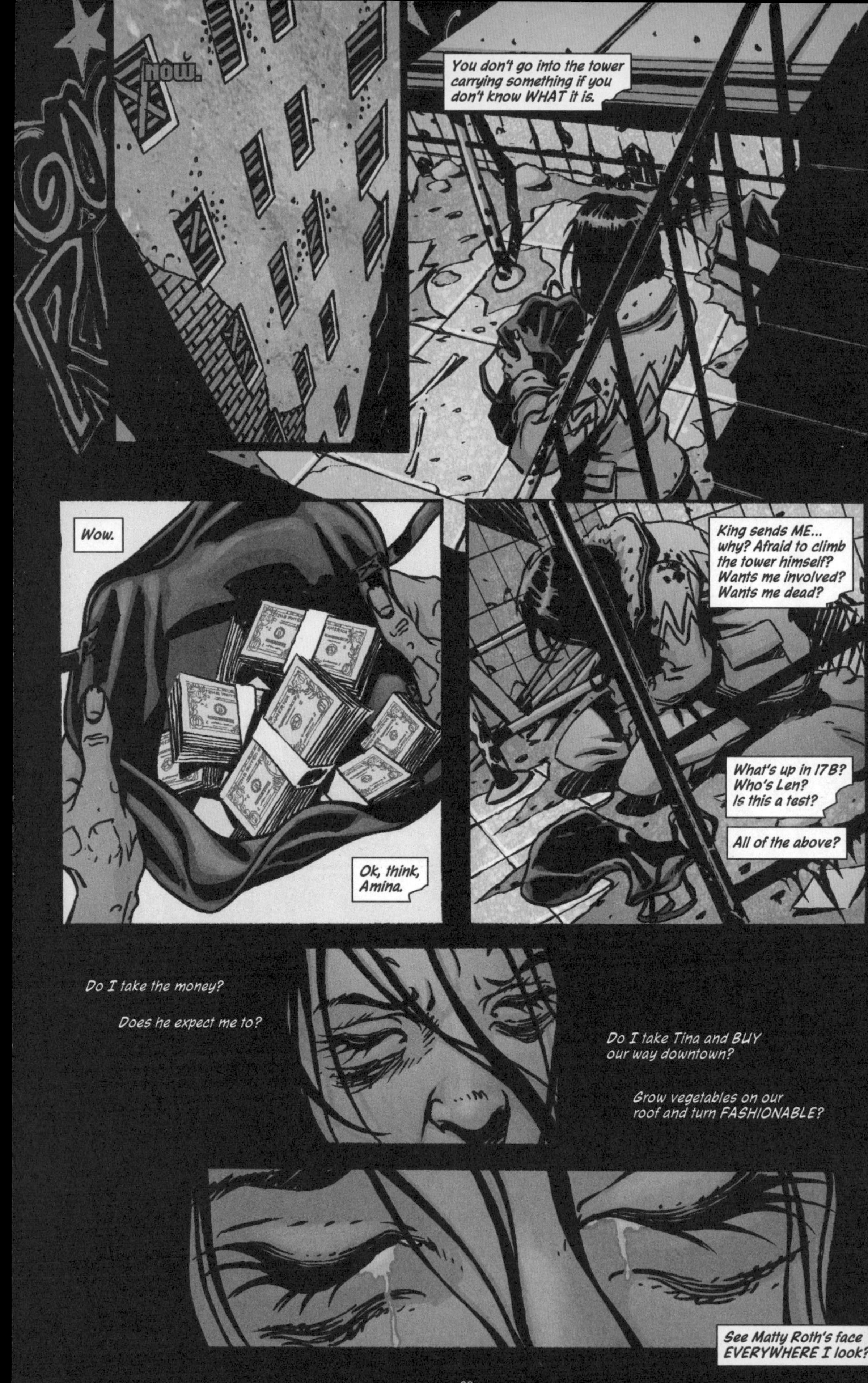
now.
You don't go into the tower carrying something if you don't know WHAT it is.
Wow.
Ok, think, Amina.
King sends ME... why? Afraid to climb the tower himself? Wants me involved? Wants me dead?
What's up in 17B? Who's Len? Is this a test?
All of the above?
Do I take the money?
Does he expect me to?
Do I take Tina and BUY our way downtown?
Grow vegetables on our roof and turn FASHIONABLE?
See Matty Roth's face EVERYWHERE I look?

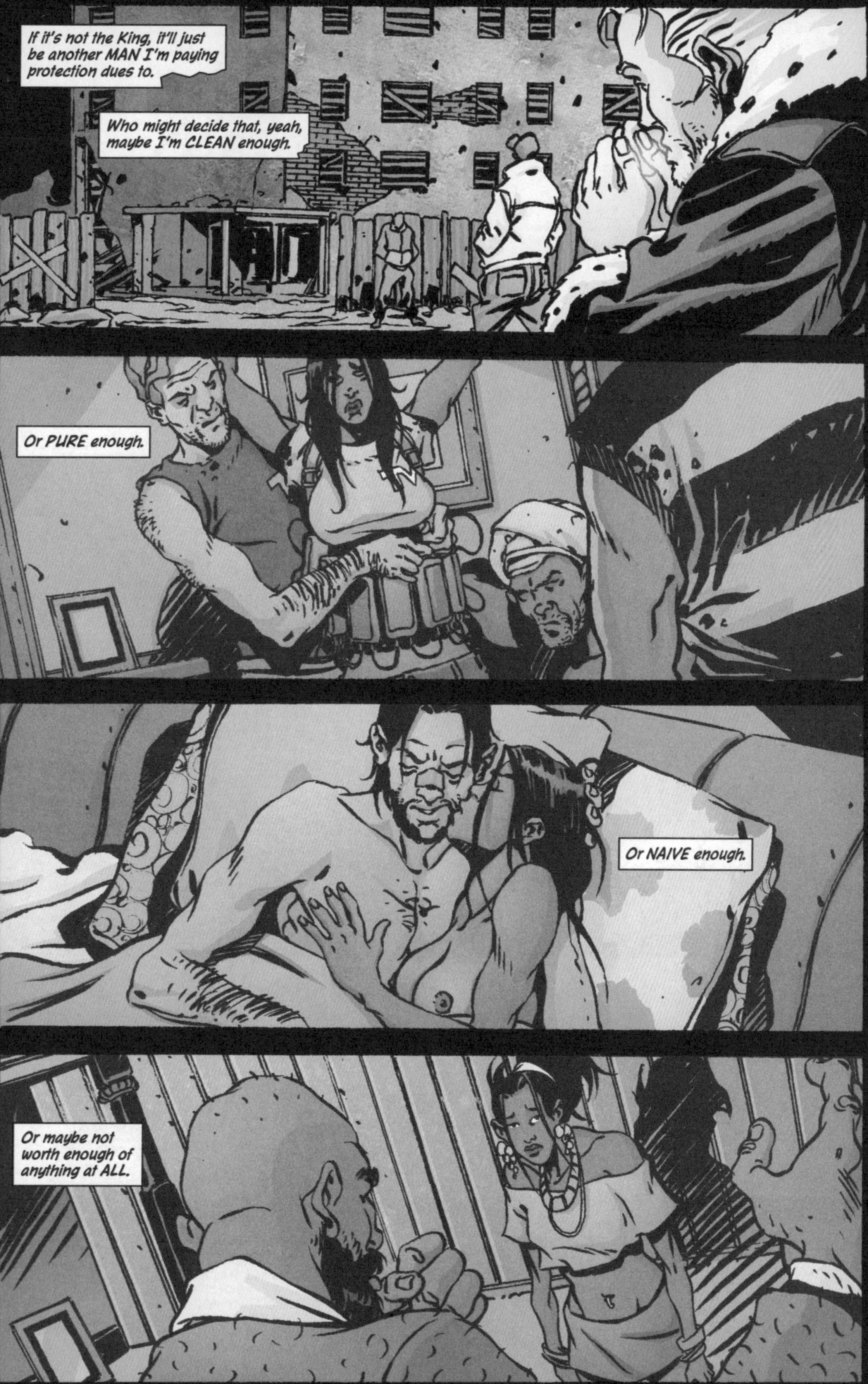

If it's not the King, it'll just be another MAN I'm paying protection dues to.
Who might decide that, yeah, maybe I'm CLEAN enough.
Or PURE enough.
Or NAIVE enough.
Or maybe not worth enough of anything at ALL.

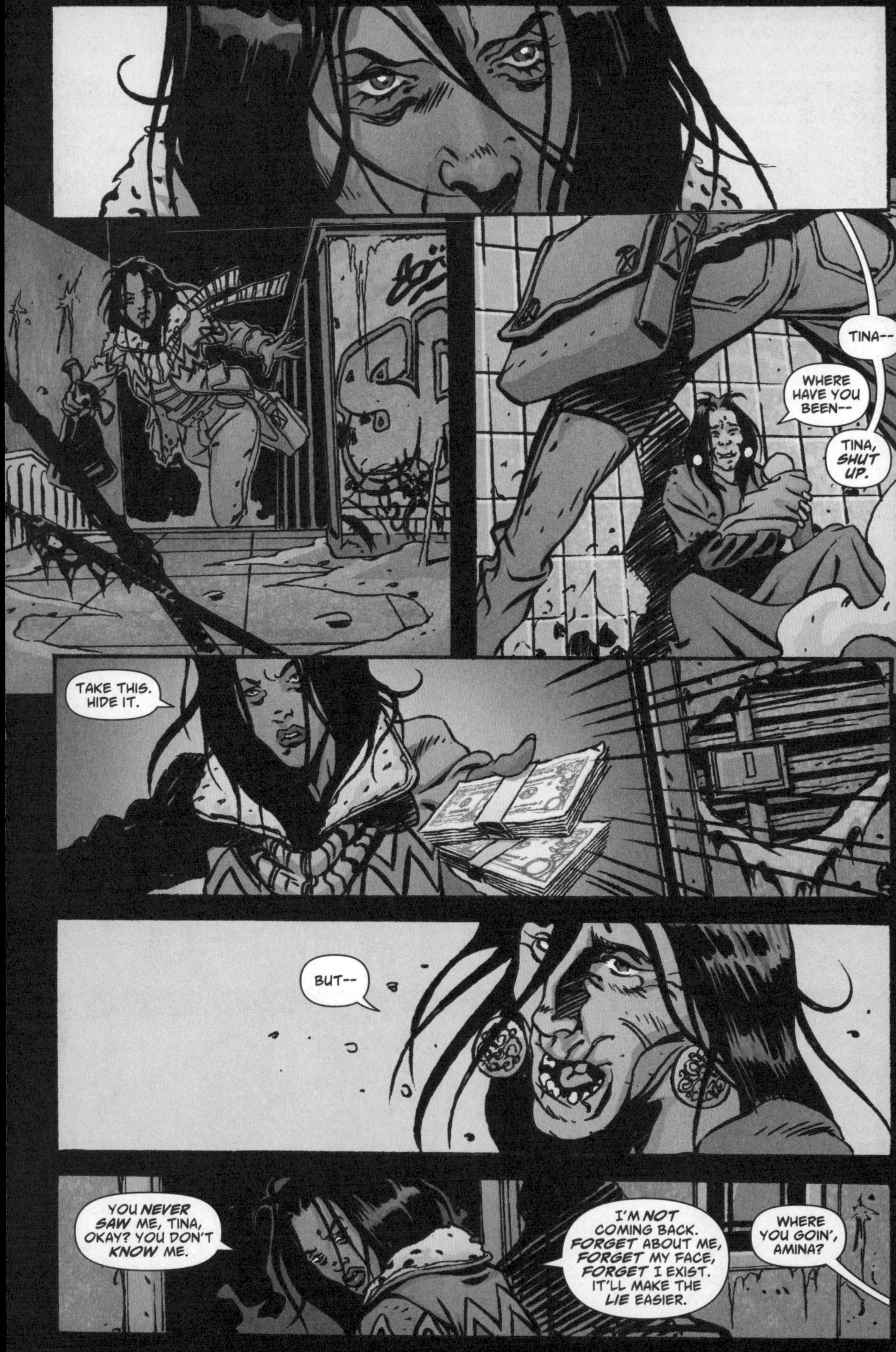
TINA--
WHERE HAVE YOU BEEN--
TINA, SHUT UP.
TAKE THIS. HIDE IT.
BUT--
YOU NEVER SAW ME, TINA, OKAY? YOU DON'T KNOW ME.
I'M NOT COMING BACK. FORGET ABOUT ME, FORGET MY FACE, FORGET I EXIST. IT'LL MAKE THE LIE EASIER.
WHERE YOU GOIN', AMINA?

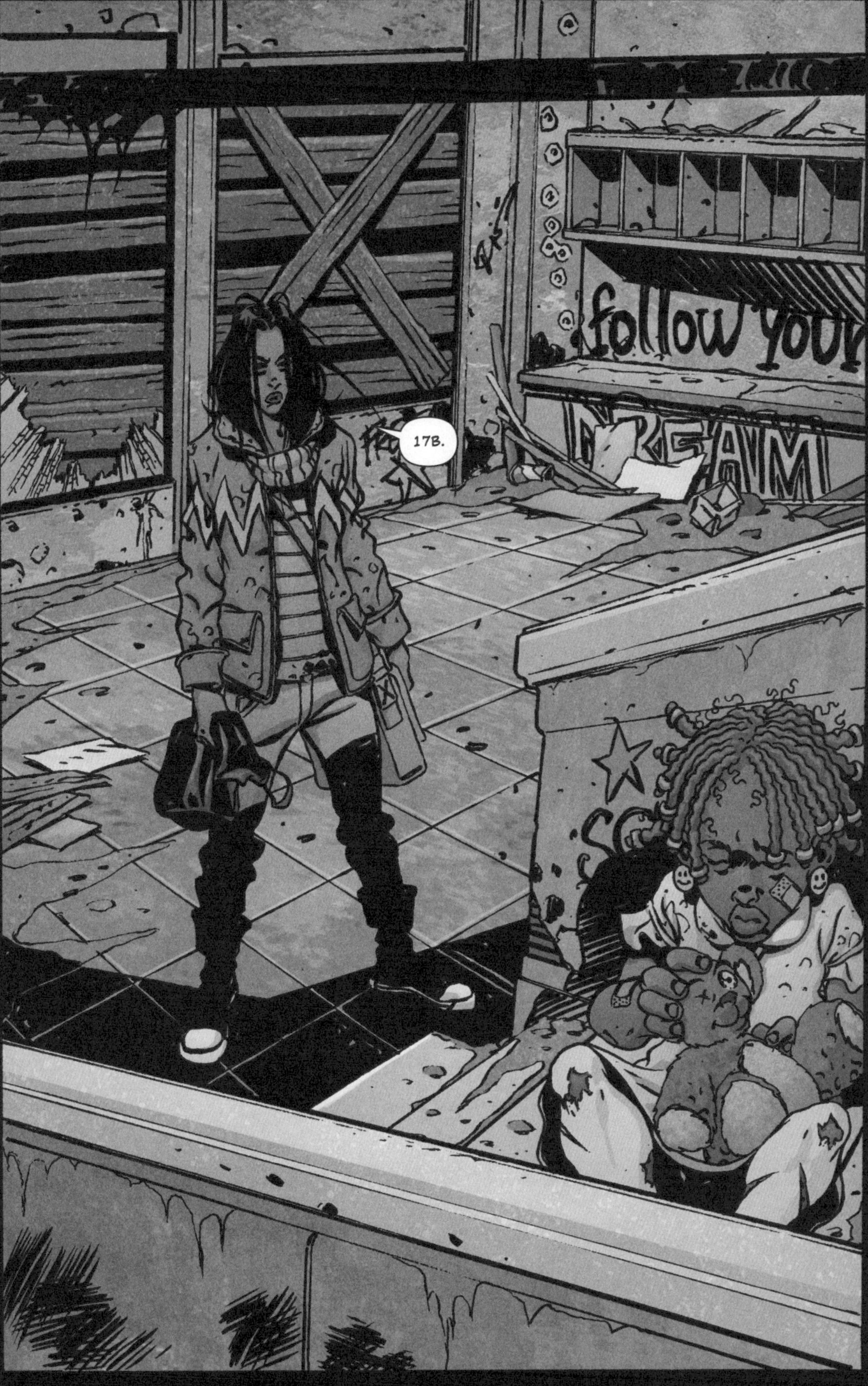
17B.
follow you

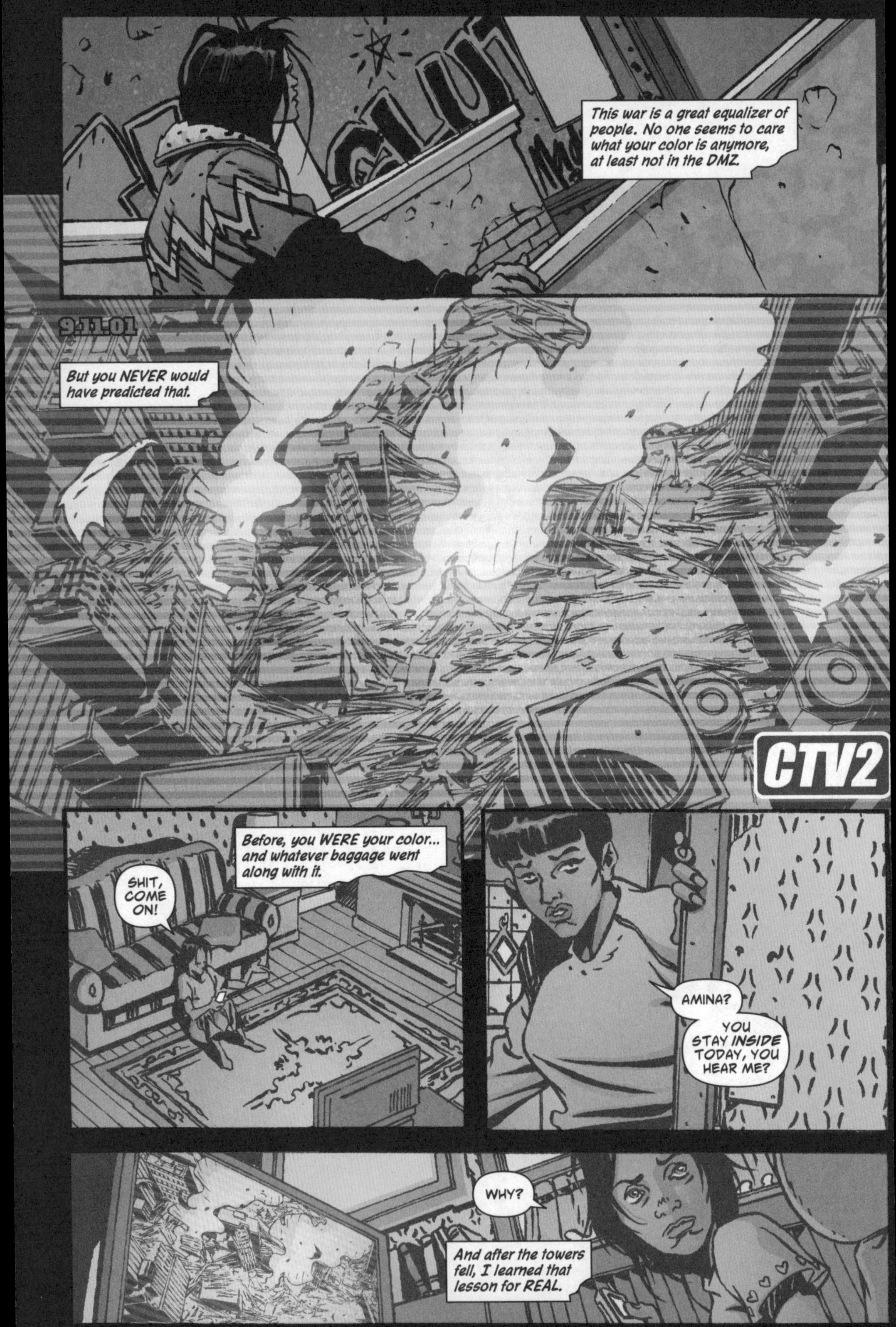
This war is a great equalizer of people. No one seems to care what your color is anymore, at least not in the DMZ.
9.11.01
But you NEVER would have predicted that.
CTV2
Before, you WERE your color... and whatever baggage went along with it.
SHIT, COME ON!
AMINA?
YOU STAY INSIDE TODAY, YOU HEAR ME?
WHY?
And after the towers fell, I learned that lesson for REAL.

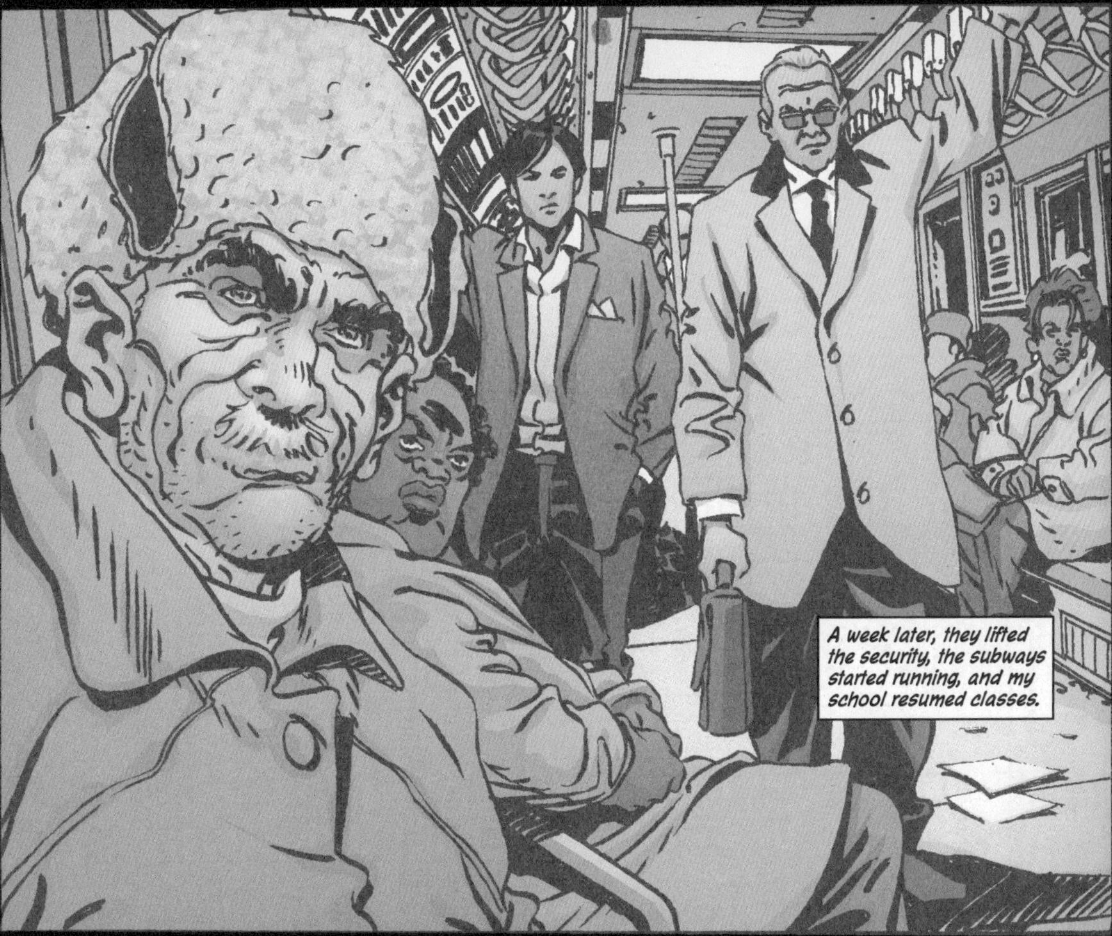
A week later, they lifted the security, the subways started running, and my school resumed classes.

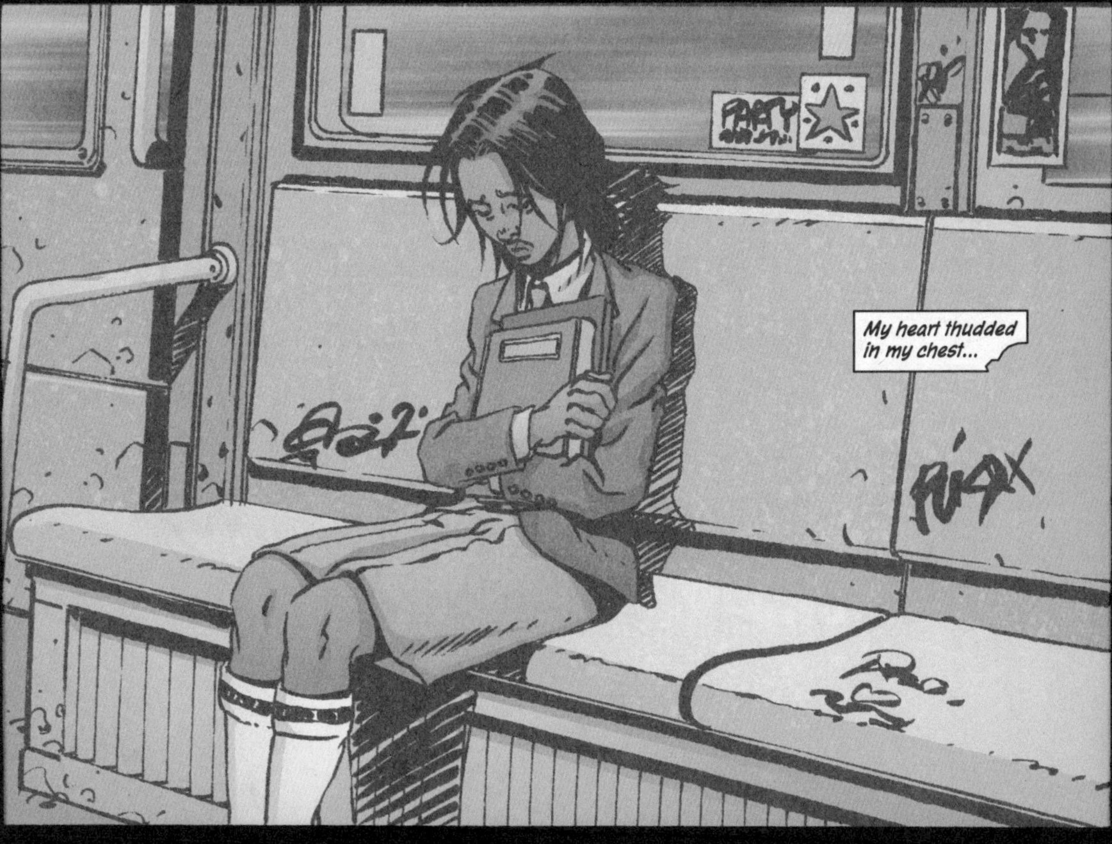
My heart thudded in my chest...

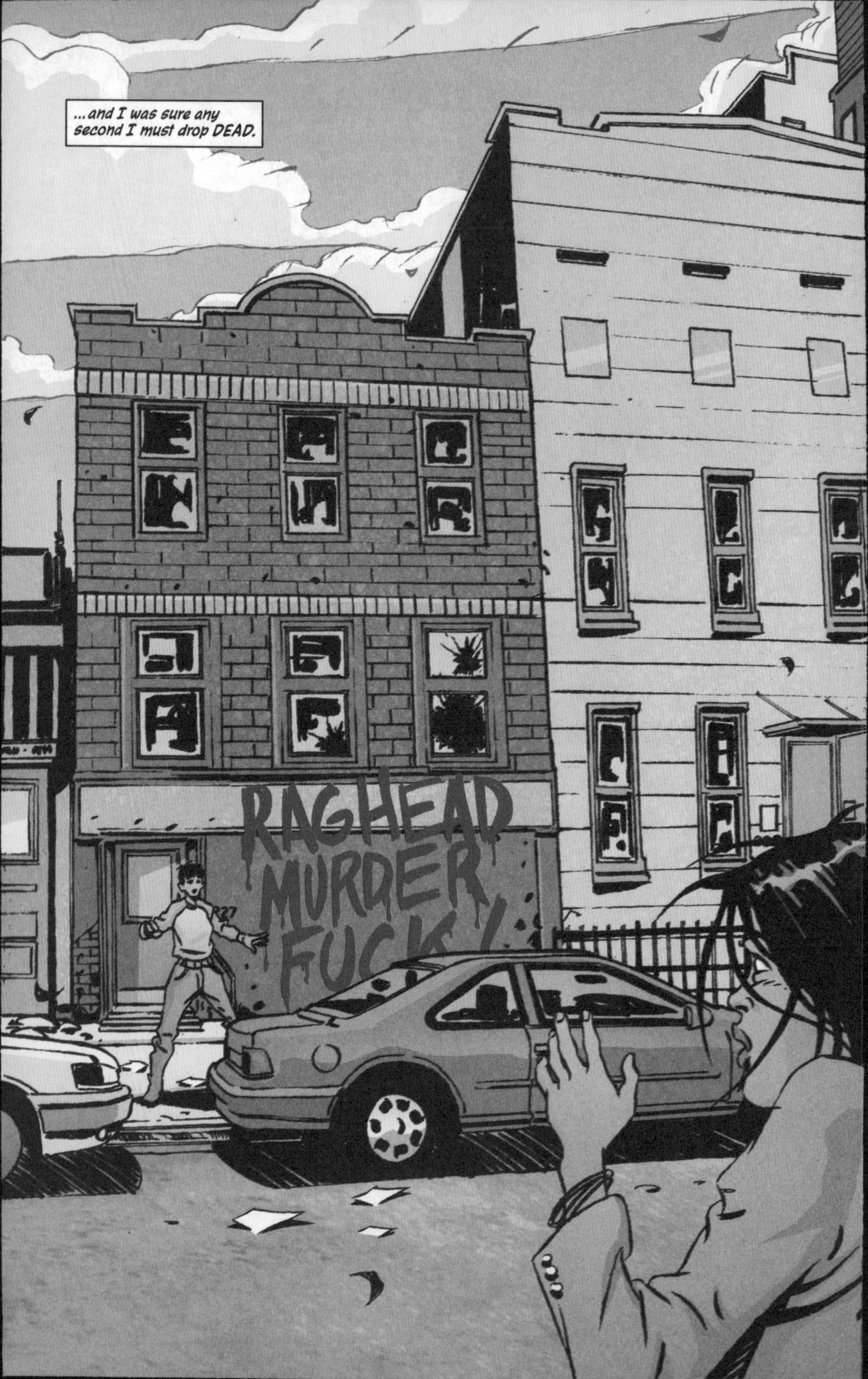
...and I was sure any second I must drop DEAD.
RAGHEAD MURDER FUCK!

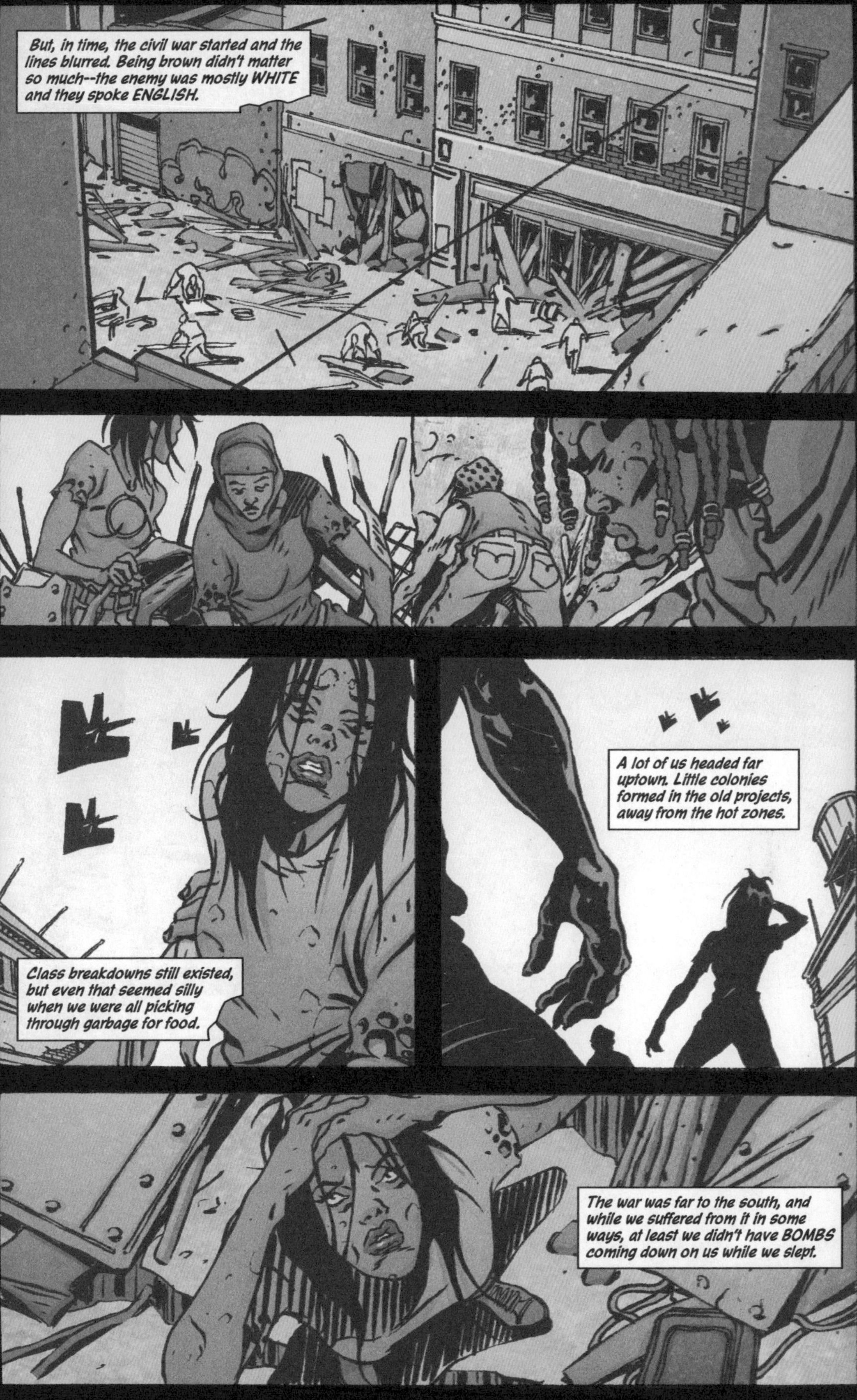
But, in time, the civil war started and the lines blurred. Being brown didn't matter so much--the enemy was mostly WHITE and they spoke ENGLISH.
Class breakdowns still existed, but even that seemed silly when we were all picking through garbage for food.
A lot of us headed far uptown. Little colonies formed in the old projects, away from the hot zones.
The war was far to the south, and while we suffered from it in some ways, at least we didn't have BOMBS coming down on us while we slept.

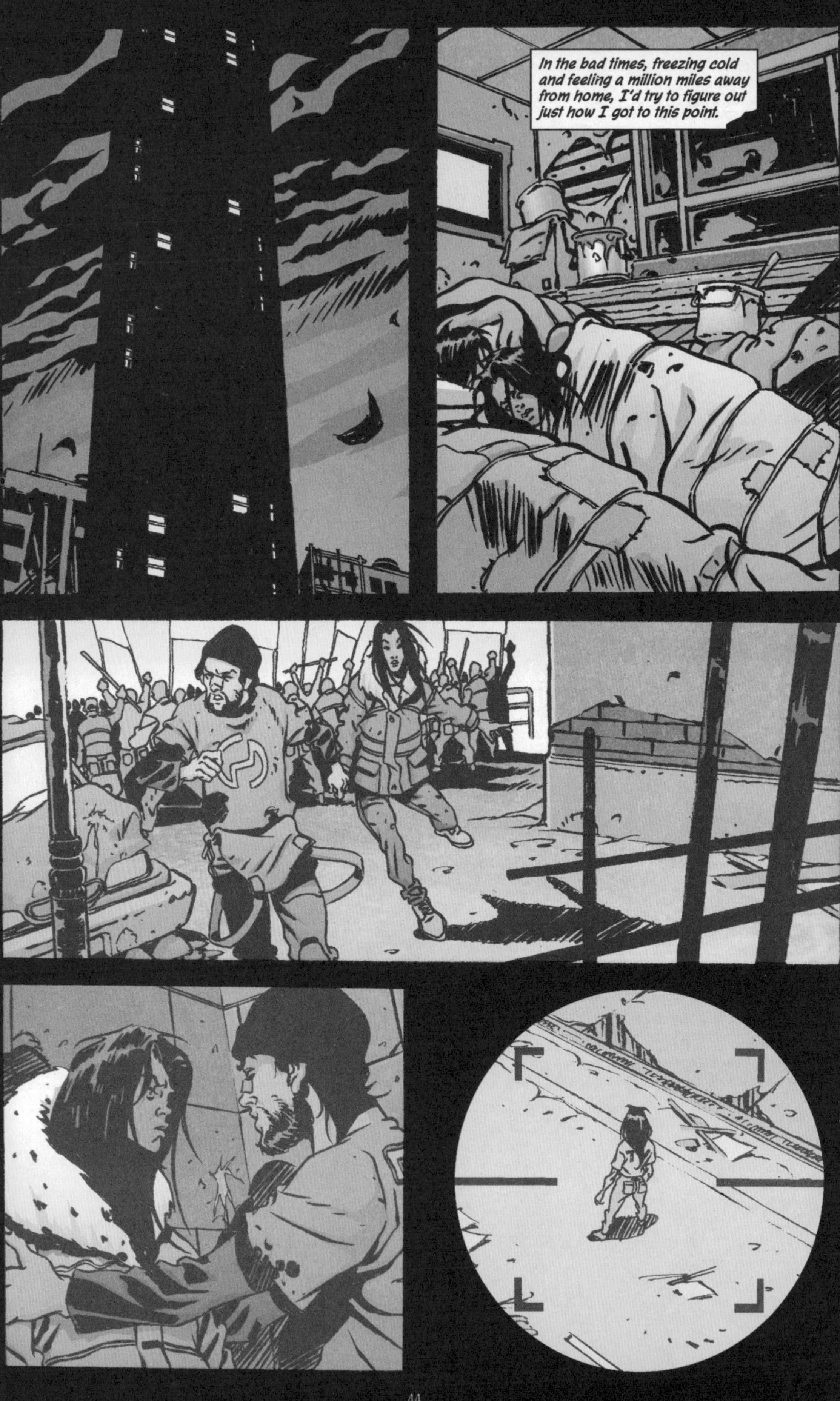
In the bad times, freezing cold and feeling a million miles away from home, I'd try to figure out just how I got to this point.

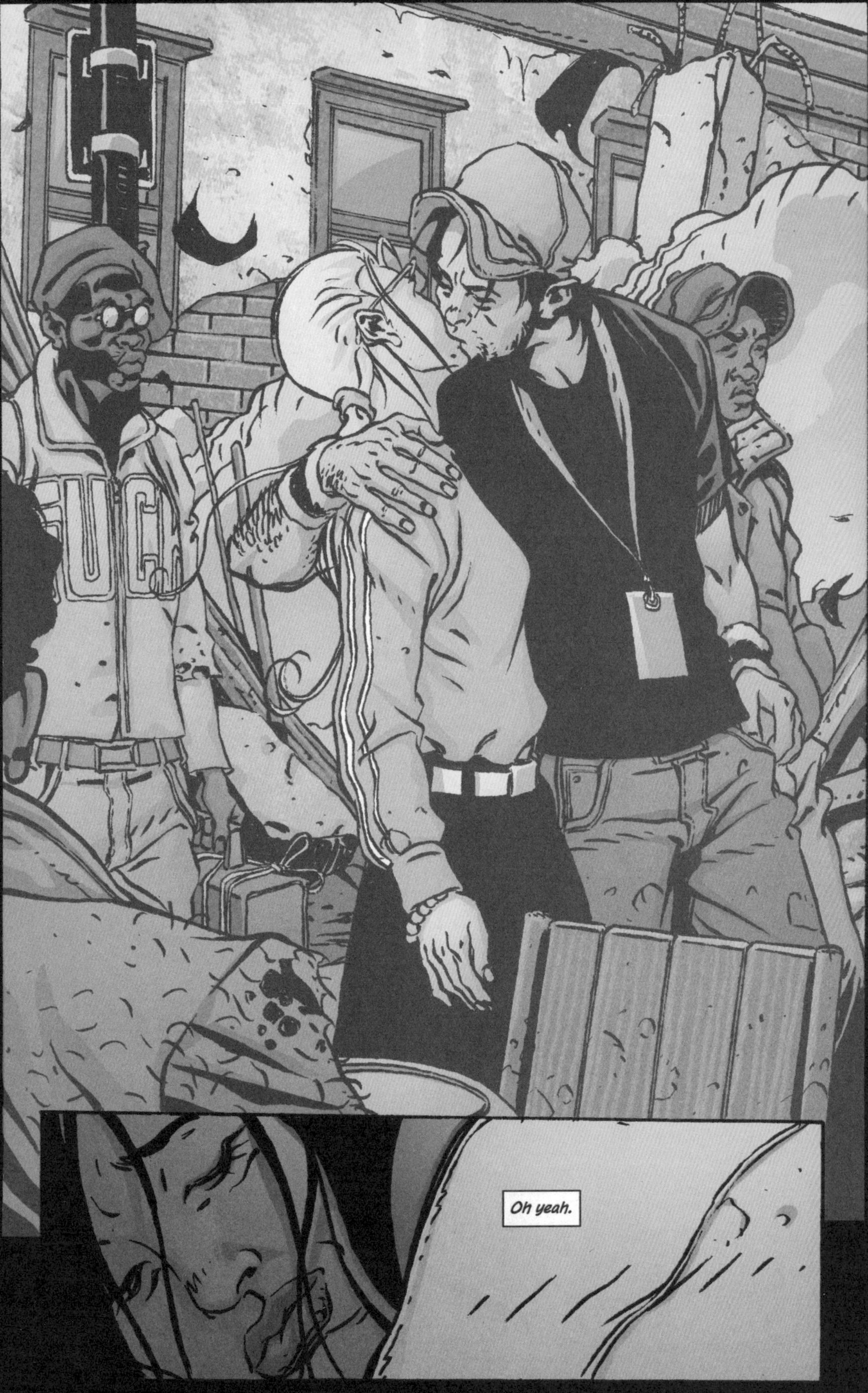
Oh yeah.

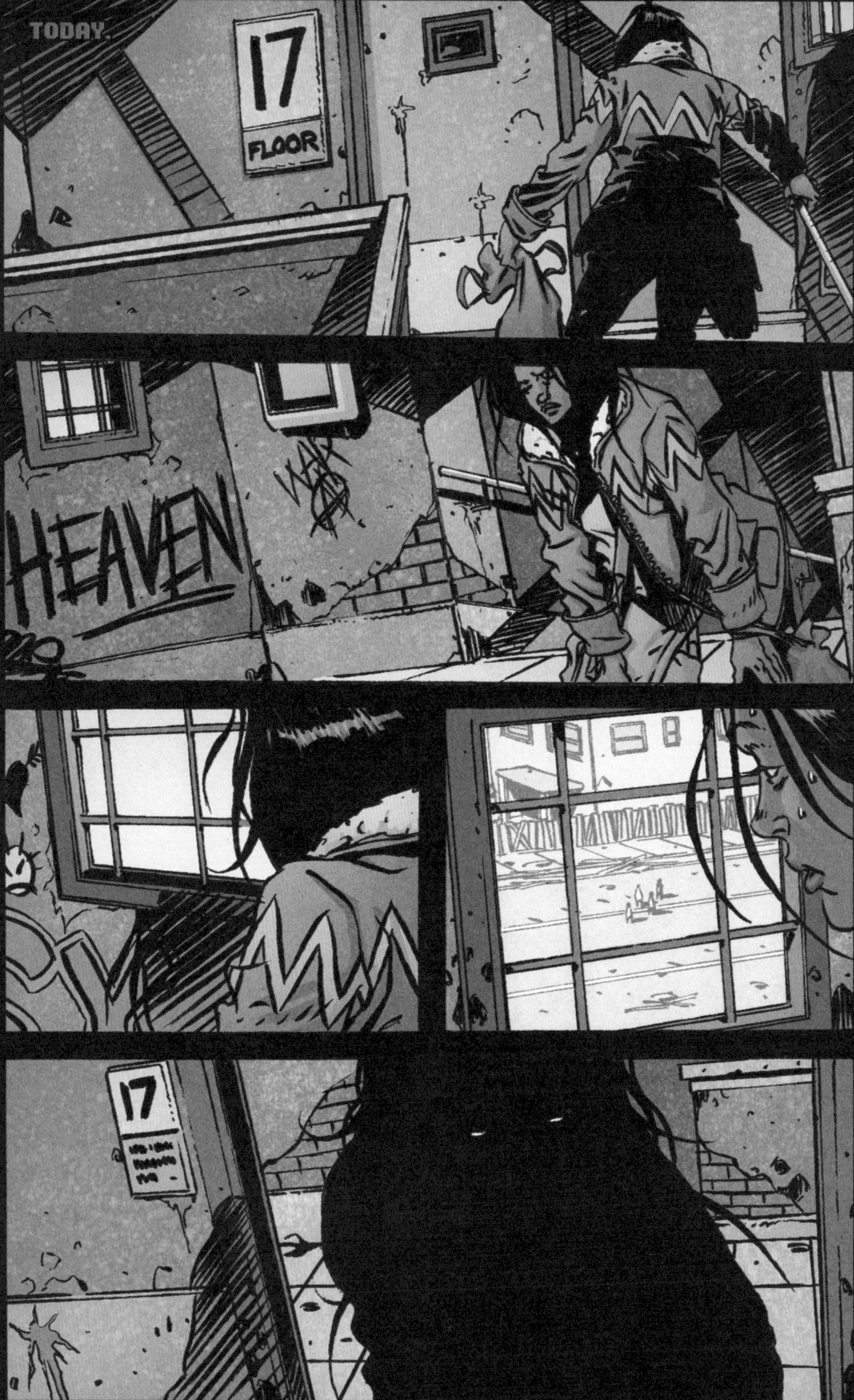
TODAY.
17
FLOOR
HEAVEN
17

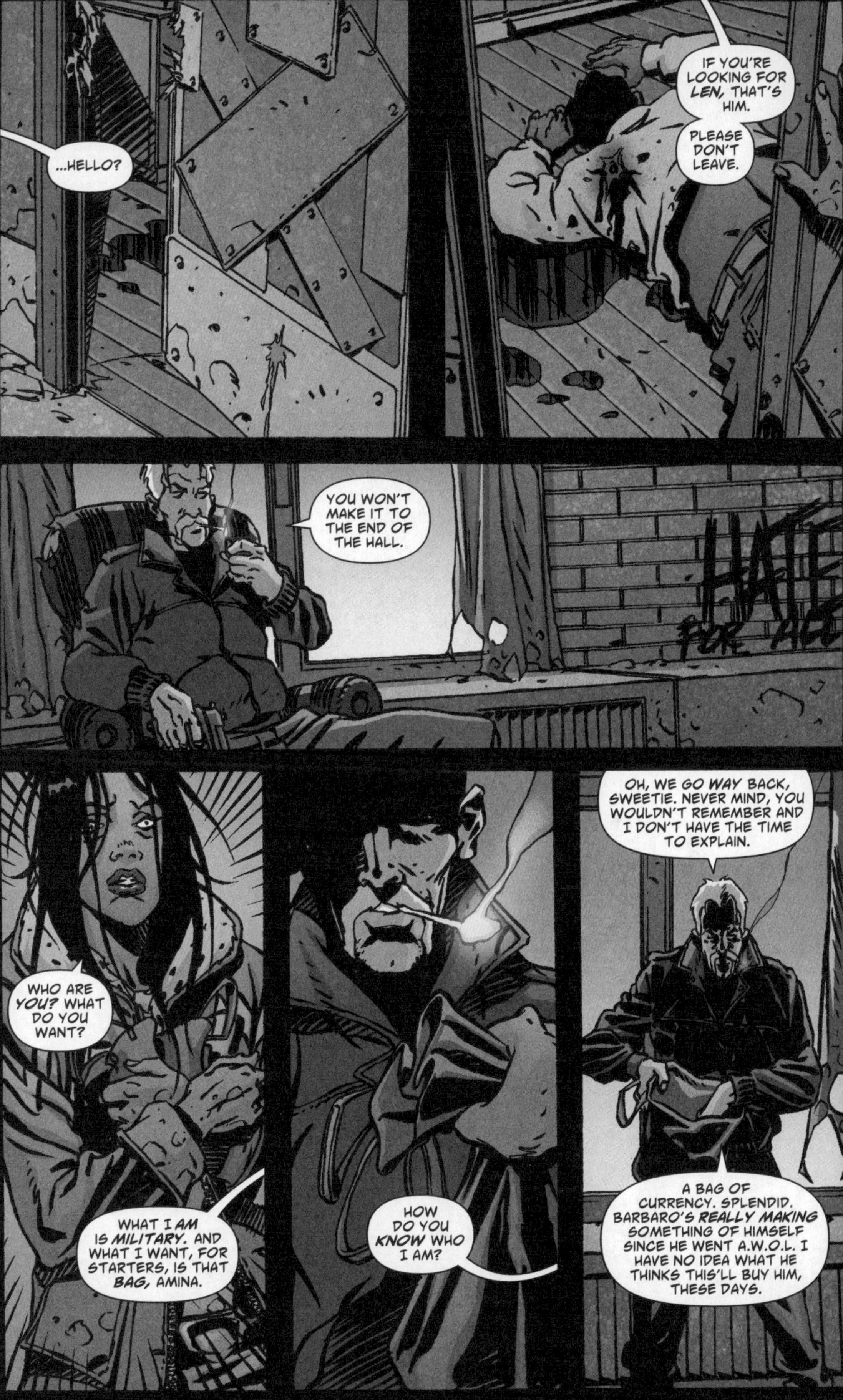

...HELLO?
IF YOU'RE LOOKING FOR LEN, THAT'S HIM.
PLEASE DON'T LEAVE.
YOU WON'T MAKE IT TO THE END OF THE HALL.
WHO ARE YOU? WHAT DO YOU WANT?
WHAT I AM IS MILITARY. AND WHAT I WANT, FOR STARTERS, IS THAT BAG, AMINA.
HOW DO YOU KNOW WHO I AM?
OH, WE GO WAY BACK, SWEETIE. NEVER MIND, YOU WOULDN'T REMEMBER AND I DON'T HAVE THE TIME TO EXPLAIN.
A BAG OF CURRENCY. SPLENDID. BARBARO'S REALLY MAKING SOMETHING OF HIMSELF SINCE HE WENT A.W.O.L. I HAVE NO IDEA WHAT HE THINKS THIS'LL BUY HIM, THESE DAYS.

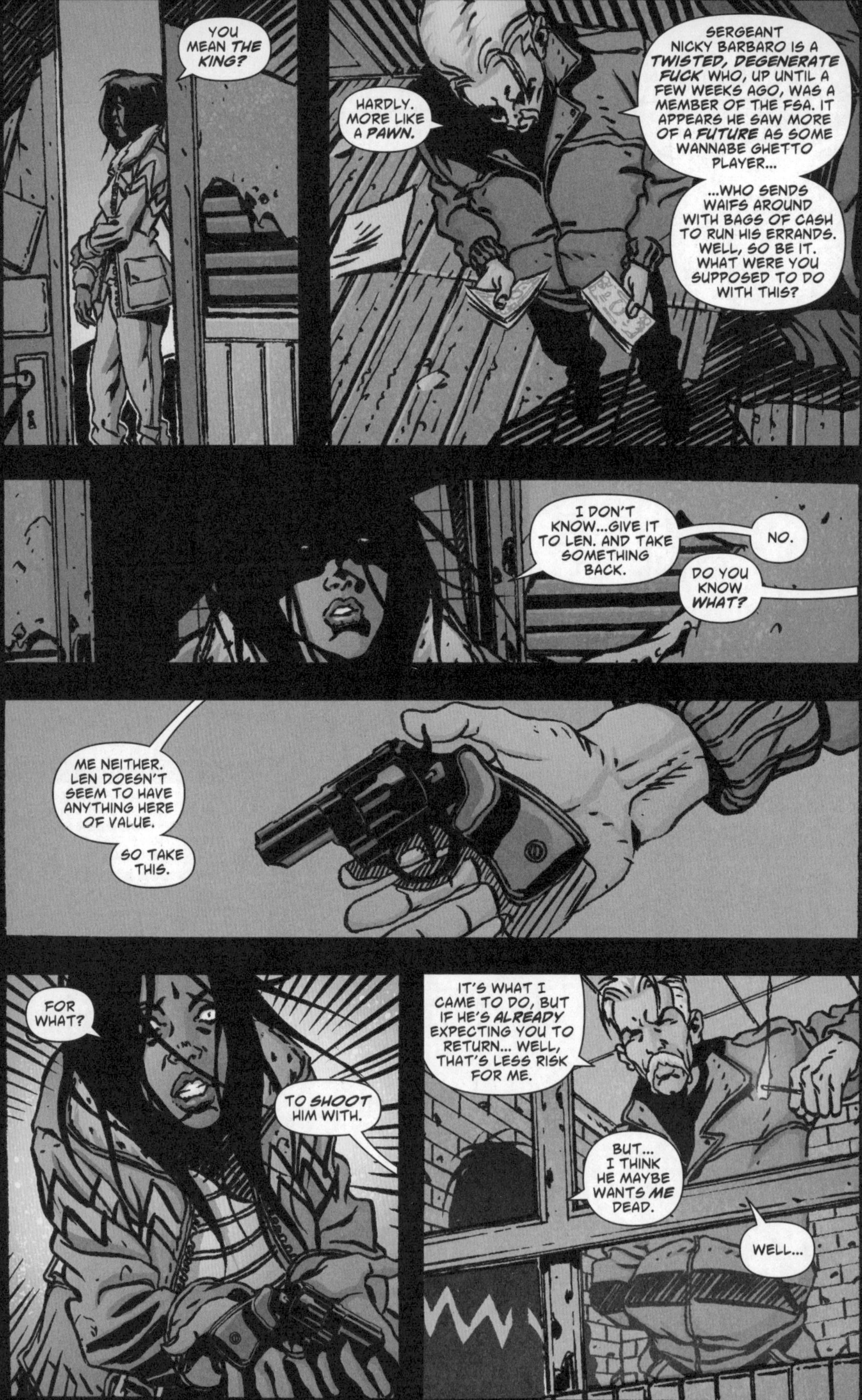
YOU MEAN THE KING?
HARDLY. MORE LIKE A PAWN.
SERGEANT NICKY BARBARO IS A TWISTED, DEGENERATE FUCK WHO, UP UNTIL A FEW WEEKS AGO, WAS A MEMBER OF THE FSA. IT APPEARS HE SAW MORE OF A FUTURE AS SOME WANNABE GHETTO PLAYER...
...WHO SENDS WAIFS AROUND WITH BAGS OF CASH TO RUN HIS ERRANDS. WELL, SO BE IT. WHAT WERE YOU SUPPOSED TO DO WITH THIS?
I DON'T KNOW...GIVE IT TO LEN. AND TAKE SOMETHING BACK.
NO.
DO YOU KNOW WHAT?
ME NEITHER. LEN DOESN'T SEEM TO HAVE ANYTHING HERE OF VALUE.
SO TAKE THIS.
FOR WHAT?
TO SHOOT HIM WITH.
IT'S WHAT I CAME TO DO, BUT IF HE'S ALREADY EXPECTING YOU TO RETURN... WELL, THAT'S LESS RISK FOR ME.
BUT... I THINK HE MAYBE WANTS ME DEAD.
WELL...

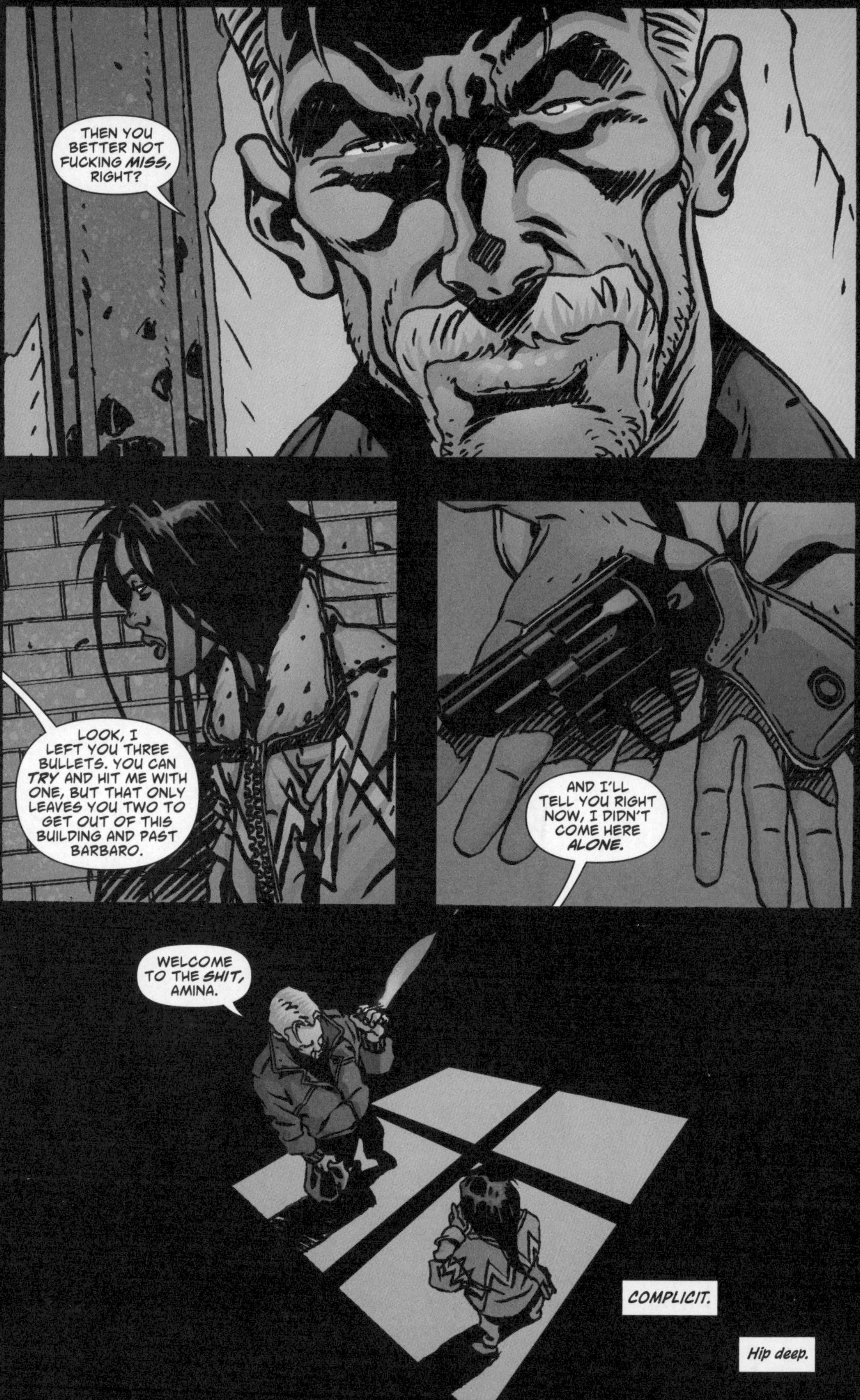
THEN YOU BETTER NOT FUCKING *MISS*, RIGHT?
LOOK, I LEFT YOU THREE BULLETS. YOU CAN *TRY* AND HIT ME WITH ONE, BUT THAT ONLY LEAVES YOU TWO TO GET OUT OF THIS BUILDING AND PAST BARBARO.
AND I'LL TELL YOU RIGHT NOW, I DIDN'T COME HERE *ALONE*.
WELCOME TO THE *SHIT*, AMINA.
COMPLICIT.
Hip deep.

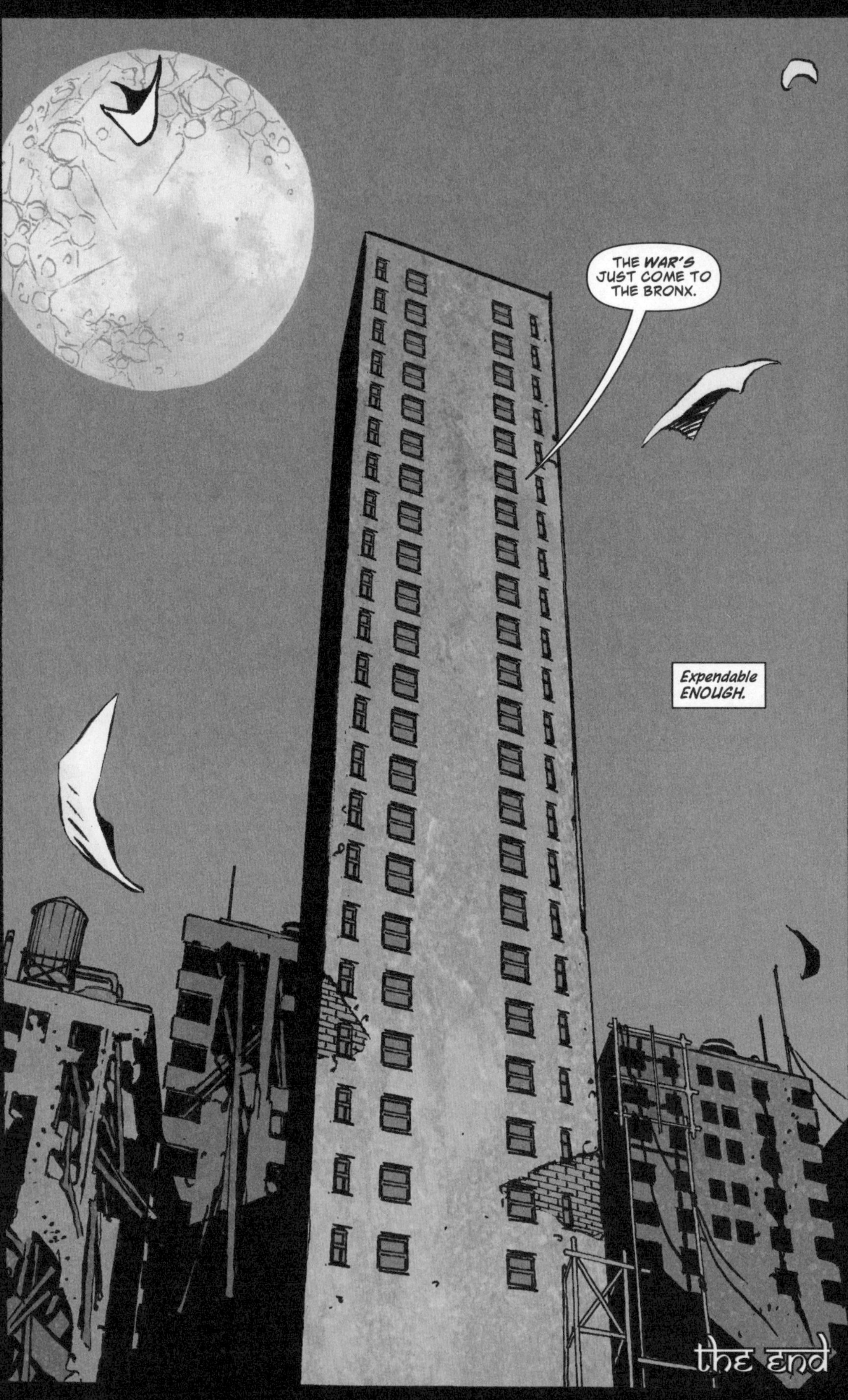
THE WAR'S JUST COME TO THE BRONX.
Expendable ENOUGH.
THE END

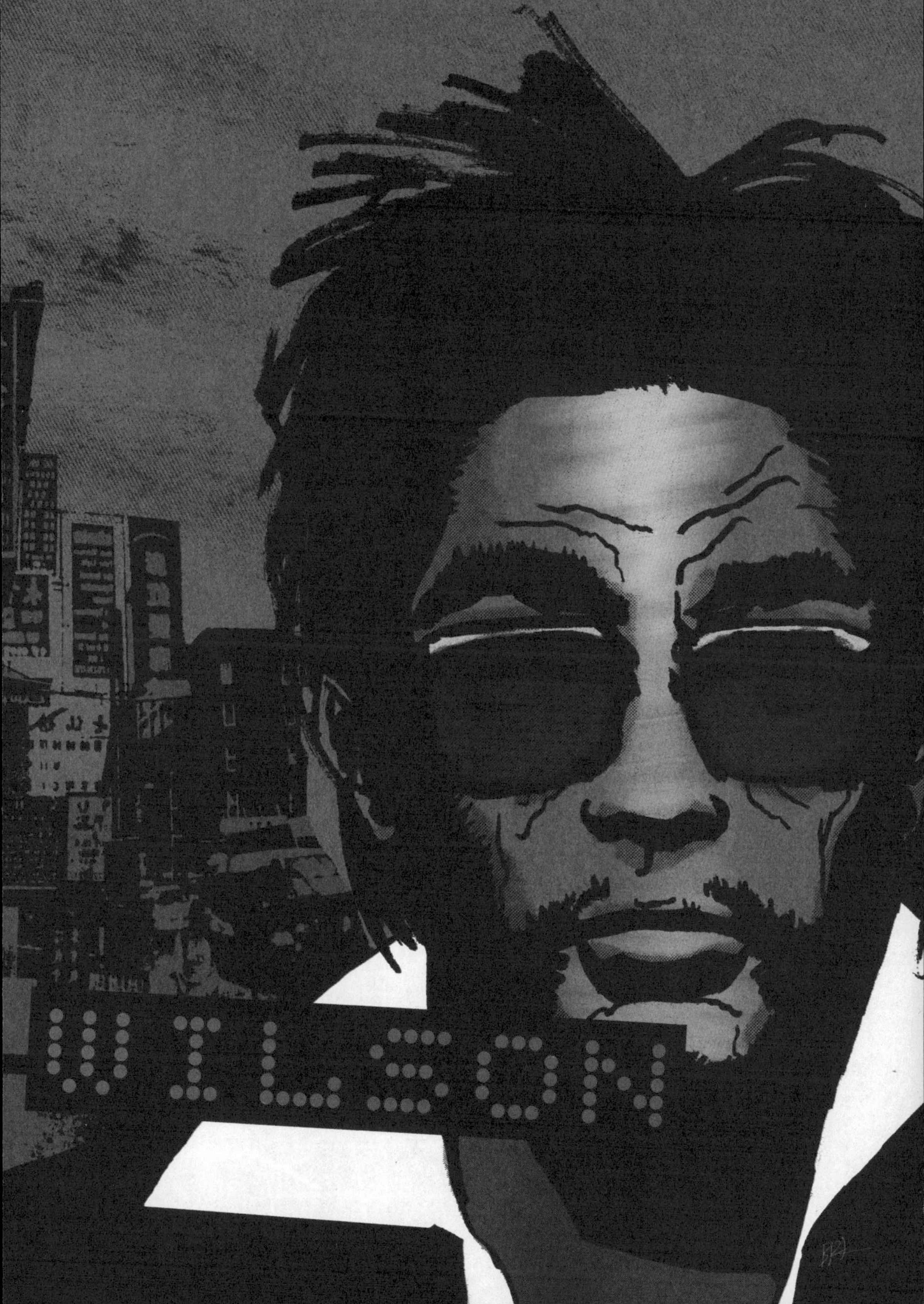
WILSON

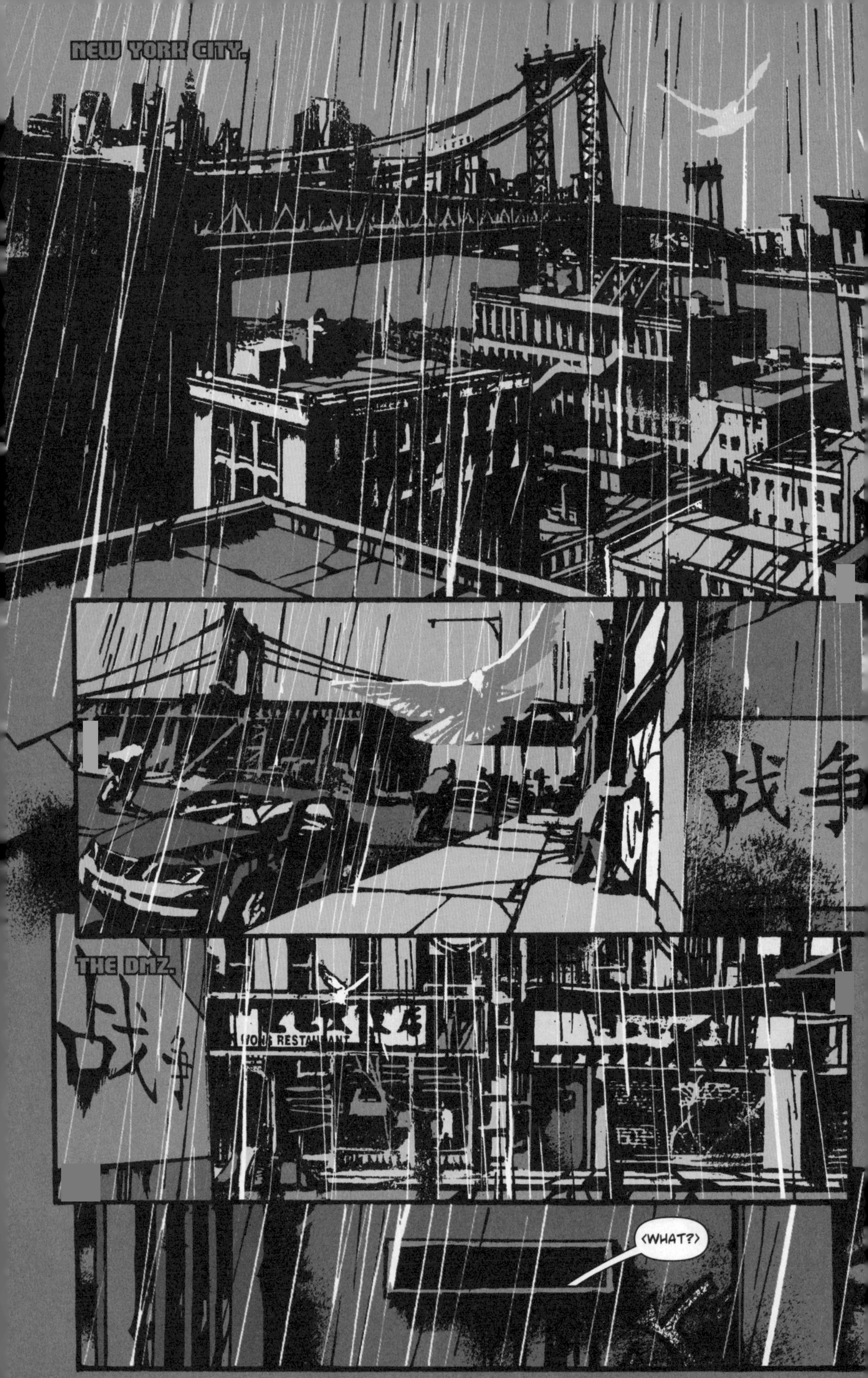
NEW YORK CITY.
战争
THE DMZ.
战争
<WHAT?>

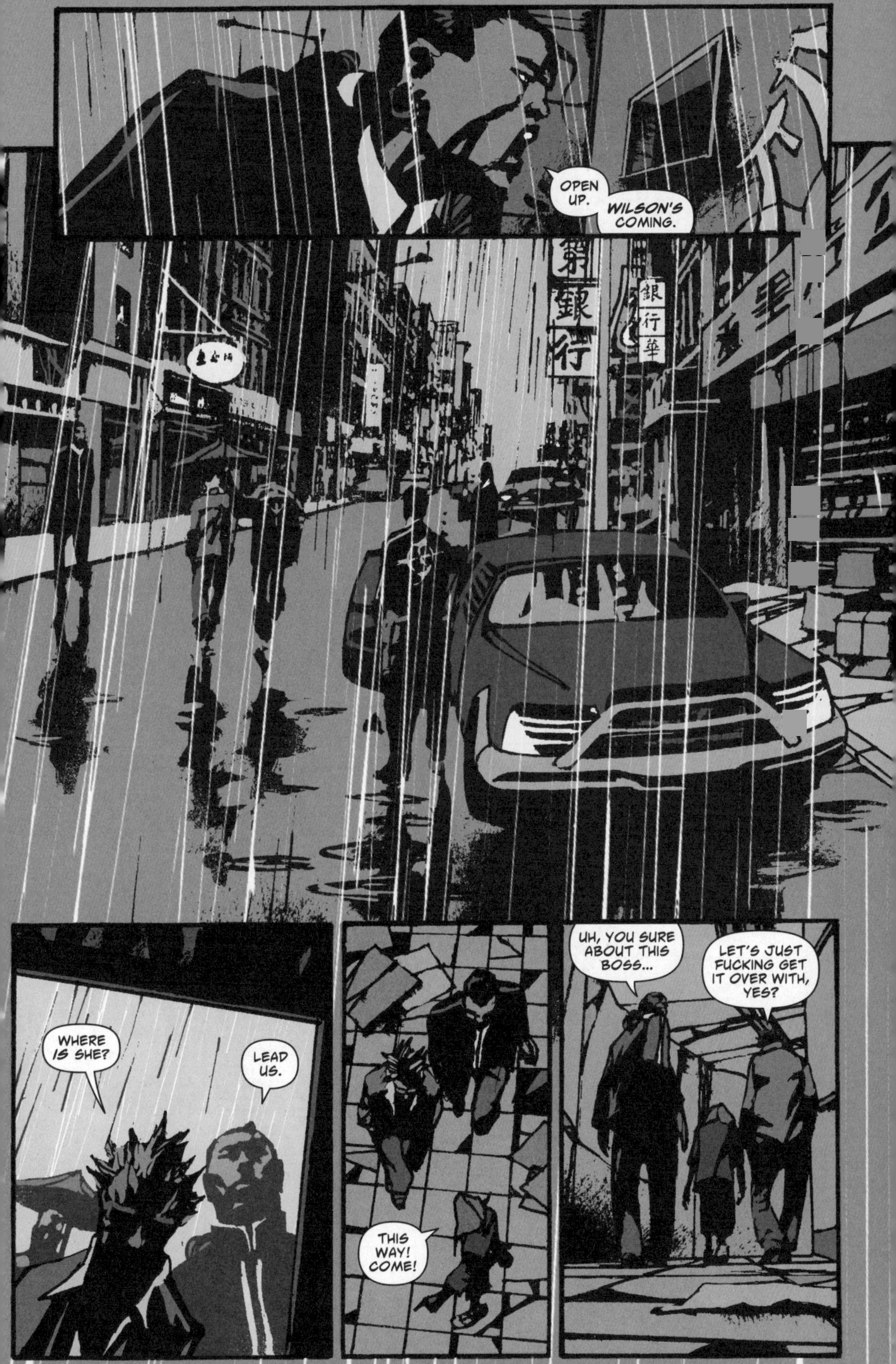
OPEN UP.
WILSON'S COMING.
WHERE IS SHE?
LEAD US.
THIS WAY! COME!
UH, YOU SURE ABOUT THIS BOSS...
LET'S JUST FUCKING GET IT OVER WITH, YES?

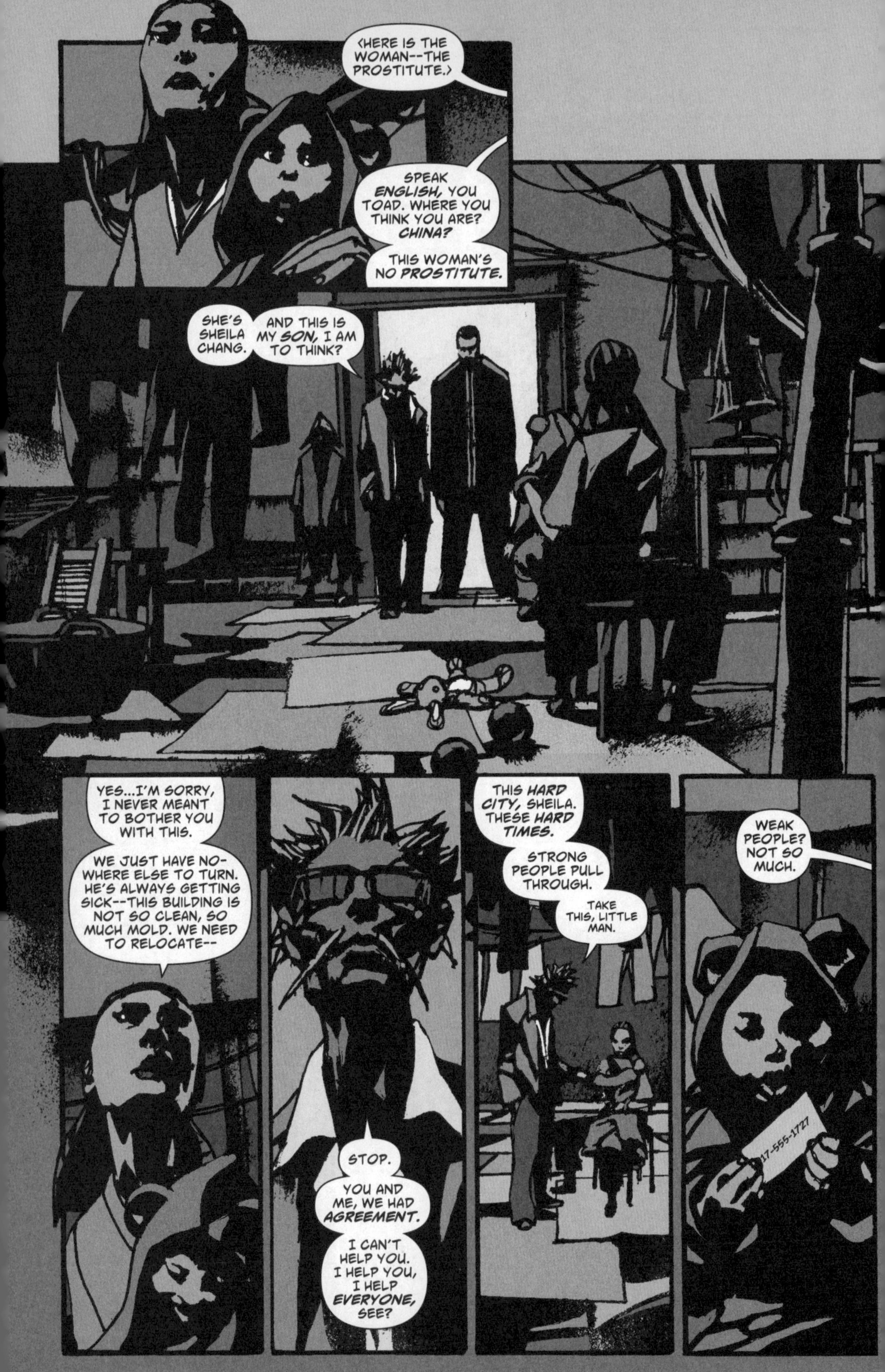
<HERE IS THE WOMAN--THE PROSTITUTE.>
SPEAK ENGLISH, YOU TOAD. WHERE YOU THINK YOU ARE? CHINA?
THIS WOMAN'S NO PROSTITUTE.
SHE'S SHEILA CHANG.
AND THIS IS MY SON, I AM TO THINK?
YES...I'M SORRY, I NEVER MEANT TO BOTHER YOU WITH THIS.
WE JUST HAVE NOWHERE ELSE TO TURN. HE'S ALWAYS GETTING SICK--THIS BUILDING IS NOT SO CLEAN, SO MUCH MOLD. WE NEED TO RELOCATE--
STOP.
YOU AND ME, WE HAD AGREEMENT.
I CAN'T HELP YOU. I HELP YOU, I HELP EVERYONE, SEE?
THIS HARD CITY, SHEILA. THESE HARD TIMES.
STRONG PEOPLE PULL THROUGH.
TAKE THIS, LITTLE MAN.
WEAK PEOPLE? NOT SO MUCH.
17-555-1727

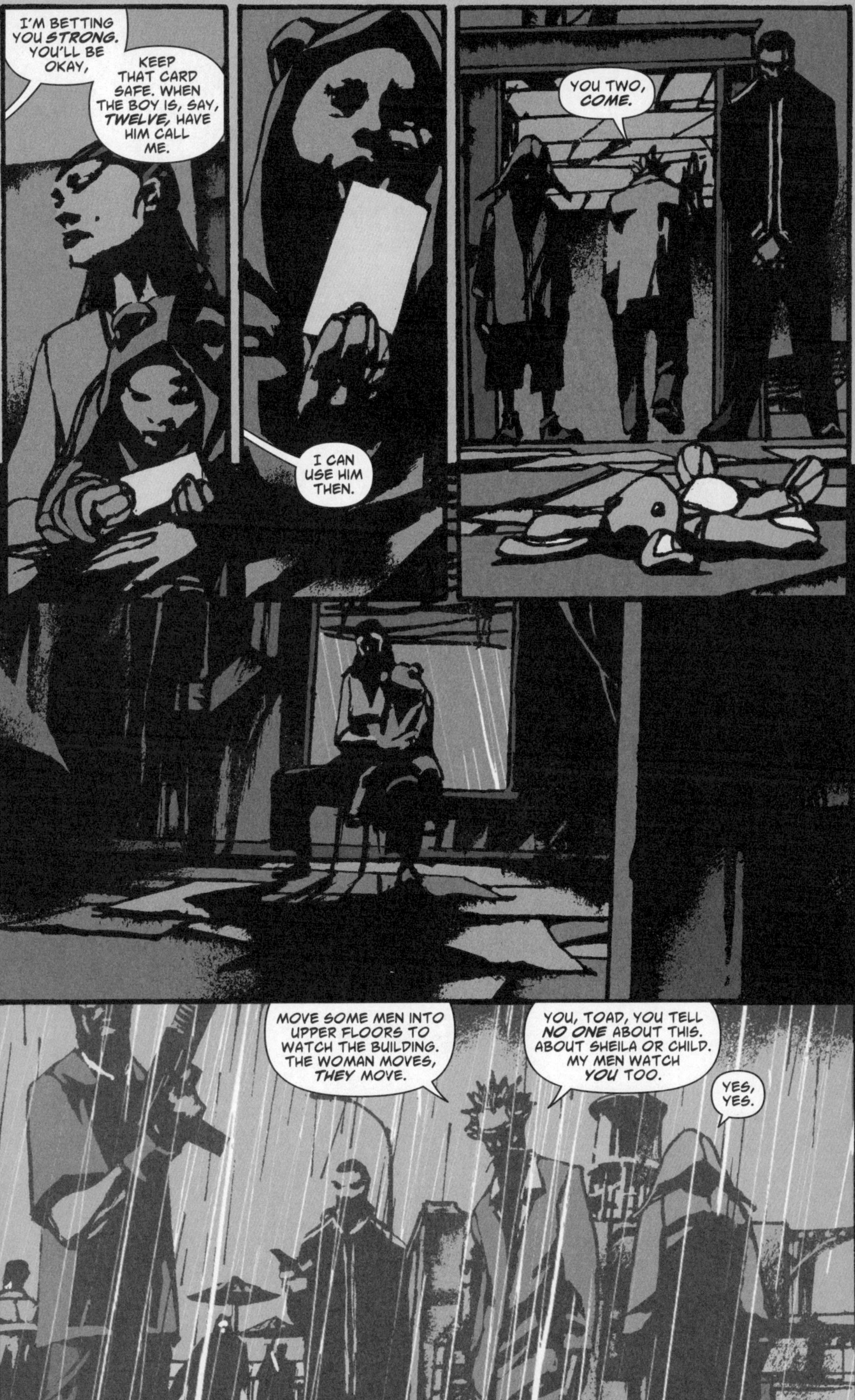
I'M BETTING YOU STRONG. YOU'LL BE OKAY,
KEEP THAT CARD SAFE. WHEN THE BOY IS, SAY, TWELVE, HAVE HIM CALL ME.
I CAN USE HIM THEN.
YOU TWO, COME.
MOVE SOME MEN INTO UPPER FLOORS TO WATCH THE BUILDING. THE WOMAN MOVES, THEY MOVE.
YOU, TOAD, YOU TELL NO ONE ABOUT THIS. ABOUT SHEILA OR CHILD. MY MEN WATCH YOU TOO.
YES, YES.

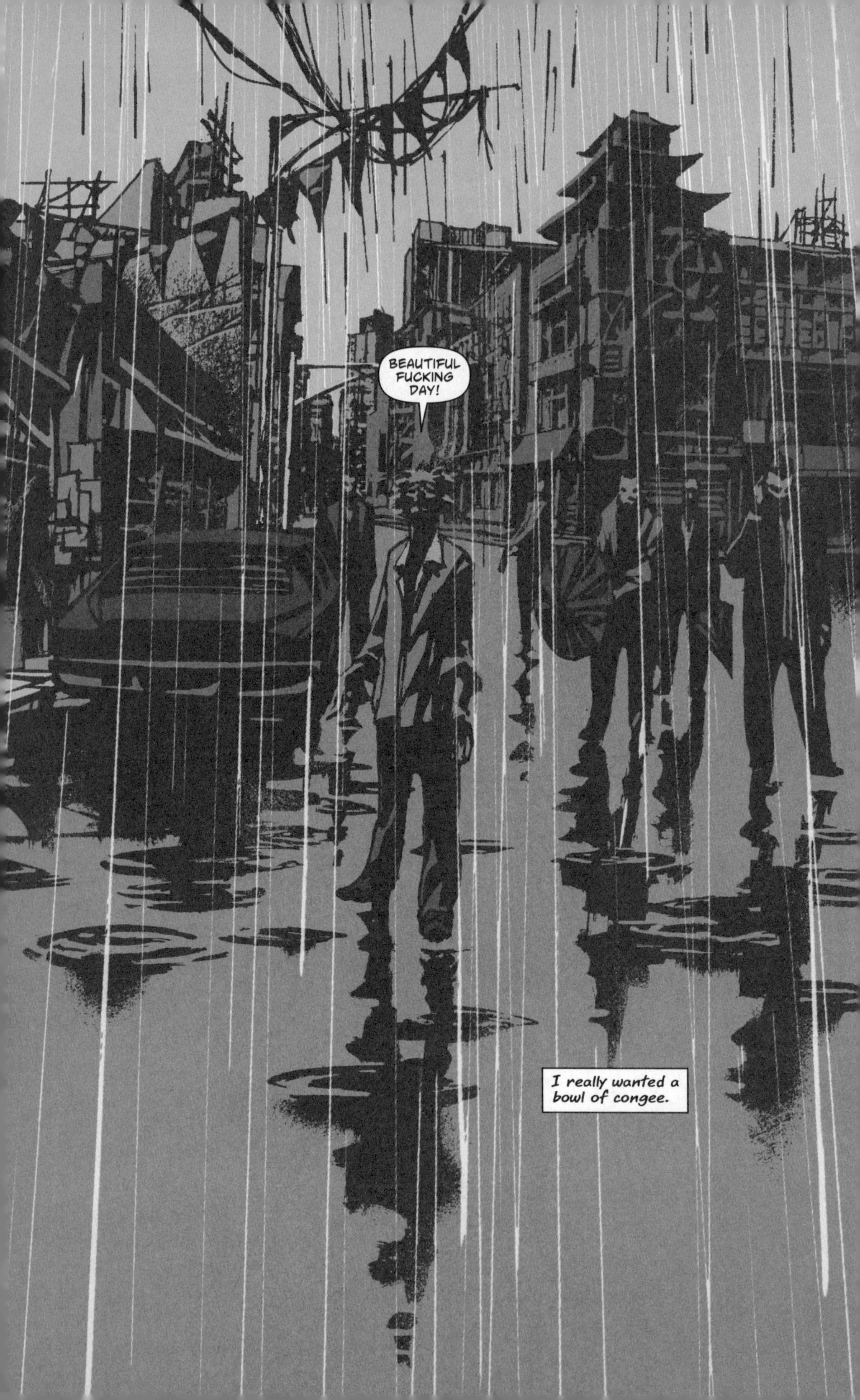
BEAUTIFUL FUCKING DAY!
I really wanted a bowl of congee.

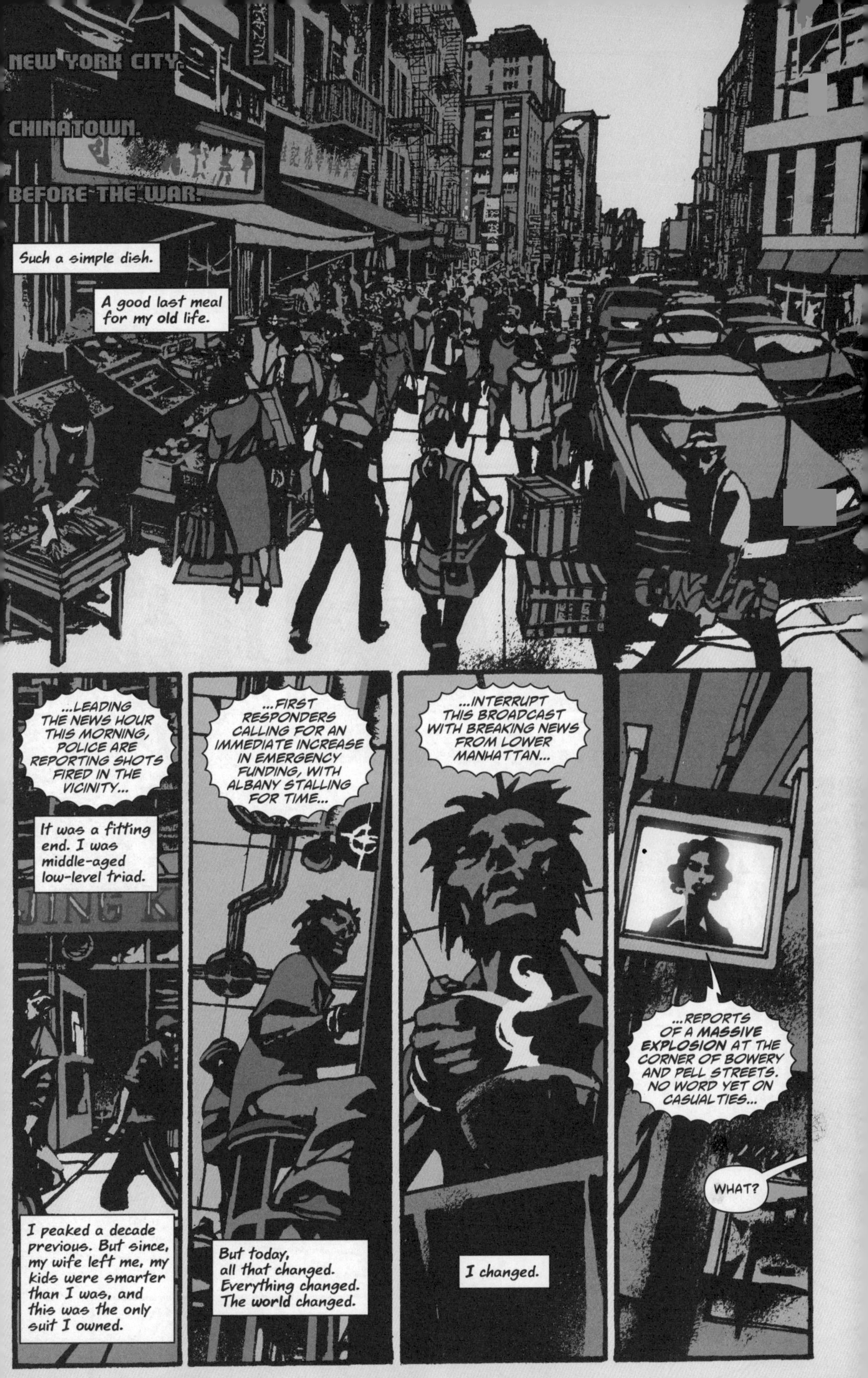
NEW YORK CITY.
CHINATOWN.
BEFORE THE WAR.
Such a simple dish.
A good last meal for my old life.
...LEADING THE NEWS HOUR THIS MORNING, POLICE ARE REPORTING SHOTS FIRED IN THE VICINITY...
It was a fitting end. I was middle-aged low-level triad.
I peaked a decade previous. But since, my wife left me, my kids were smarter than I was, and this was the only suit I owned.
...FIRST RESPONDERS CALLING FOR AN IMMEDIATE INCREASE IN EMERGENCY FUNDING, WITH ALBANY STALLING FOR TIME...
But today, all that changed. Everything changed. The world changed.
...INTERRUPT THIS BROADCAST WITH BREAKING NEWS FROM LOWER MANHATTAN...
I changed.
...REPORTS OF A MASSIVE EXPLOSION AT THE CORNER OF BOWERY AND PELL STREETS. NO WORD YET ON CASUALTIES...
WHAT?

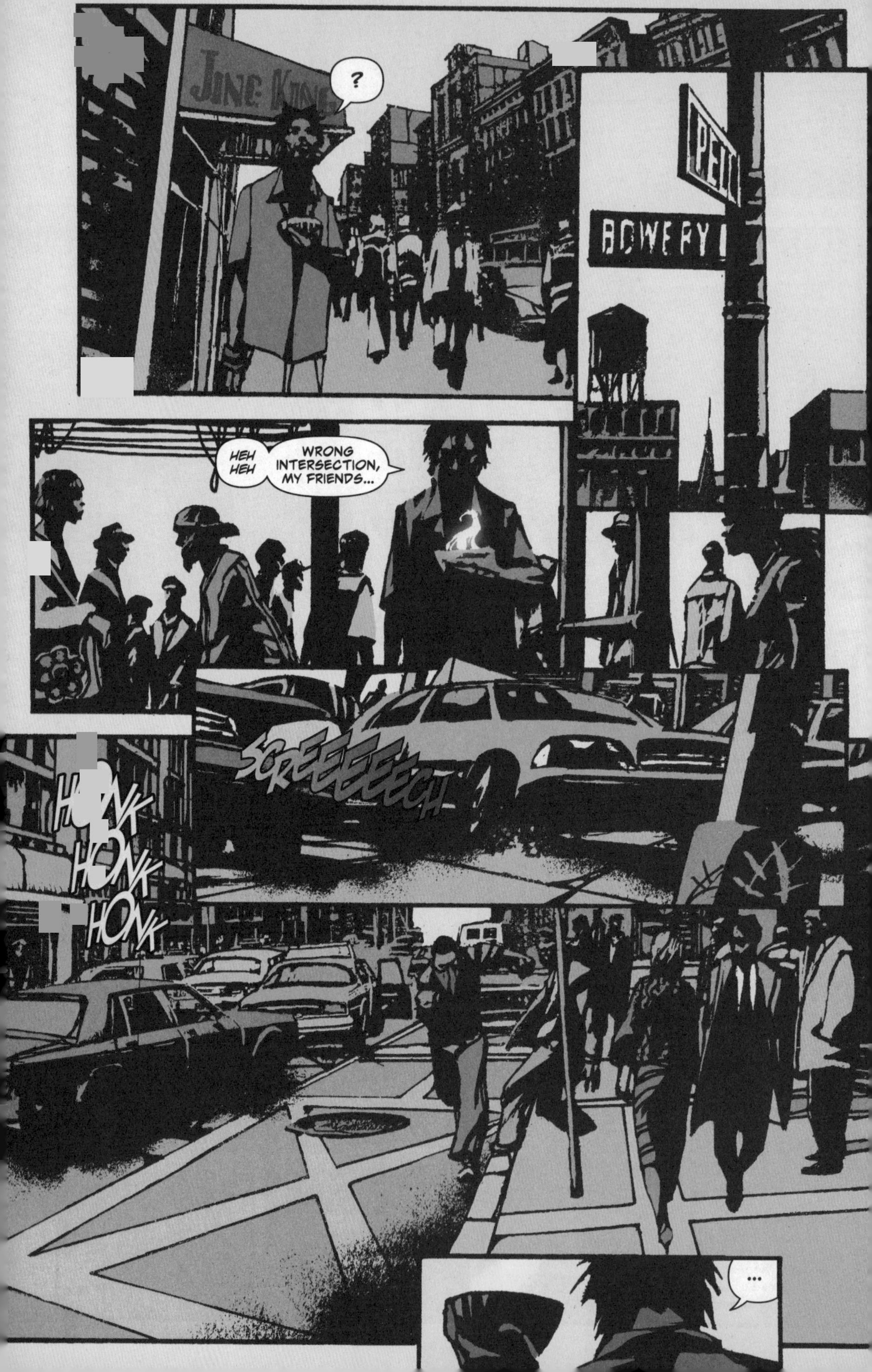

JING KING
?
BOWERY
HEH HEH
WRONG INTERSECTION, MY FRIENDS...
SCREEEEEECH
HONK
HONK
...

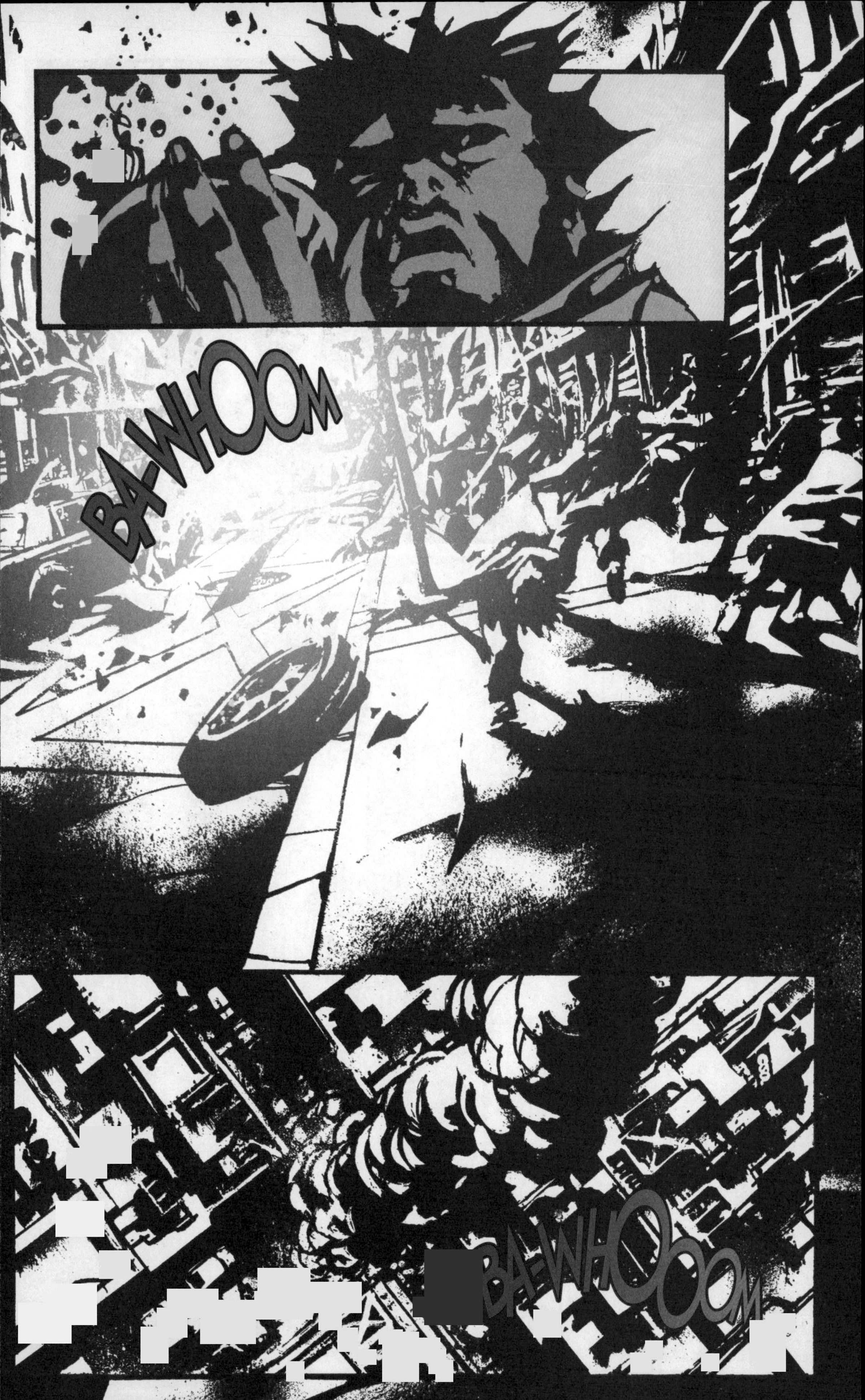
BA-WHOOM
BA-WHOOOOM

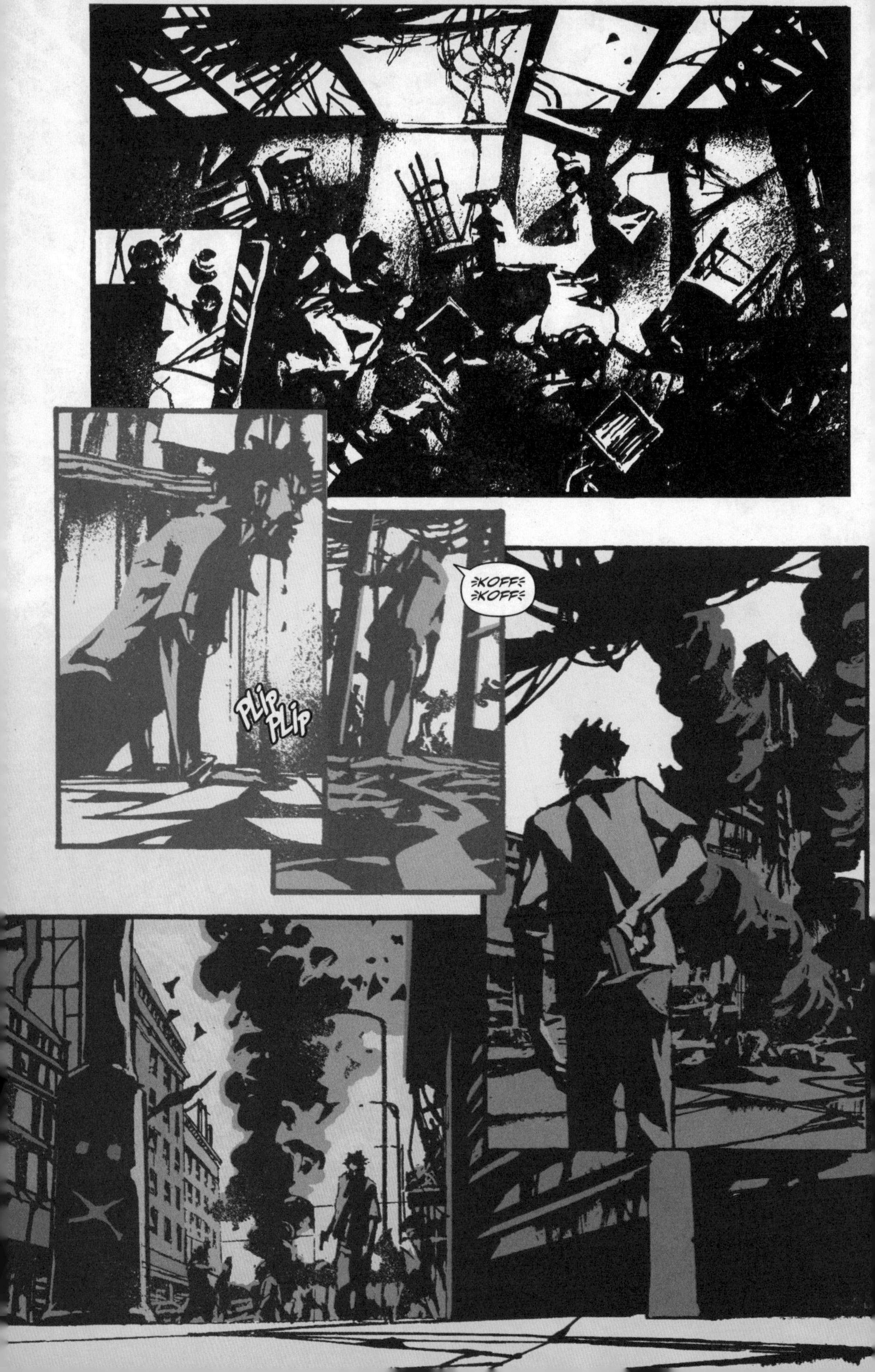
KOFF KOFF
PLIP PLIP

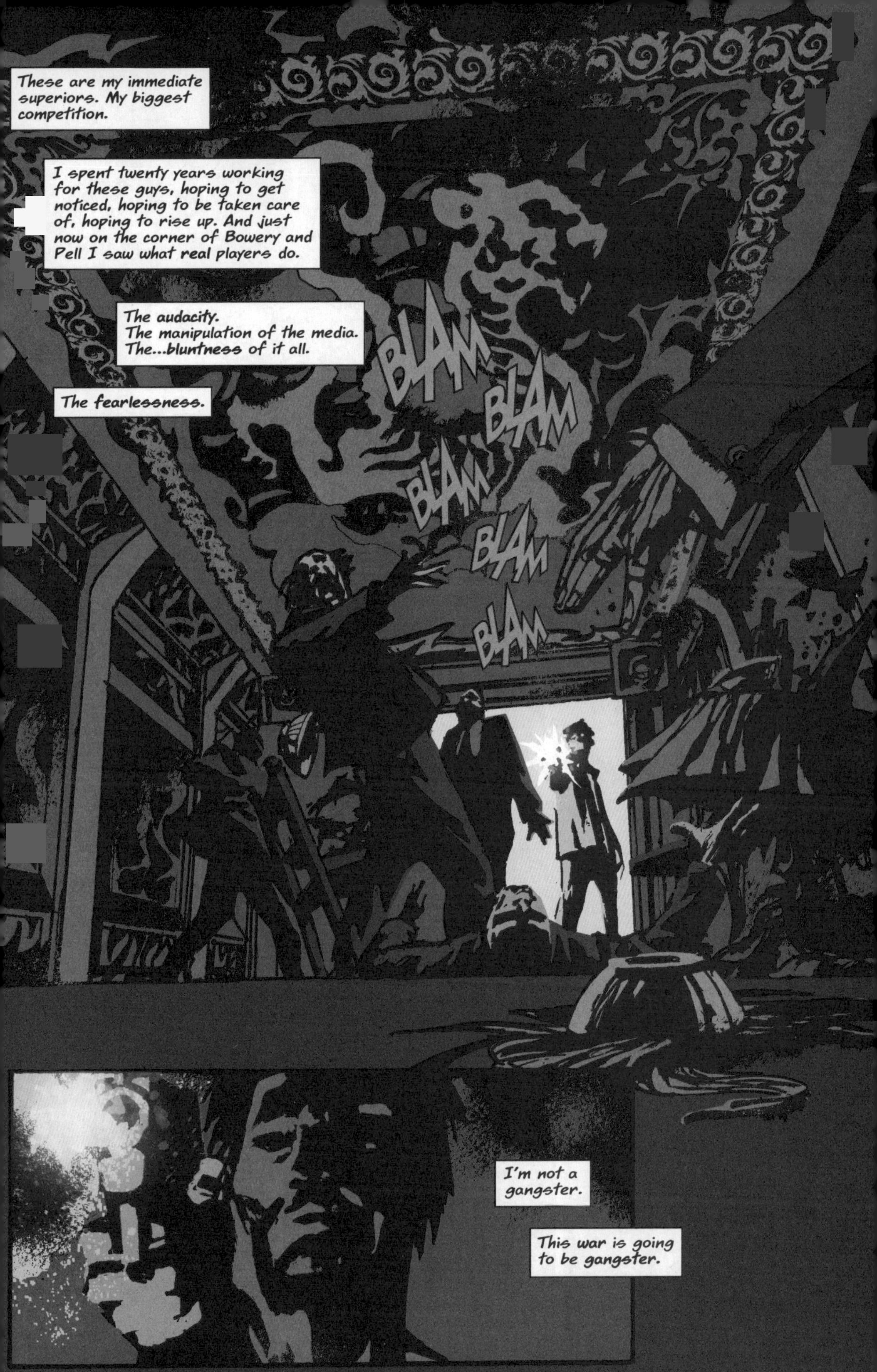
These are my immediate superiors. My biggest competition.
I spent twenty years working for these guys, hoping to get noticed, hoping to be taken care of, hoping to rise up. And just now on the corner of Bowery and Pell I saw what real players do.
The audacity.
The manipulation of the media.
The...bluntness of it all.
The fearlessness.
BLAM
BLAM
BLAM
BLAM
BLAM
I'm not a gangster.
This war is going to be gangster.

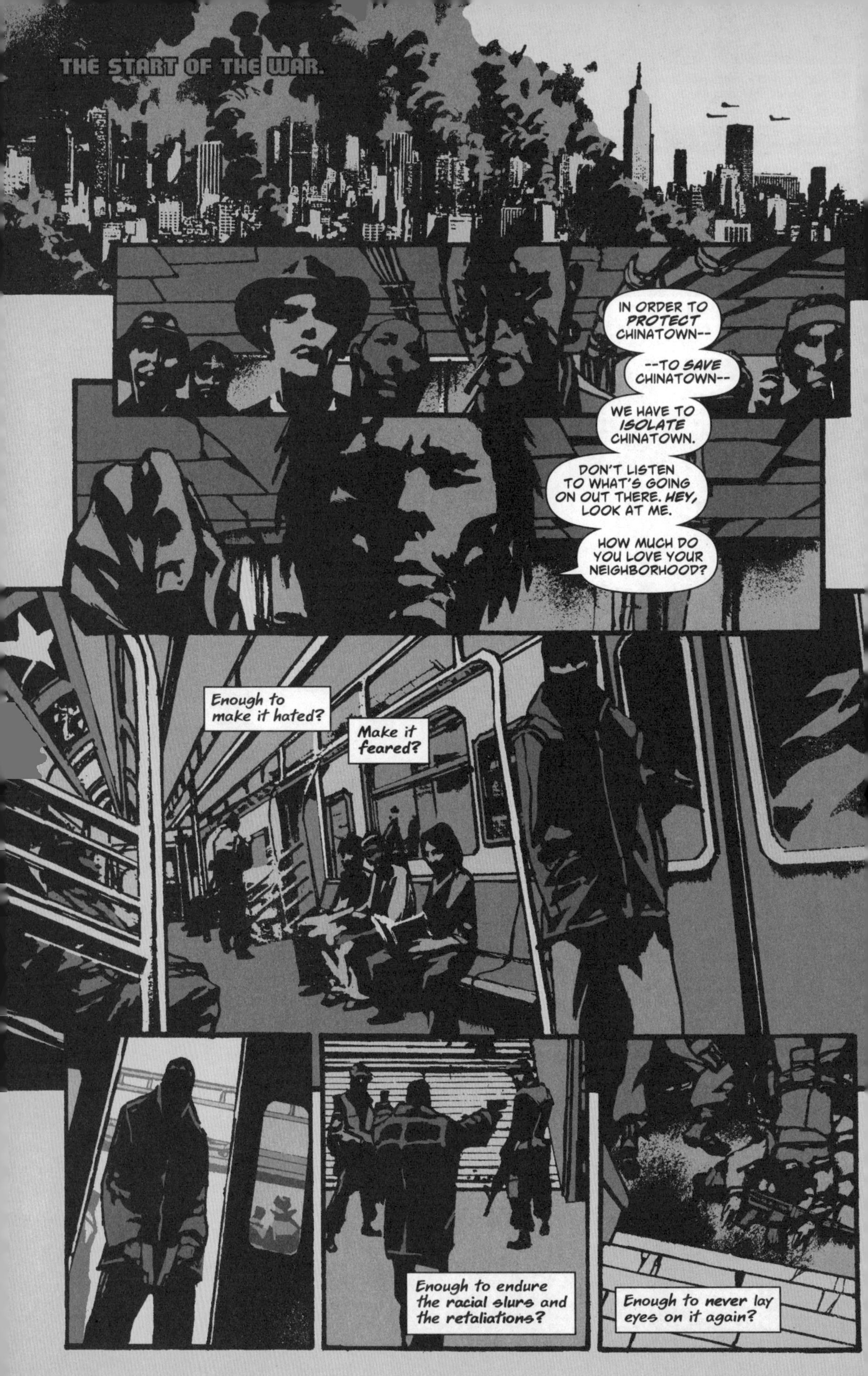
THE START OF THE WAR.
IN ORDER TO PROTECT CHINATOWN--
--TO SAVE CHINATOWN--
WE HAVE TO ISOLATE CHINATOWN.
DON'T LISTEN TO WHAT'S GOING ON OUT THERE. HEY, LOOK AT ME.
HOW MUCH DO YOU LOVE YOUR NEIGHBORHOOD?
Enough to make it hated?
Make it feared?
Enough to endure the racial slurs and the retaliations?
Enough to never lay eyes on it again?

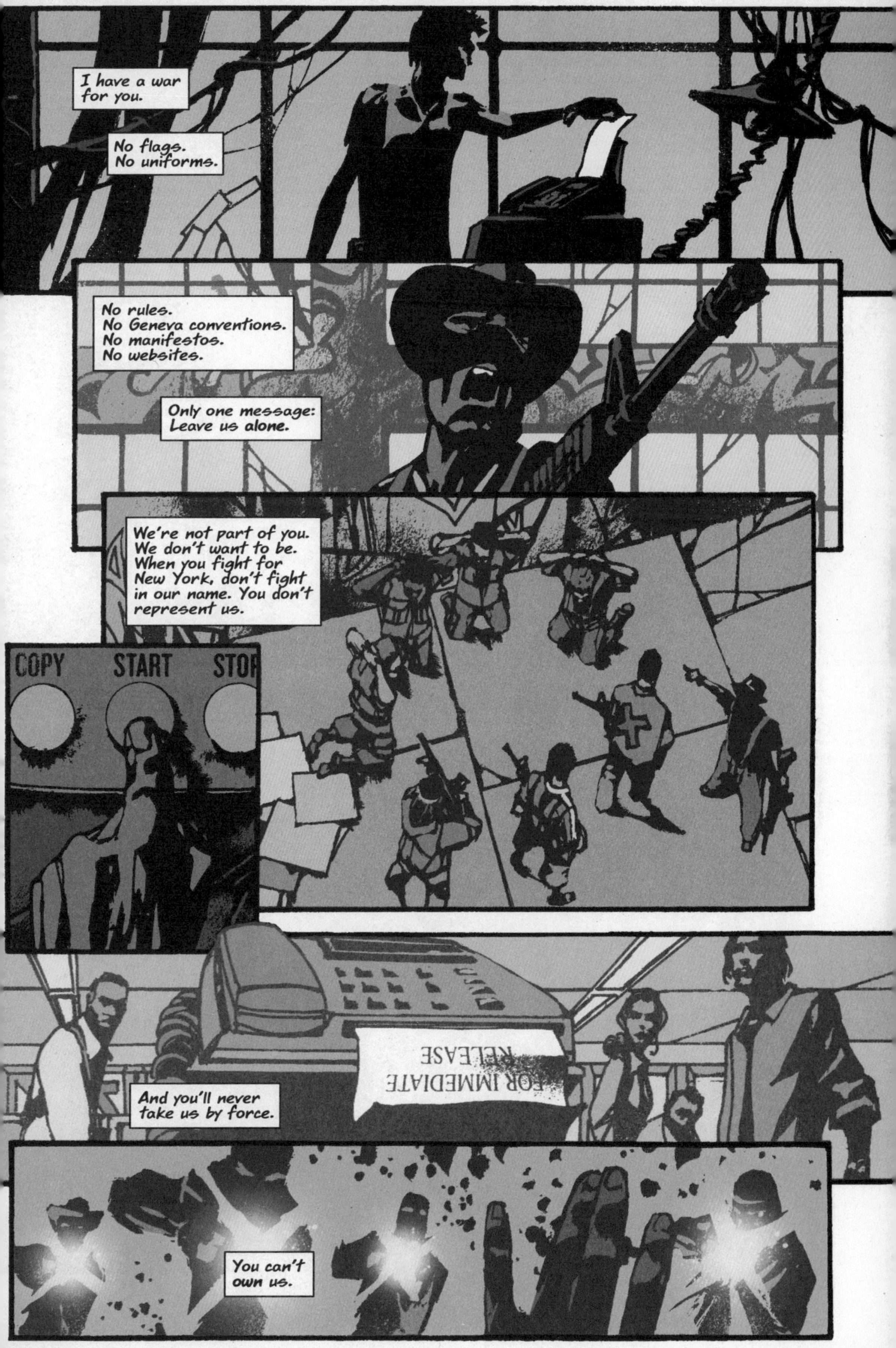
I have a war for you.
No flags. No uniforms.
No rules. No Geneva conventions. No manifestos. No websites.
Only one message: Leave us alone.
We're not part of you. We don't want to be. When you fight for New York, don't fight in our name. You don't represent us.
COPY
START
STO
And you'll never take us by force.
FOR IMMEDIATE RELEASE
You can't own us.

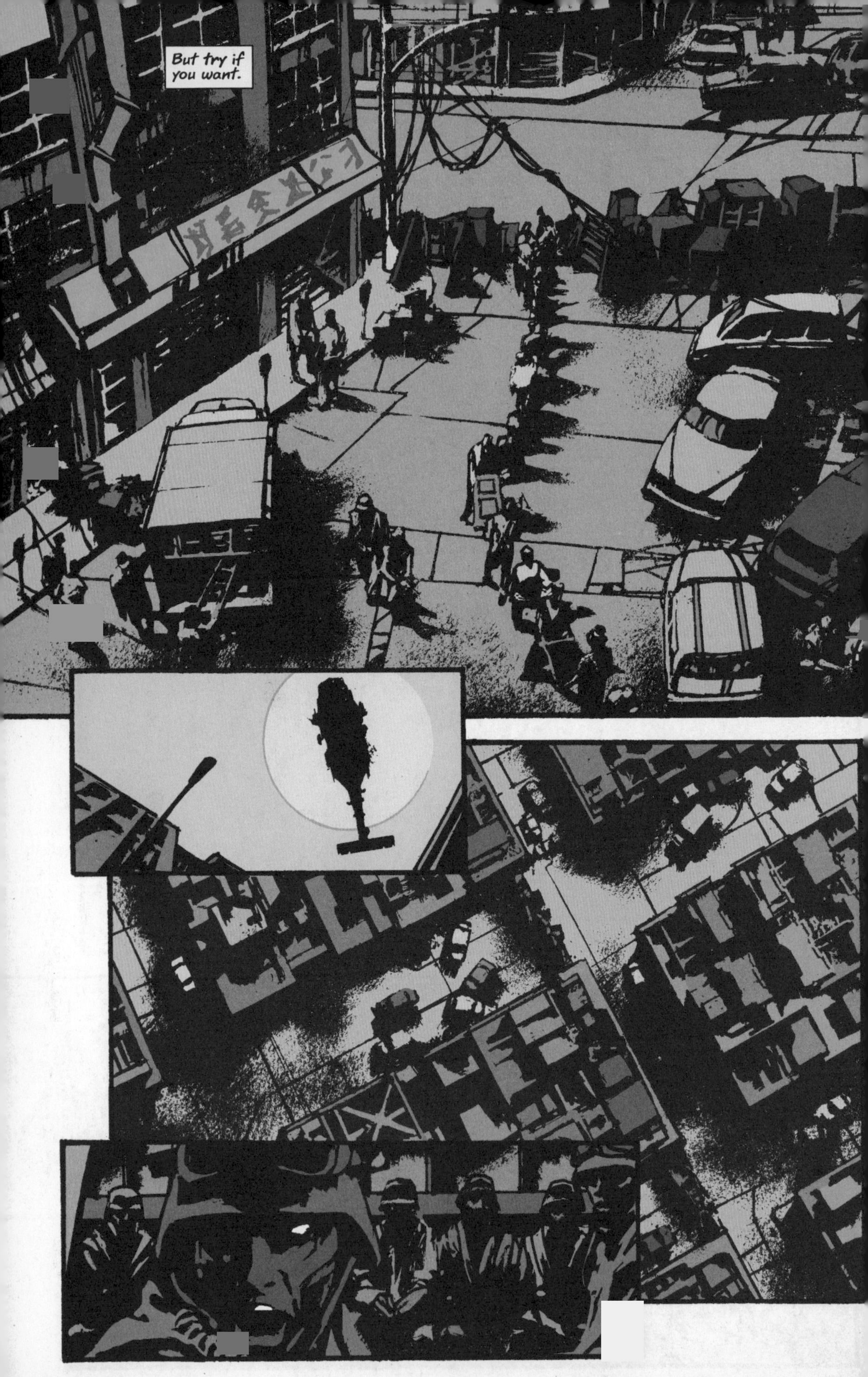
But try if
you want.

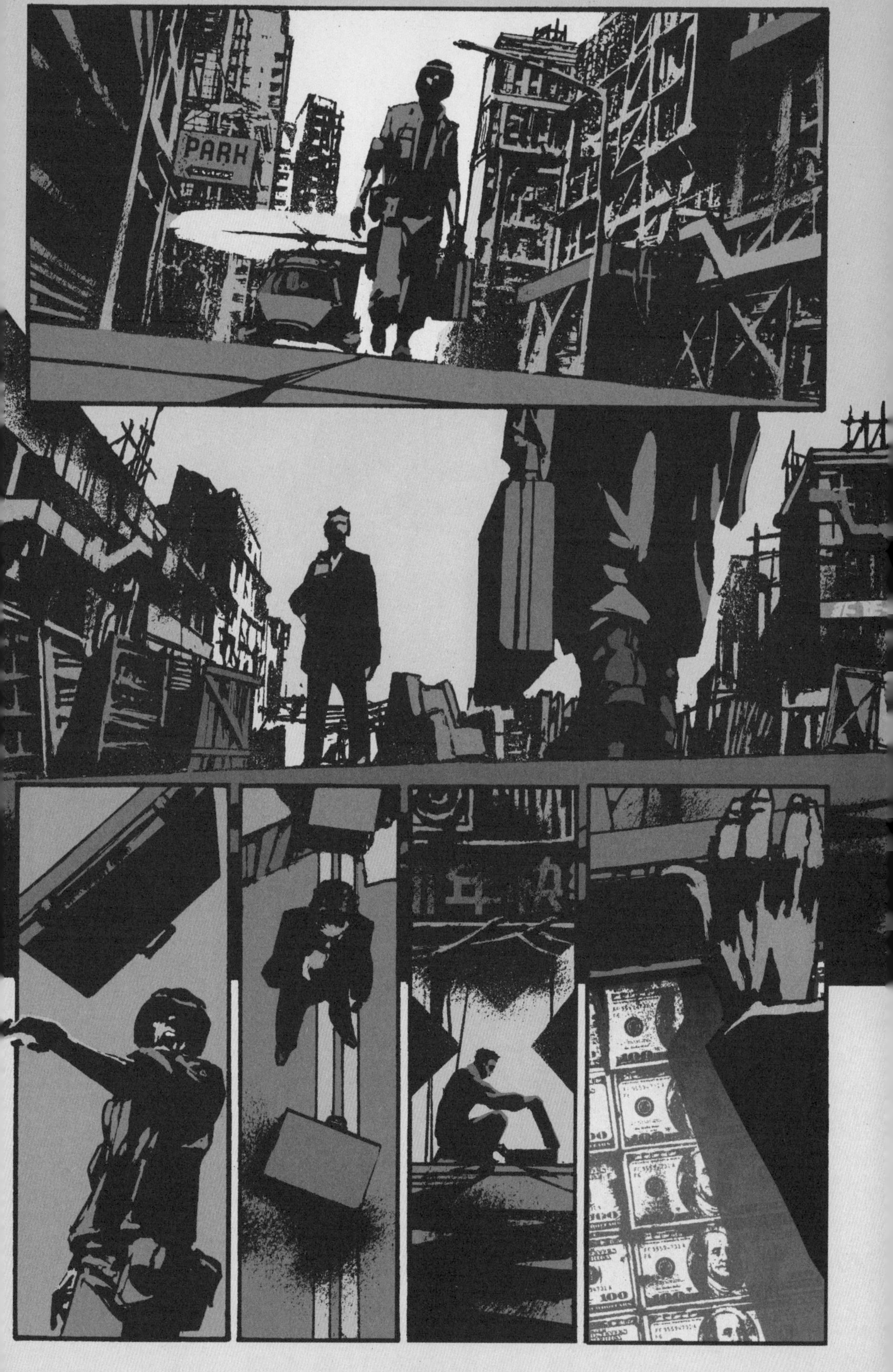
PARK

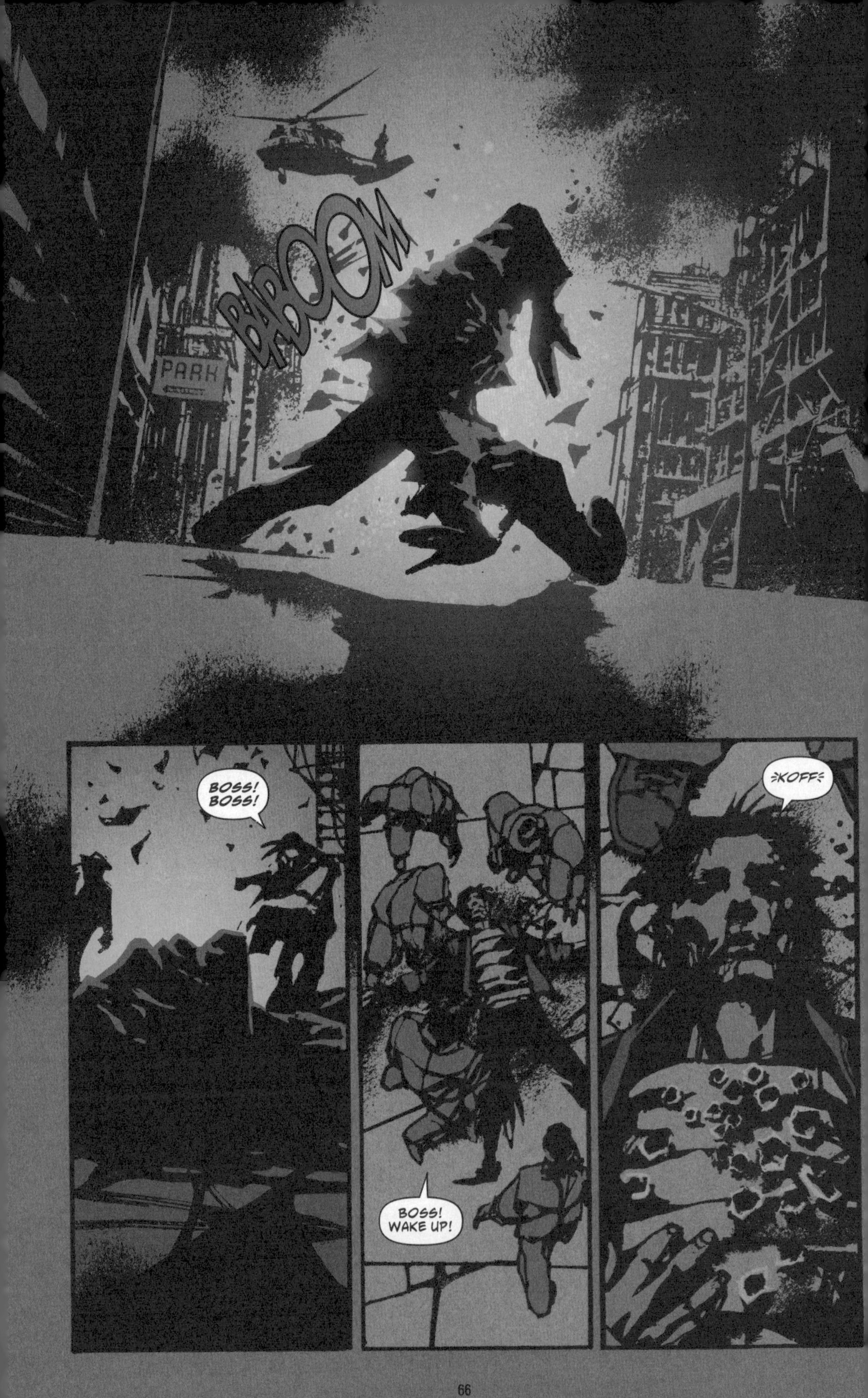
BABOOM
PARK
BOSS! BOSS!
BOSS! WAKE UP!
KOFF

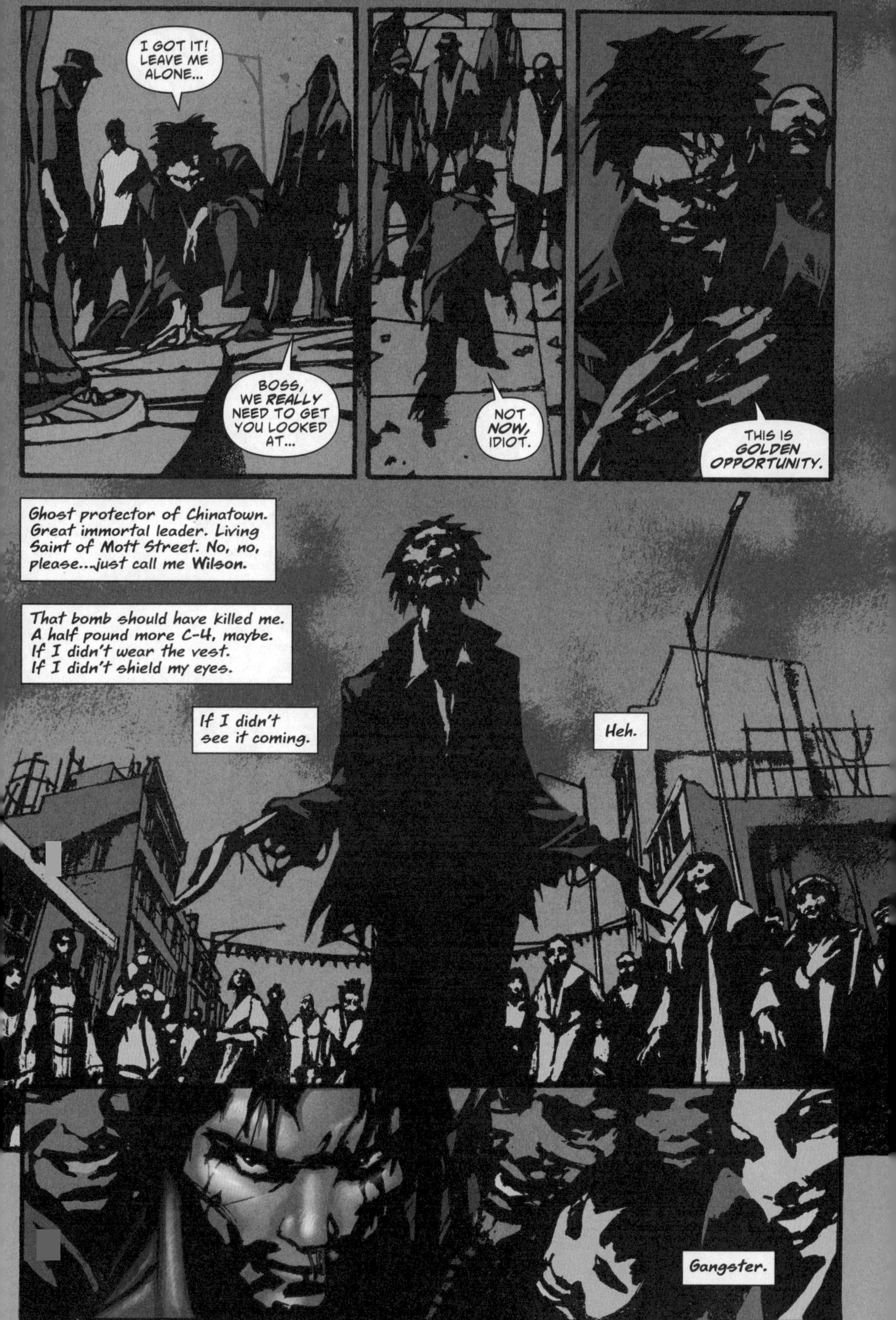
I GOT IT! LEAVE ME ALONE...
BOSS, WE REALLY NEED TO GET YOU LOOKED AT...
NOT NOW, IDIOT.
THIS IS GOLDEN OPPORTUNITY.
Ghost protector of Chinatown. Great immortal leader. Living Saint of Mott Street. No, no, please...just call me Wilson.
That bomb should have killed me. A half pound more C-4, maybe. If I didn't wear the vest. If I didn't shield my eyes.
If I didn't see it coming.
Heh.
Gangster.

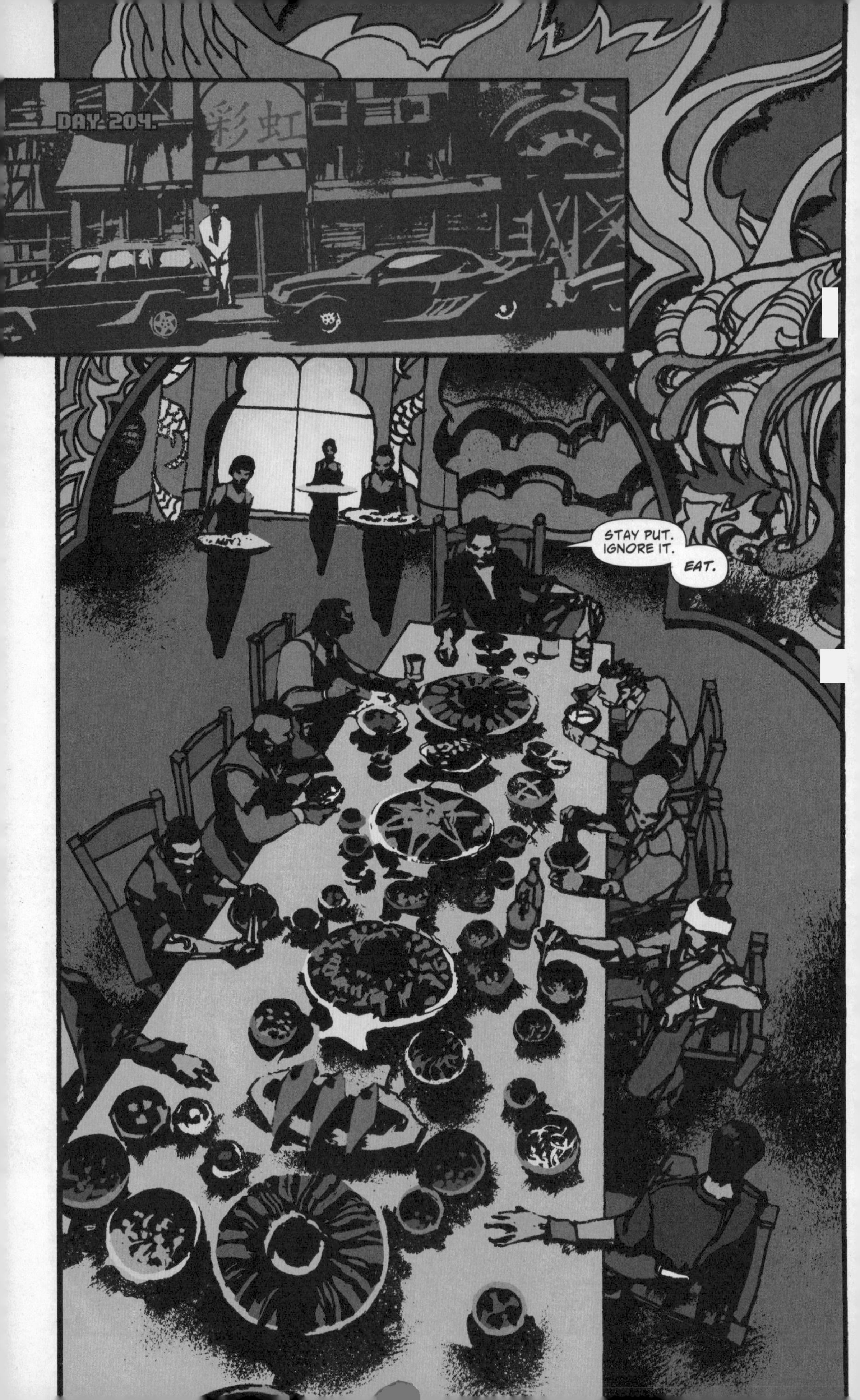
DAY 204.
彩虹
STAY PUT. IGNORE IT.
EAT.

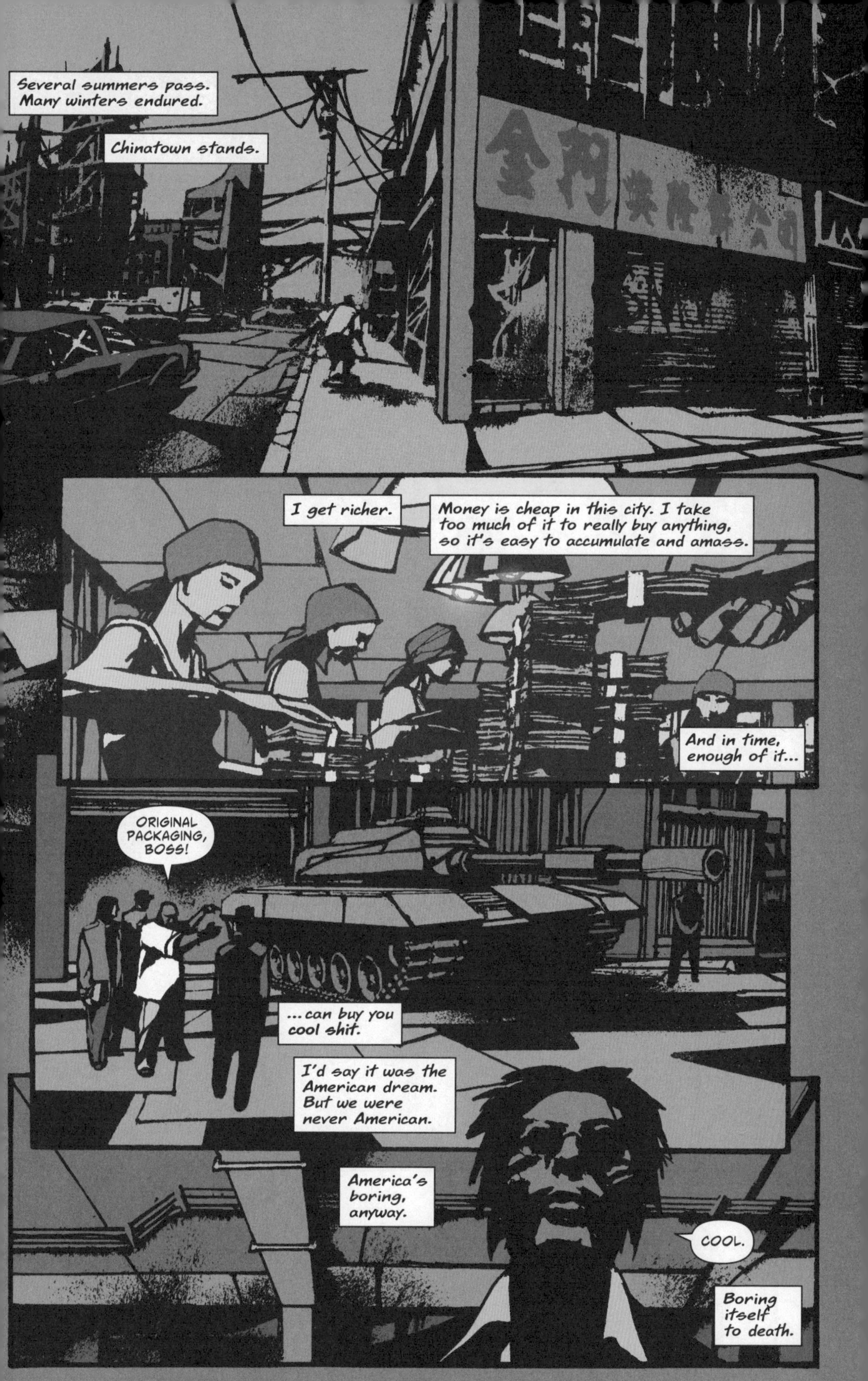
Several summers pass. Many winters endured.
Chinatown stands.
I get richer.
Money is cheap in this city. I take too much of it to really buy anything, so it's easy to accumulate and amass.
And in time, enough of it...
ORIGINAL PACKAGING, BOSS!
...can buy you cool shit.
I'd say it was the American dream. But we were never American.
America's boring, anyway.
COOL.
Boring itself to death.

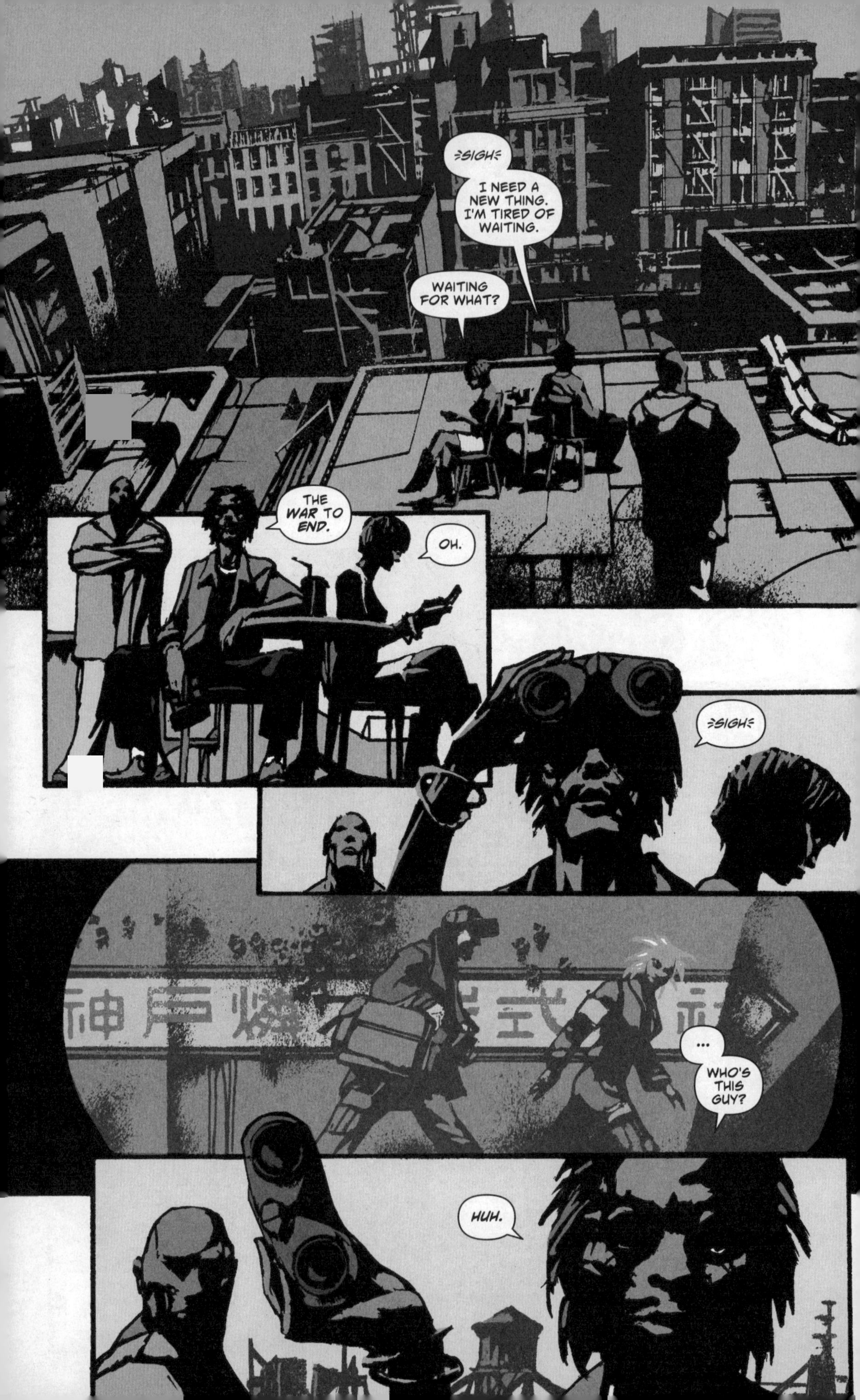

SIGH
I NEED A NEW THING. I'M TIRED OF WAITING.
WAITING FOR WHAT?
THE WAR TO END.
OH.
SIGH
...
WHO'S THIS GUY?
HUH.

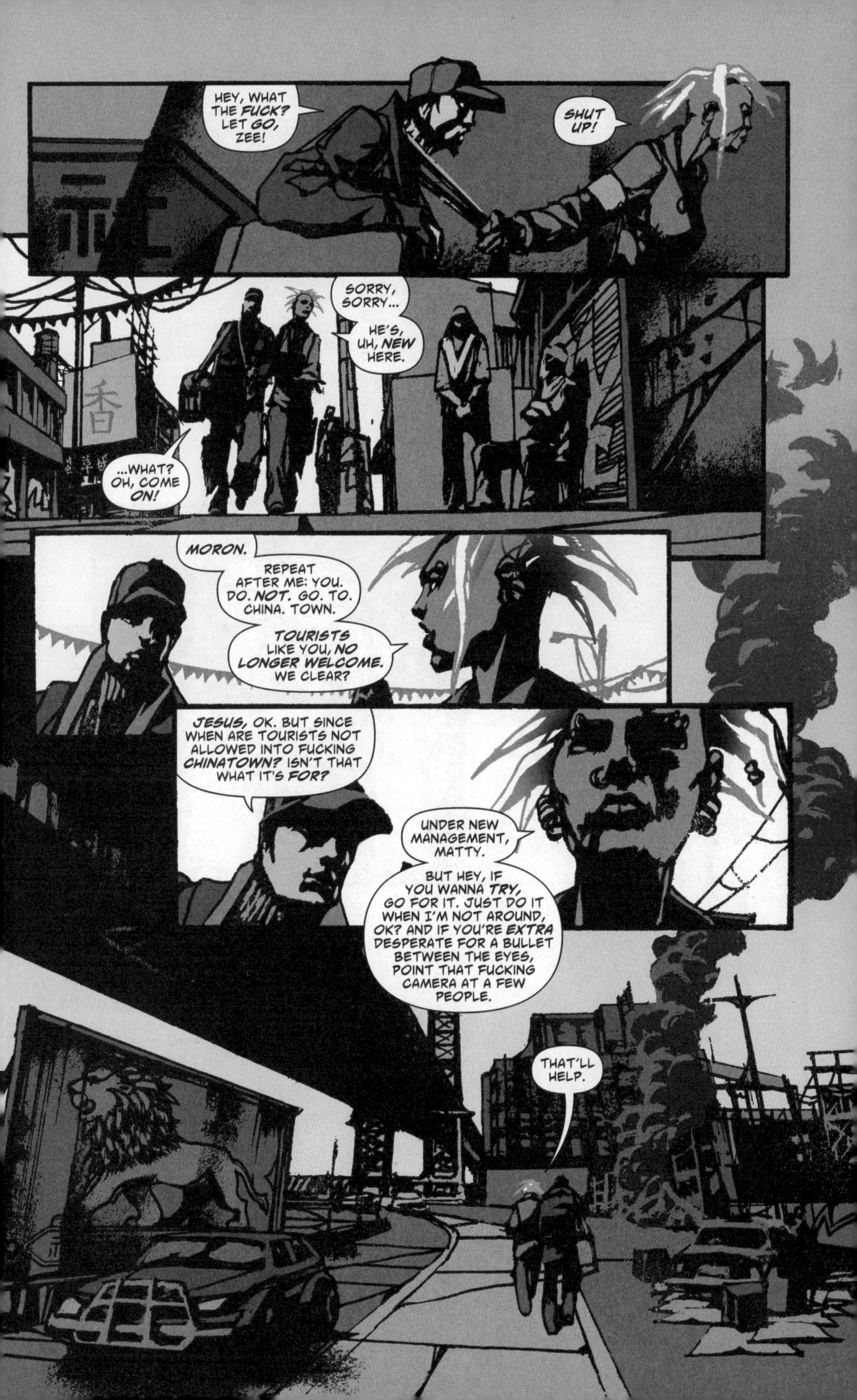
HEY, WHAT THE FUCK? LET GO, ZEE!
SHUT UP!
SORRY, SORRY...
HE'S, UH, NEW HERE.
...WHAT? OH, COME ON!
MORON.
REPEAT AFTER ME: YOU. DO. NOT. GO. TO. CHINA. TOWN.
TOURISTS LIKE YOU, NO LONGER WELCOME. WE CLEAR?
JESUS, OK. BUT SINCE WHEN ARE TOURISTS NOT ALLOWED INTO FUCKING CHINATOWN? ISN'T THAT WHAT IT'S FOR?
UNDER NEW MANAGEMENT, MATTY.
BUT HEY, IF YOU WANNA TRY, GO FOR IT. JUST DO IT WHEN I'M NOT AROUND, OK? AND IF YOU'RE EXTRA DESPERATE FOR A BULLET BETWEEN THE EYES, POINT THAT FUCKING CAMERA AT A FEW PEOPLE.
THAT'LL HELP.

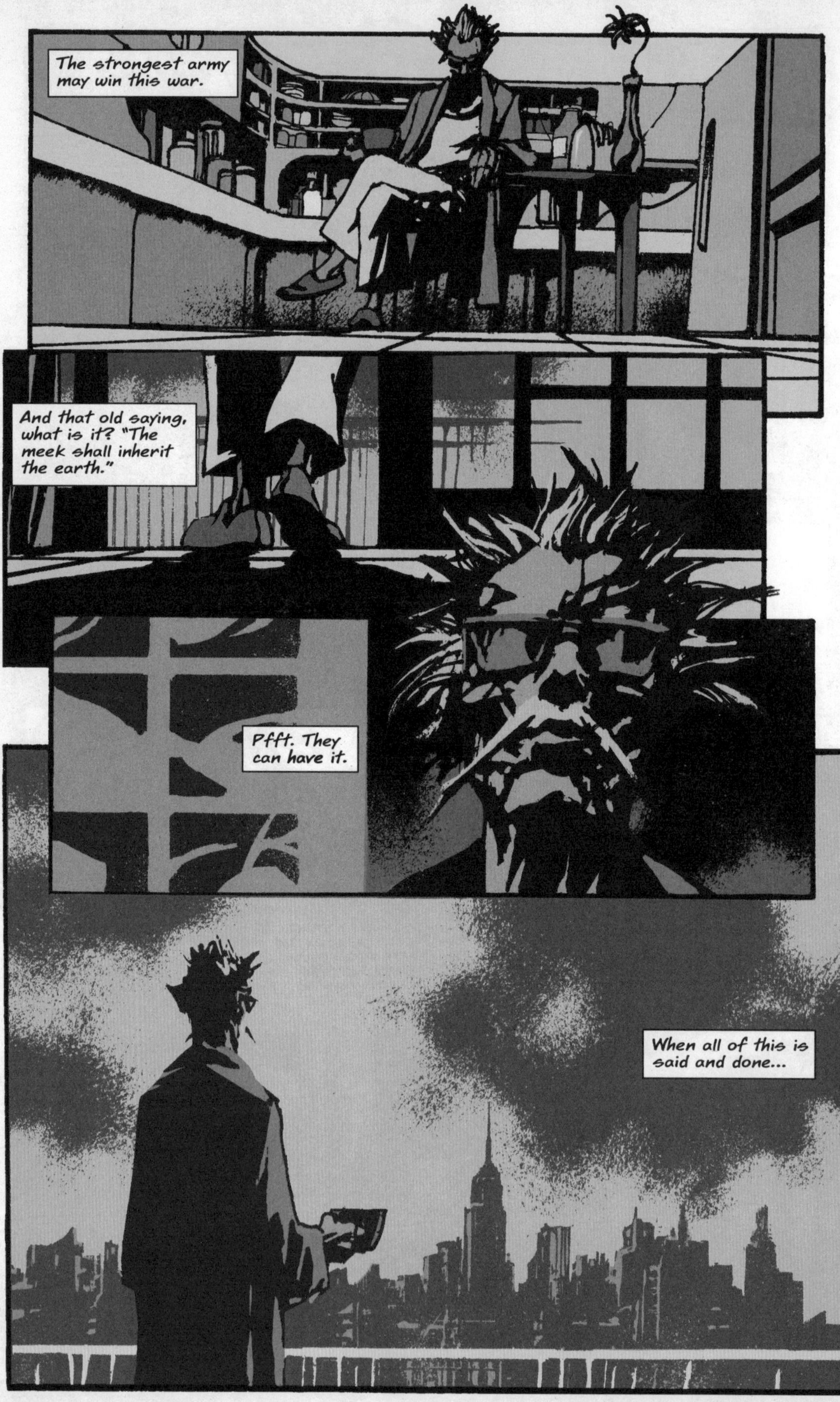
The strongest army may win this war.
And that old saying, what is it? "The meek shall inherit the earth."
Pfft. They can have it.
When all of this is said and done...

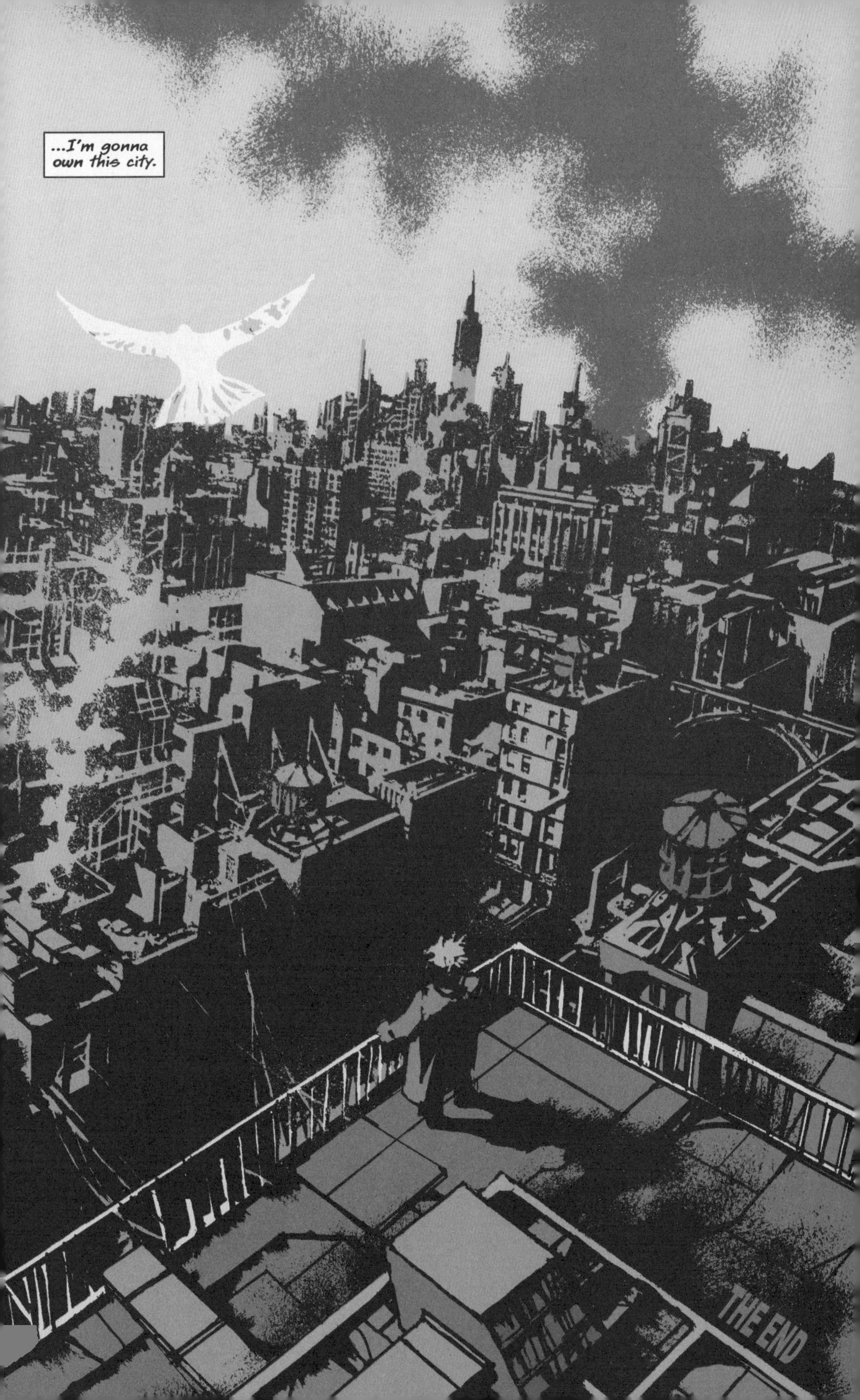
...I'm gonna own this city.
THE END

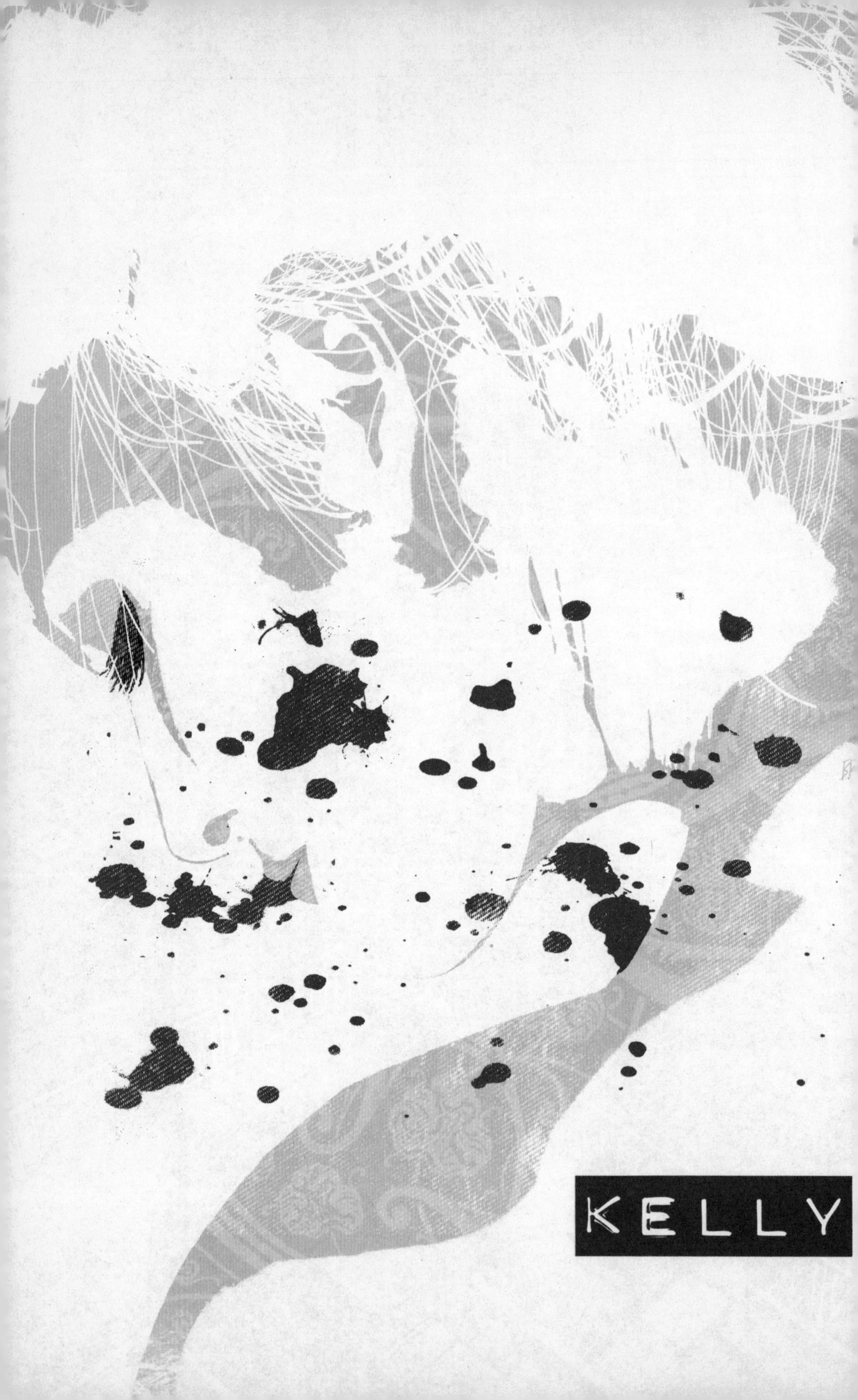
KELLY

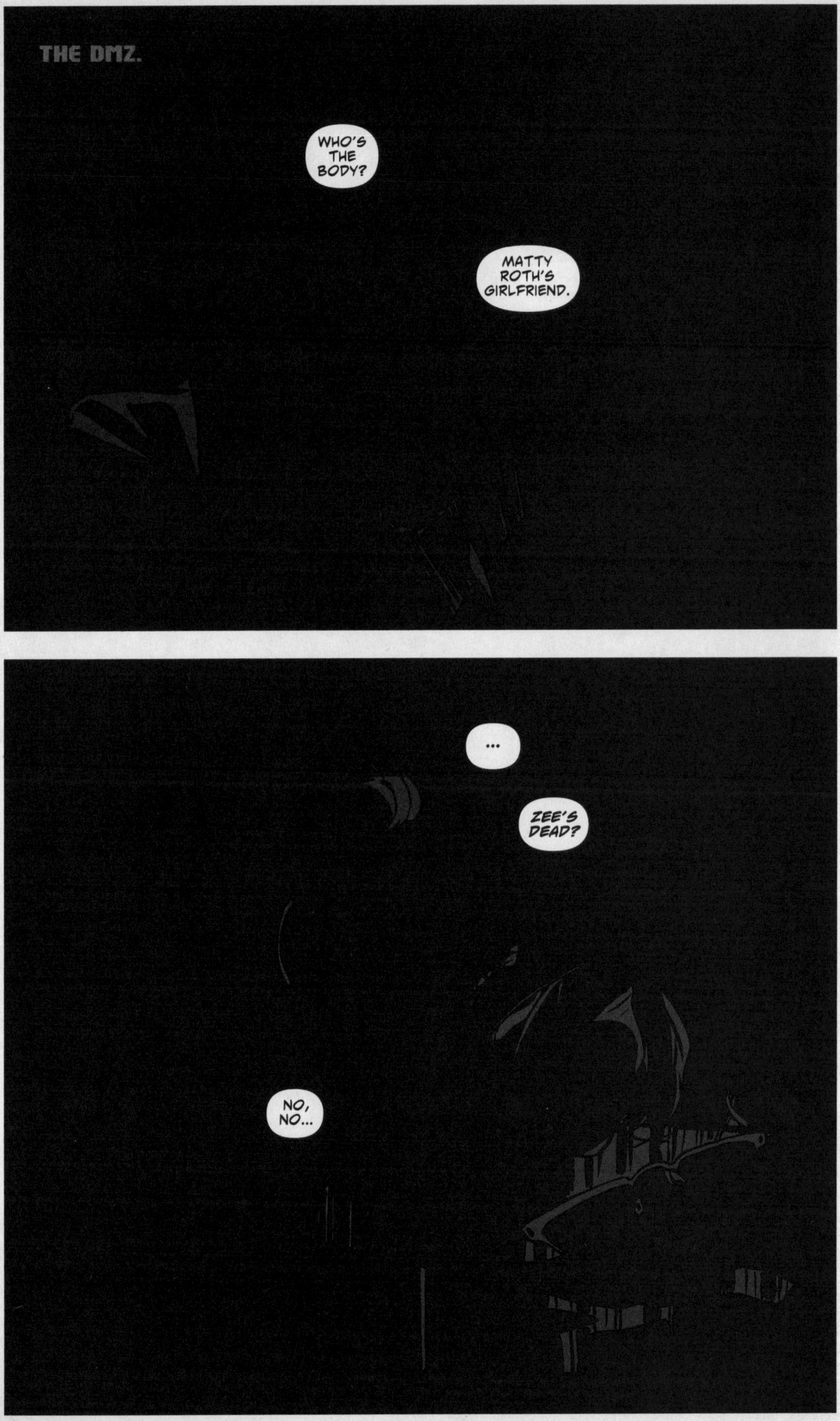
THE DMZ.
WHO'S THE BODY?
MATTY ROTH'S GIRLFRIEND.
...
ZEE'S DEAD?
NO, NO...

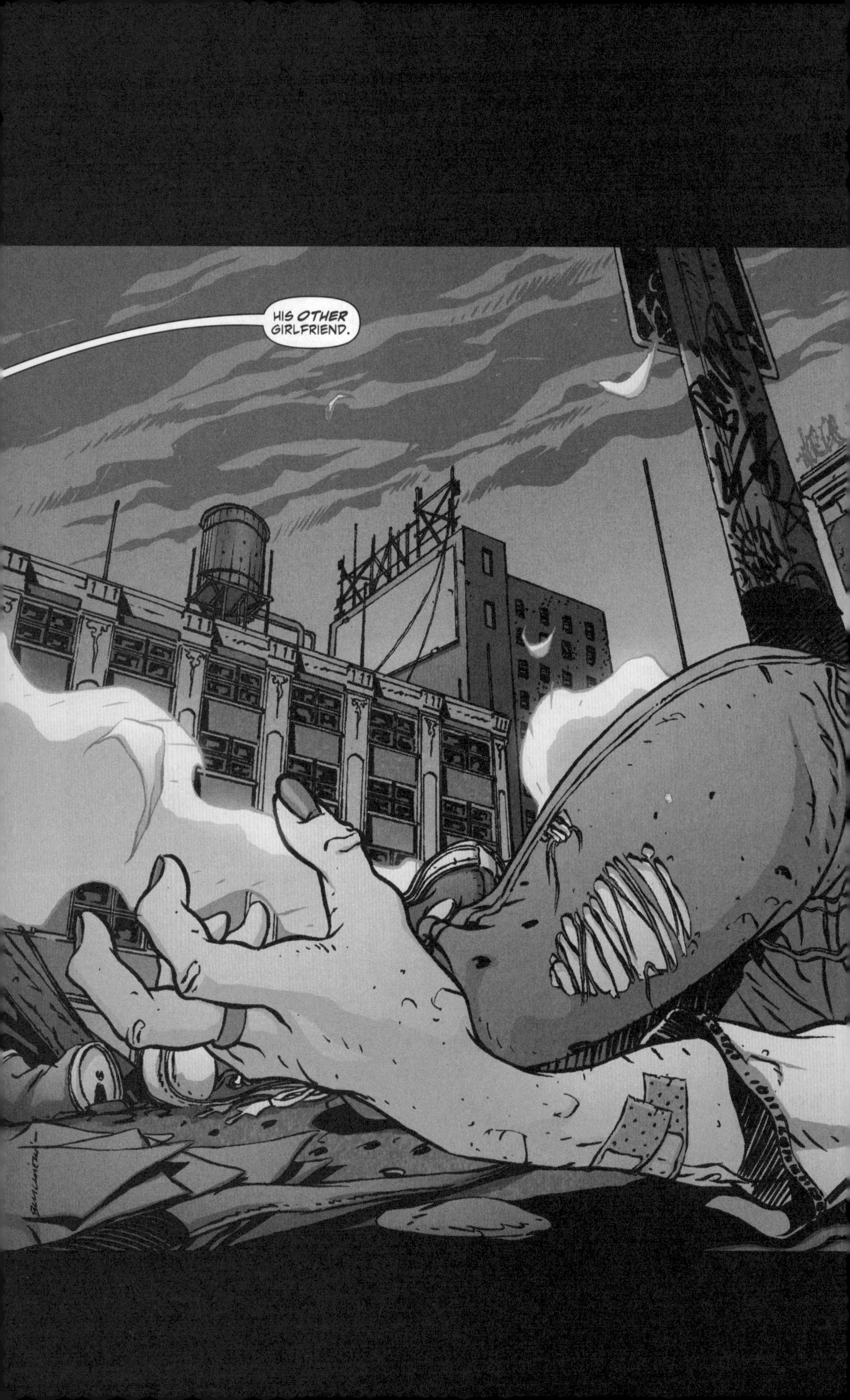
HIS *OTHER* GIRLFRIEND.

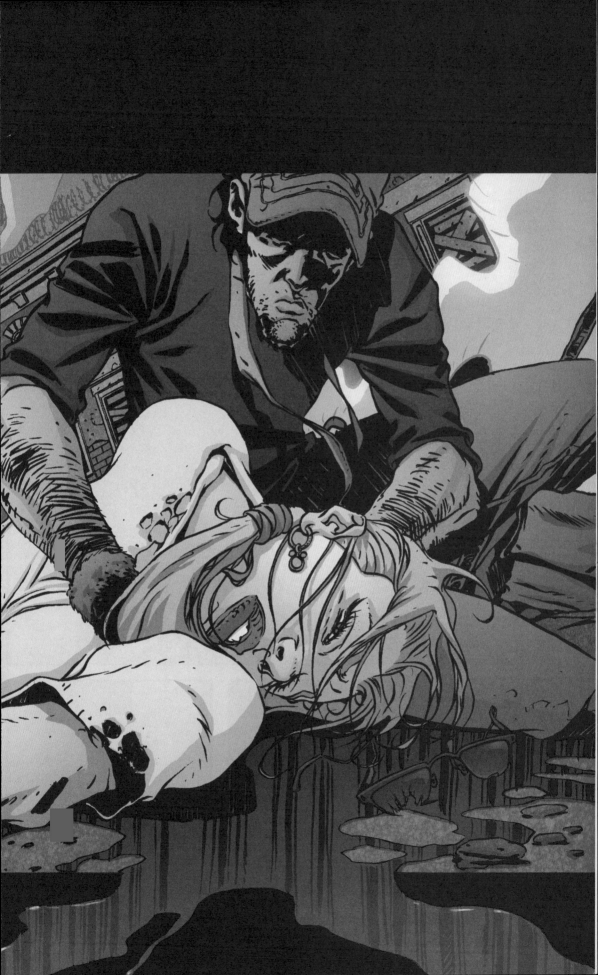

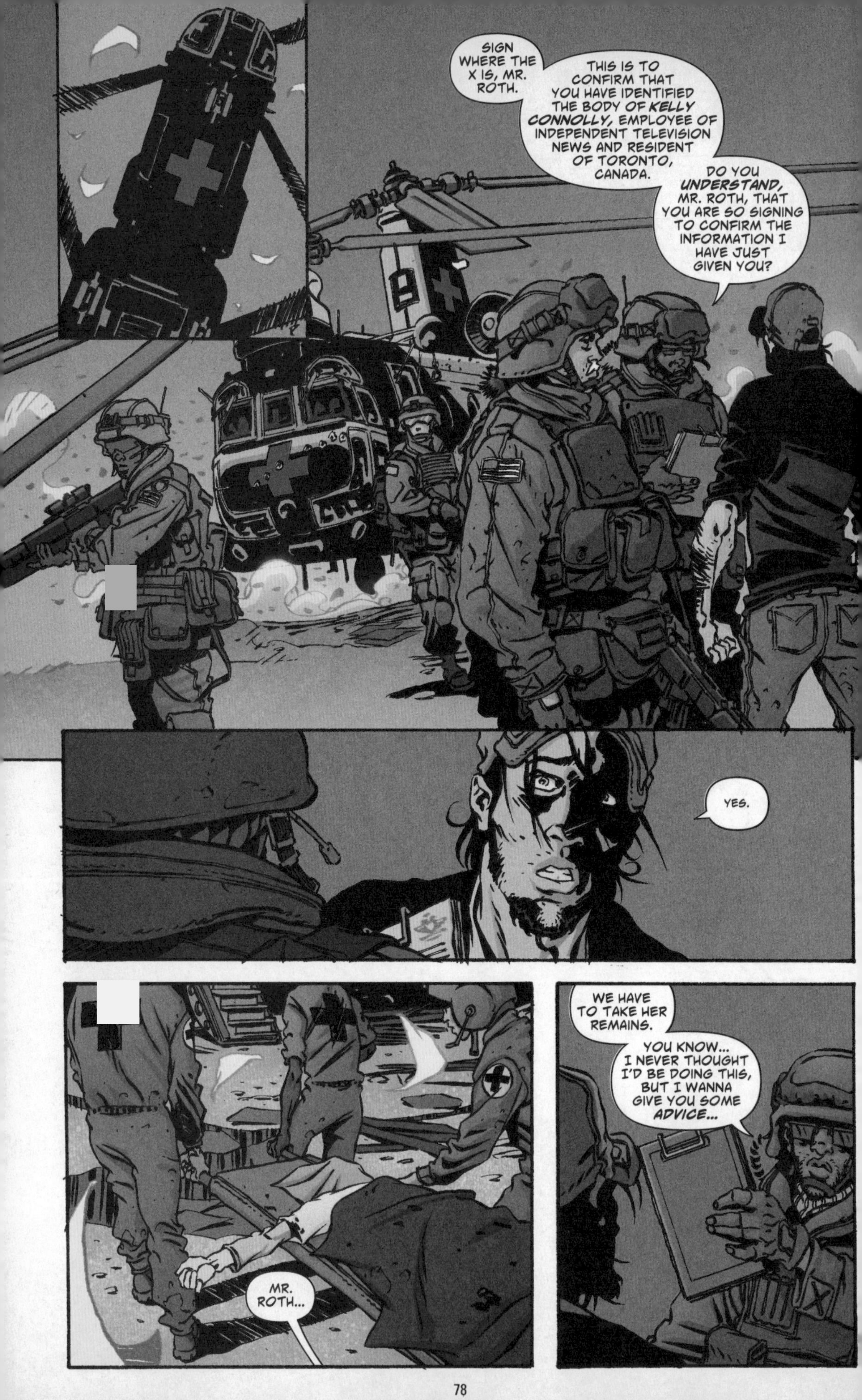
SIGN WHERE THE X IS, MR. ROTH.
THIS IS TO CONFIRM THAT YOU HAVE IDENTIFIED THE BODY OF KELLY CONNOLLY, EMPLOYEE OF INDEPENDENT TELEVISION NEWS AND RESIDENT OF TORONTO, CANADA.
DO YOU UNDERSTAND, MR. ROTH, THAT YOU ARE SO SIGNING TO CONFIRM THE INFORMATION I HAVE JUST GIVEN YOU?
YES.
MR. ROTH...
WE HAVE TO TAKE HER REMAINS.
YOU KNOW... I NEVER THOUGHT I'D BE DOING THIS, BUT I WANNA GIVE YOU SOME ADVICE...

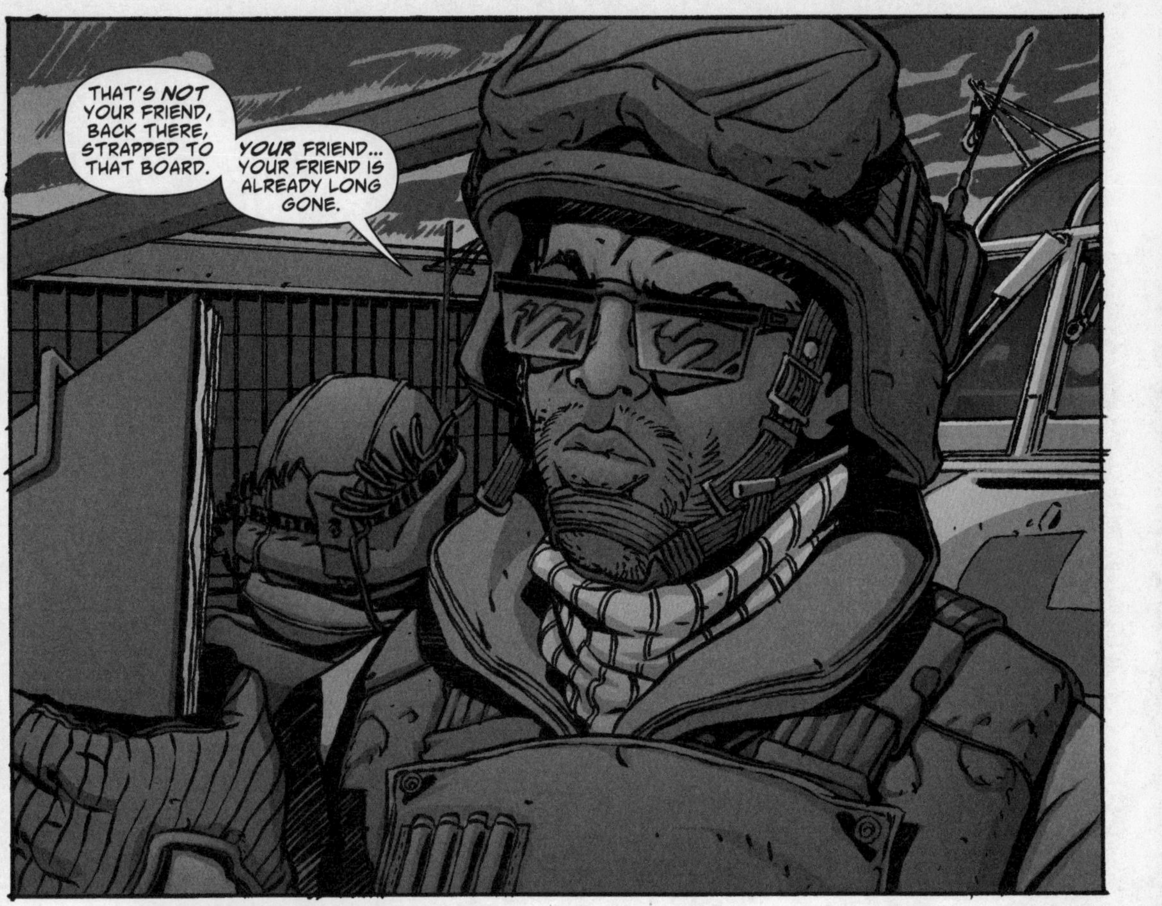
THAT'S *NOT* YOUR FRIEND, BACK THERE, STRAPPED TO THAT BOARD.
YOUR FRIEND... YOUR FRIEND IS ALREADY LONG GONE.

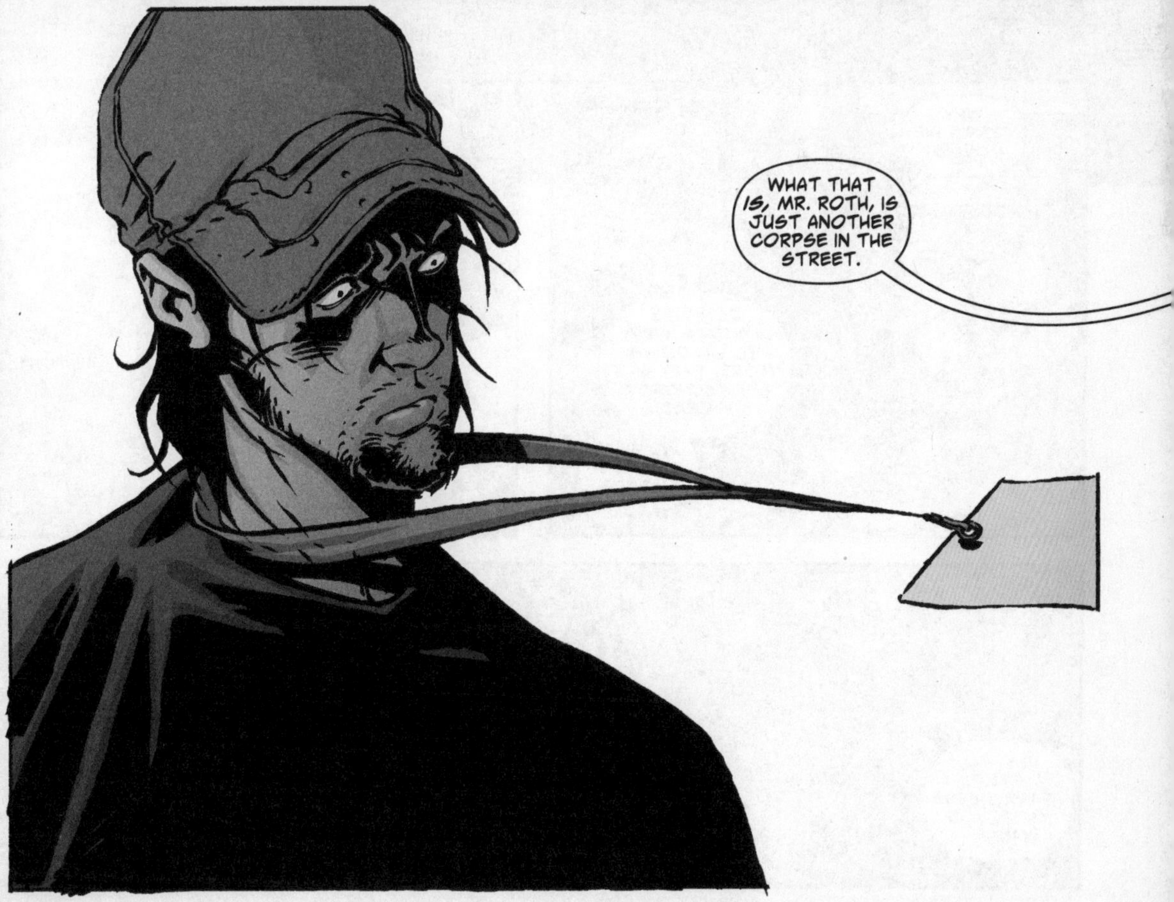
WHAT THAT *IS*, MR. ROTH, IS JUST ANOTHER CORPSE IN THE STREET.

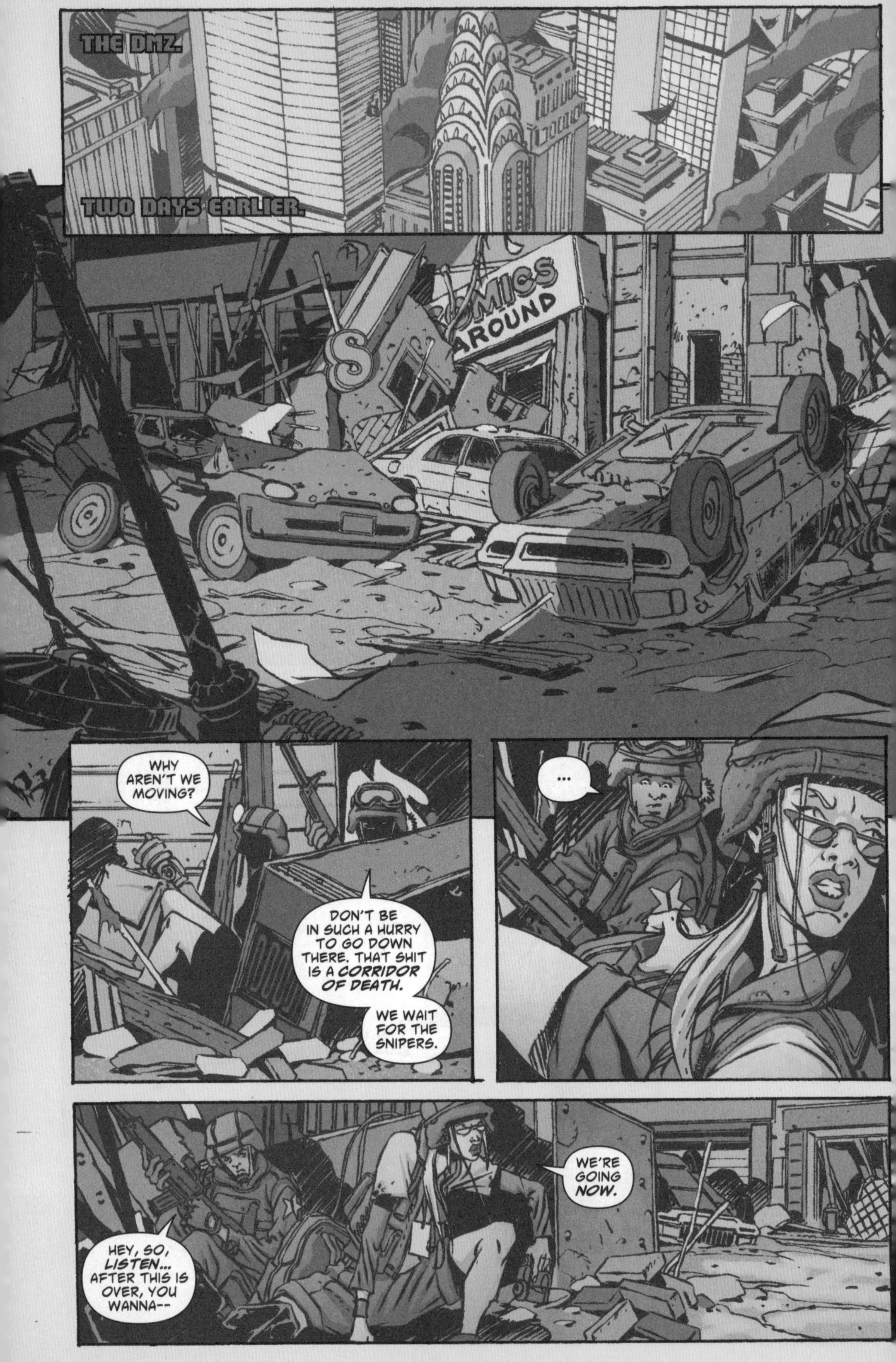
THE DMZ.
TWO DAYS EARLIER.
COMICS
AROUND
WHY AREN'T WE MOVING?
DON'T BE IN SUCH A HURRY TO GO DOWN THERE. THAT SHIT IS A *CORRIDOR OF DEATH.*
WE WAIT FOR THE SNIPERS.
...
WE'RE GOING *NOW.*
HEY, SO, *LISTEN...* AFTER THIS IS OVER, YOU WANNA--

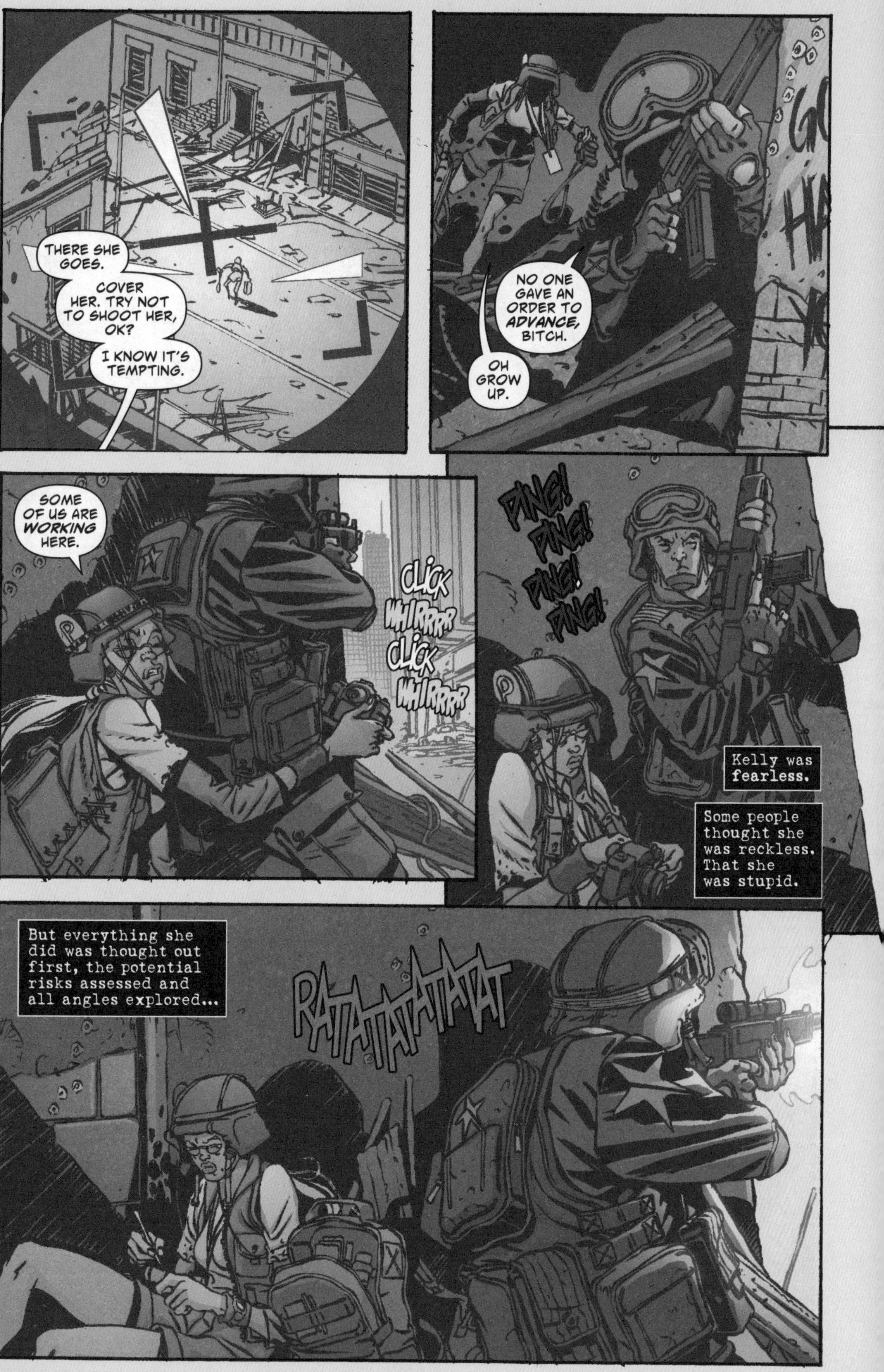
THERE SHE GOES.
COVER HER. TRY NOT TO SHOOT HER, OK?
I KNOW IT'S TEMPTING.
NO ONE GAVE AN ORDER TO *ADVANCE,* BITCH.
OH GROW UP.
SOME OF US ARE *WORKING* HERE.
CLICK
WHIRRRR
CLICK
WHIRRRR
PING! PING! PING! PING!
Kelly was **fearless.**
Some people thought she was reckless. That she was stupid.
But everything she did was thought out first, the potential risks assessed and all angles explored...
RATATATATATAT

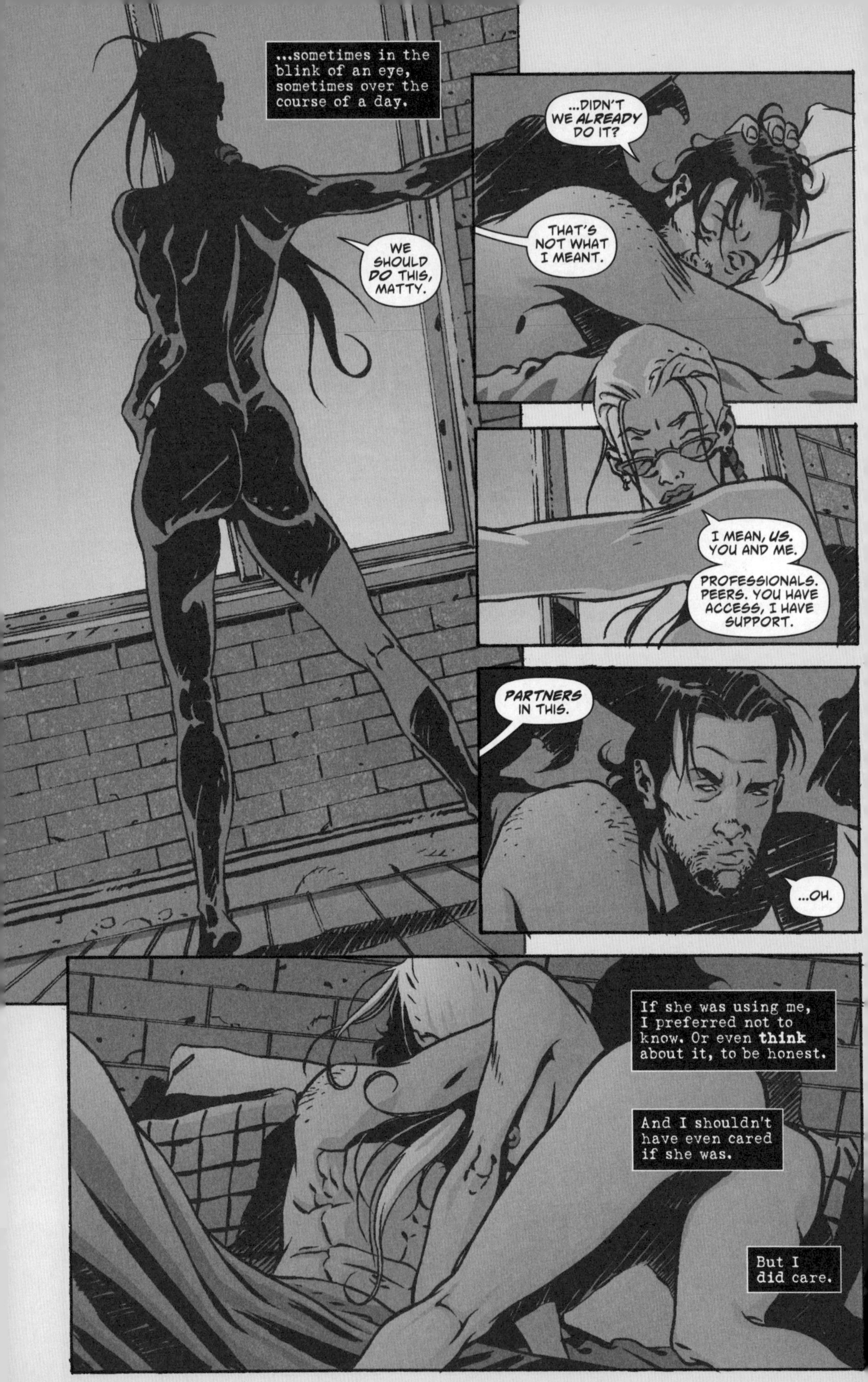
...sometimes in the blink of an eye, sometimes over the course of a day.
WE SHOULD DO THIS, MATTY.
...DIDN'T WE ALREADY DO IT?
THAT'S NOT WHAT I MEANT.
I MEAN, US. YOU AND ME.
PROFESSIONALS. PEERS. YOU HAVE ACCESS, I HAVE SUPPORT.
PARTNERS IN THIS.
...OH.
If she was using me, I preferred not to know. Or even think about it, to be honest.
And I shouldn't have even cared if she was.
But I did care.

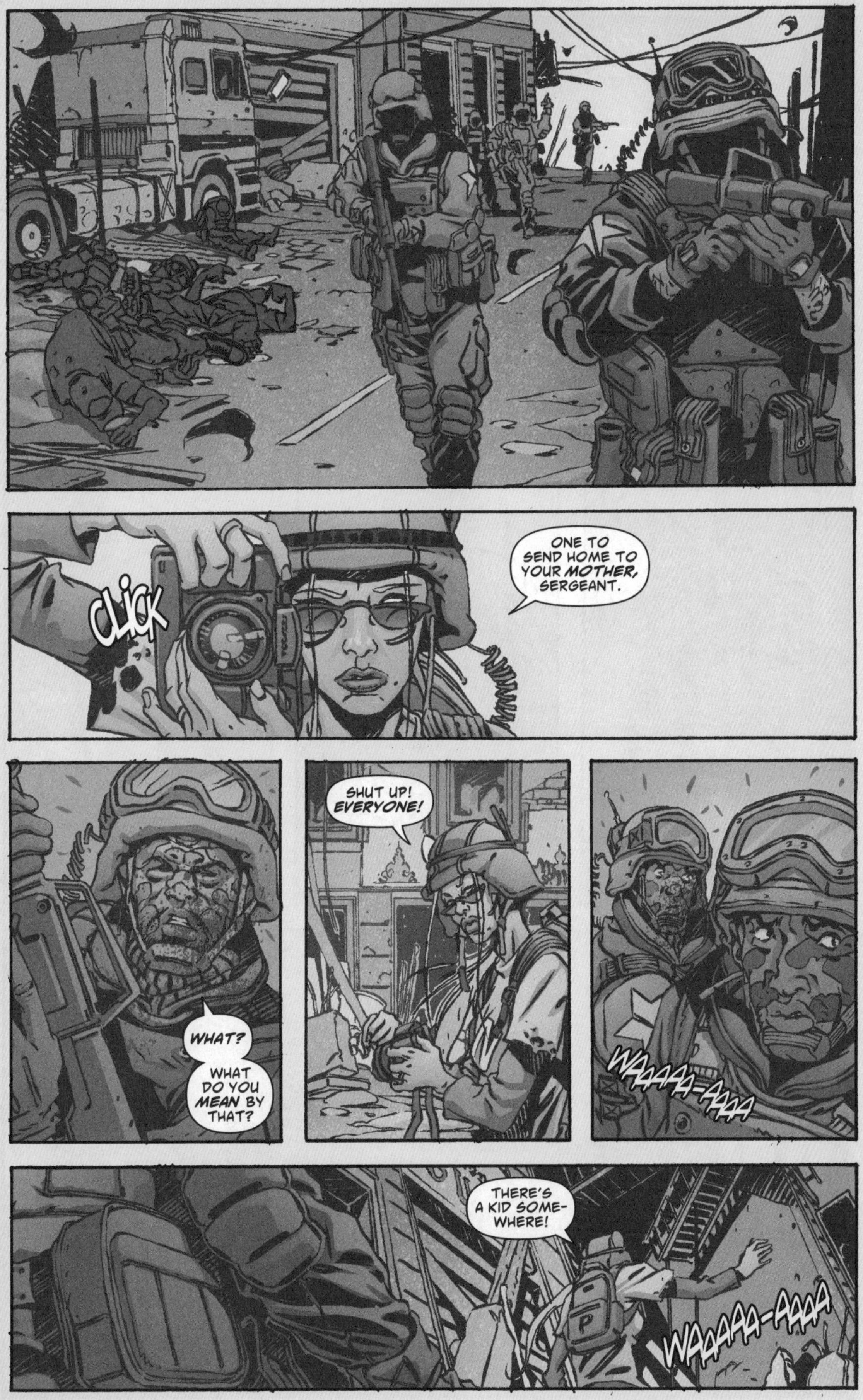
CLICK
ONE TO SEND HOME TO YOUR MOTHER, SERGEANT.
WHAT?
WHAT DO YOU MEAN BY THAT?
SHUT UP! EVERYONE!
WAAAAA-AAAA
THERE'S A KID SOME-WHERE!
WAAAAA-AAAA

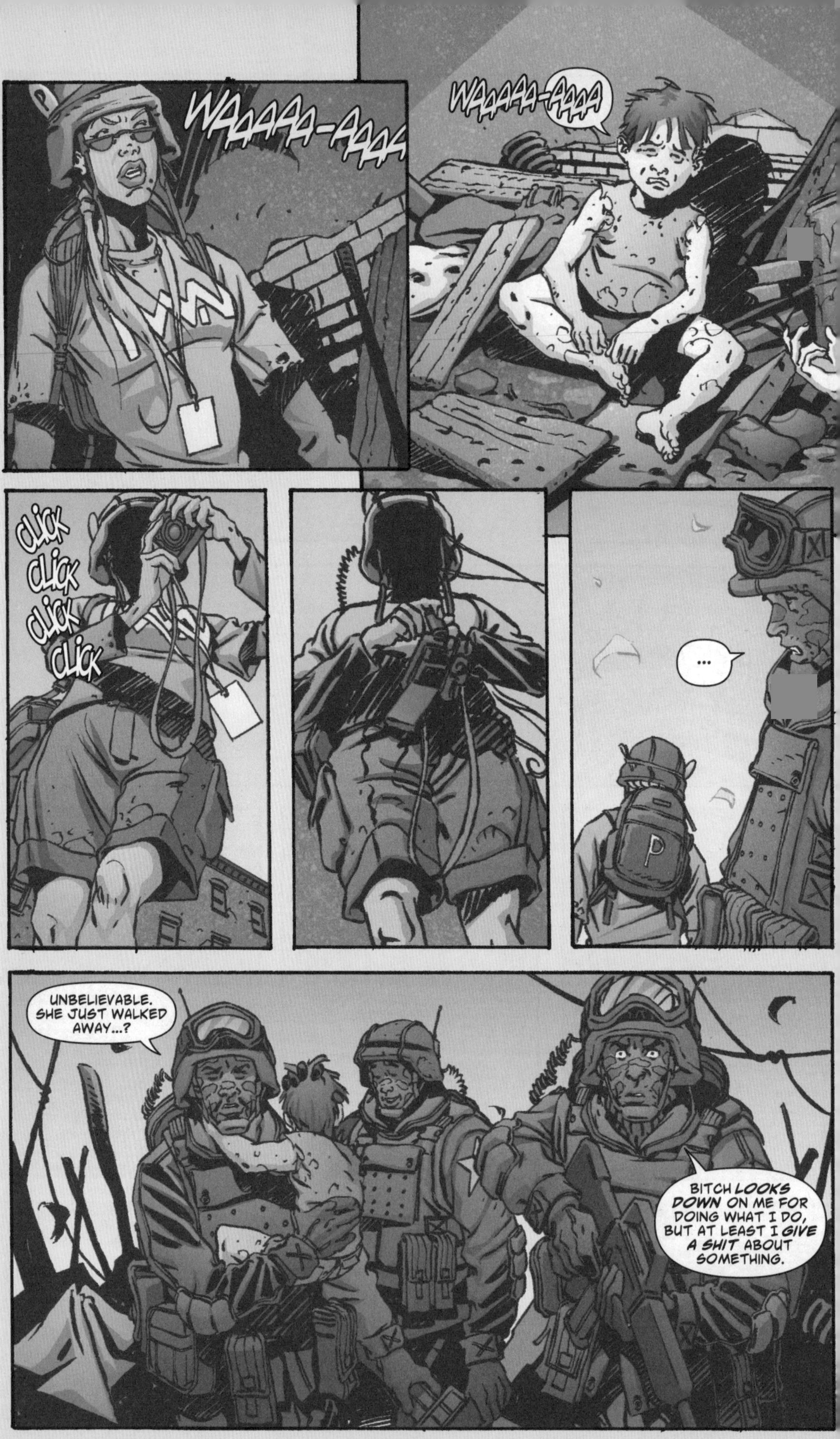
WAAAAA-AAAA
WAAAAA-AAAA
CLICK
CLICK
CLICK
CLICK
...
UNBELIEVABLE. SHE JUST WALKED AWAY...?
BITCH LOOKS DOWN ON ME FOR DOING WHAT I DO, BUT AT LEAST I GIVE A SHIT ABOUT SOMETHING.

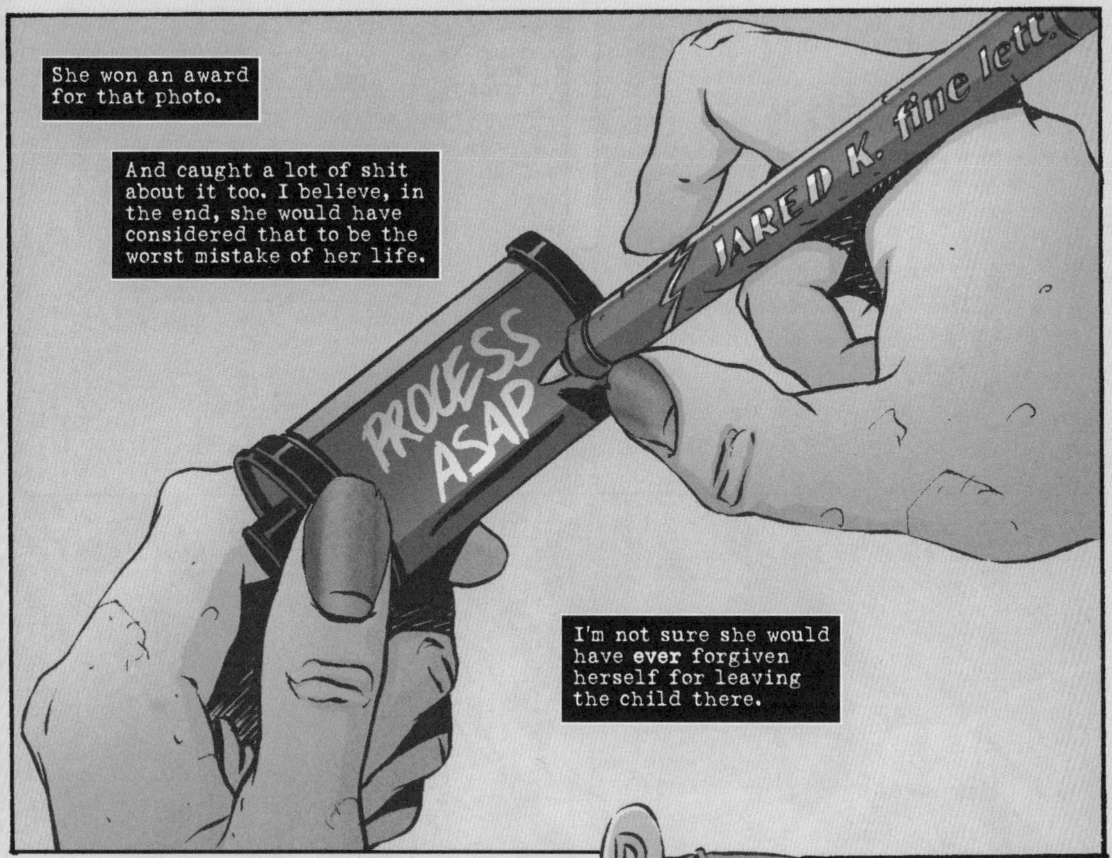
She won an award for that photo.
And caught a lot of shit about it too. I believe, in the end, she would have considered that to be the worst mistake of her life.
JARED K. fine lett
PROCESS ASAP
I'm not sure she would have **ever** forgiven herself for leaving the child there.

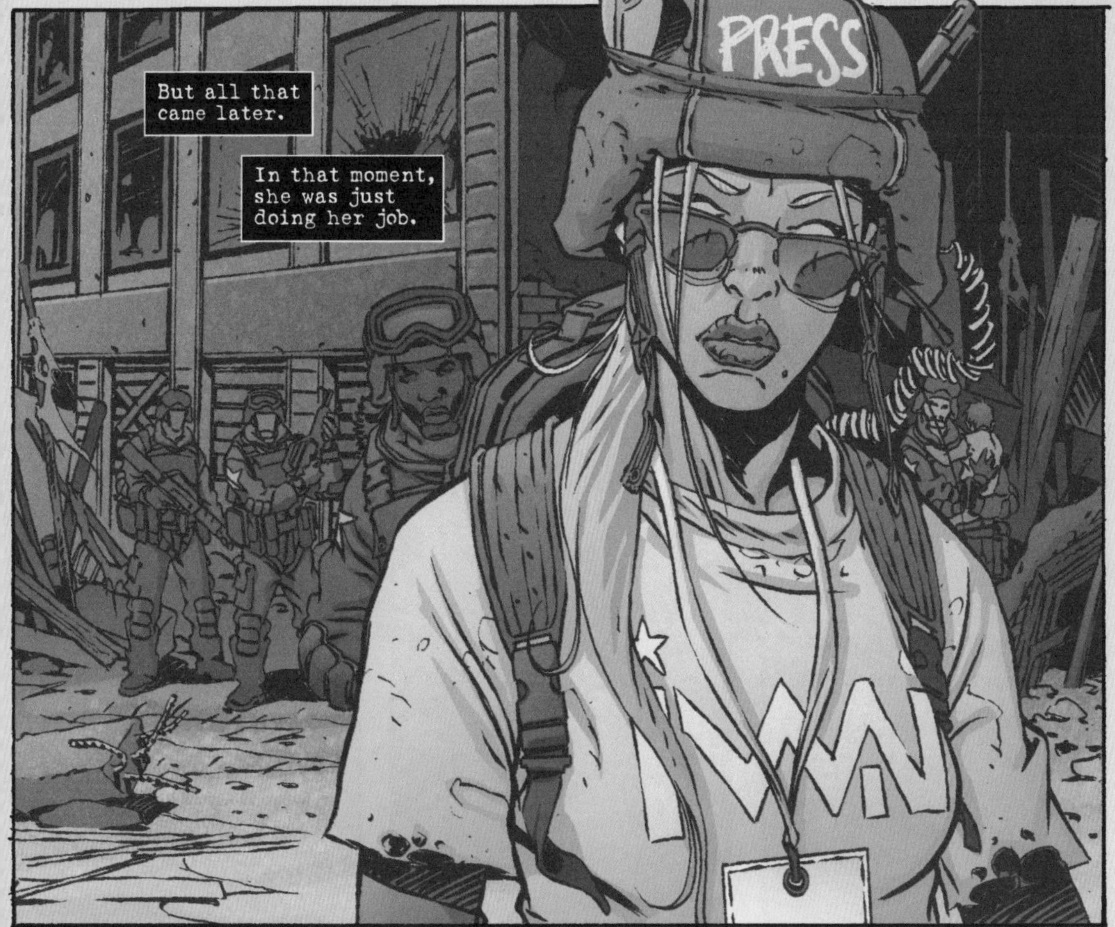
PRESS
But all that came later.
In that moment, she was just doing her job.

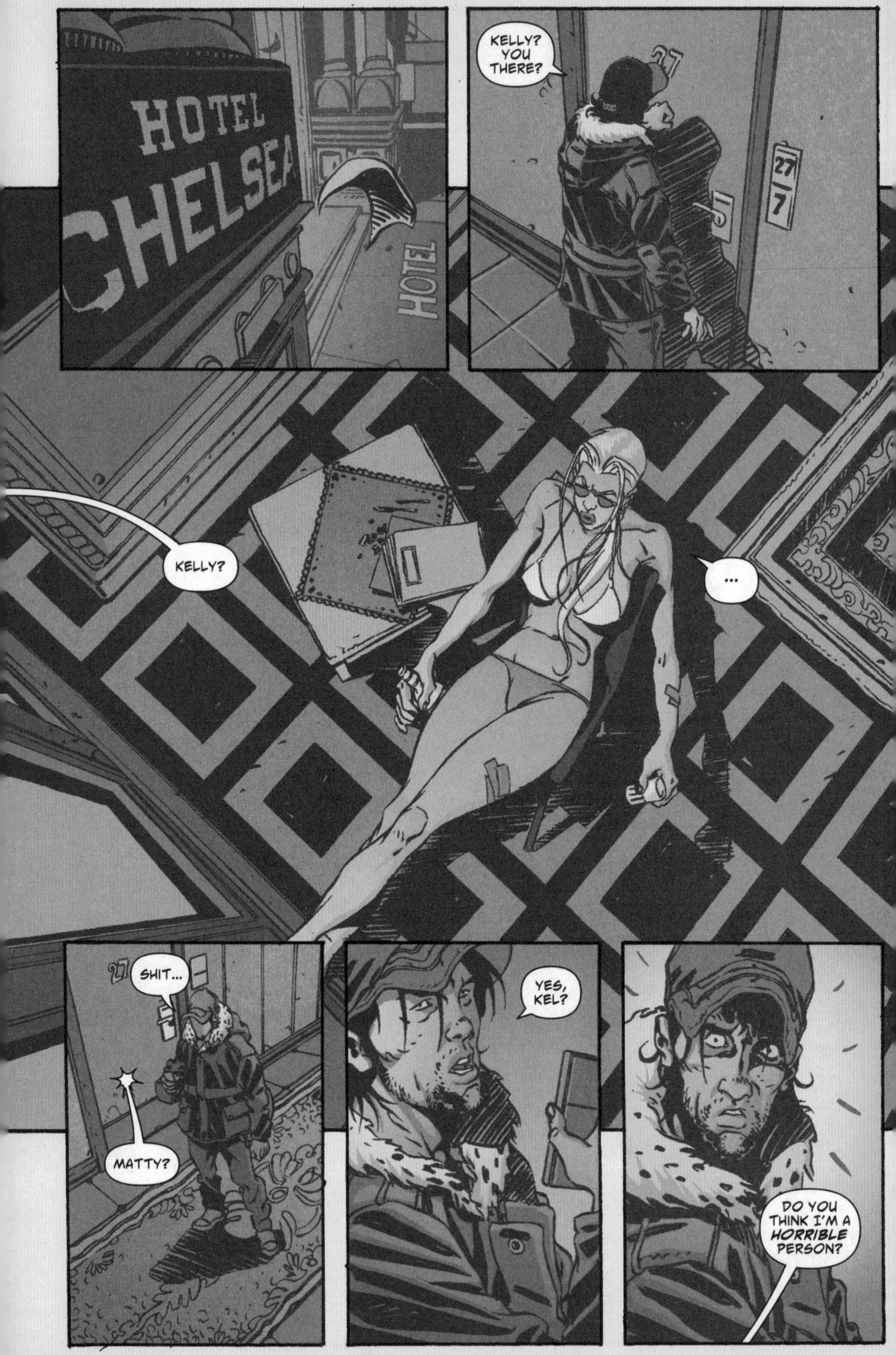
HOTEL
CHELSEA
HOTEL
KELLY? YOU THERE?
27
7
KELLY?
...
SHIT...
MATTY?
YES, KEL?
DO YOU THINK I'M A *HORRIBLE* PERSON?

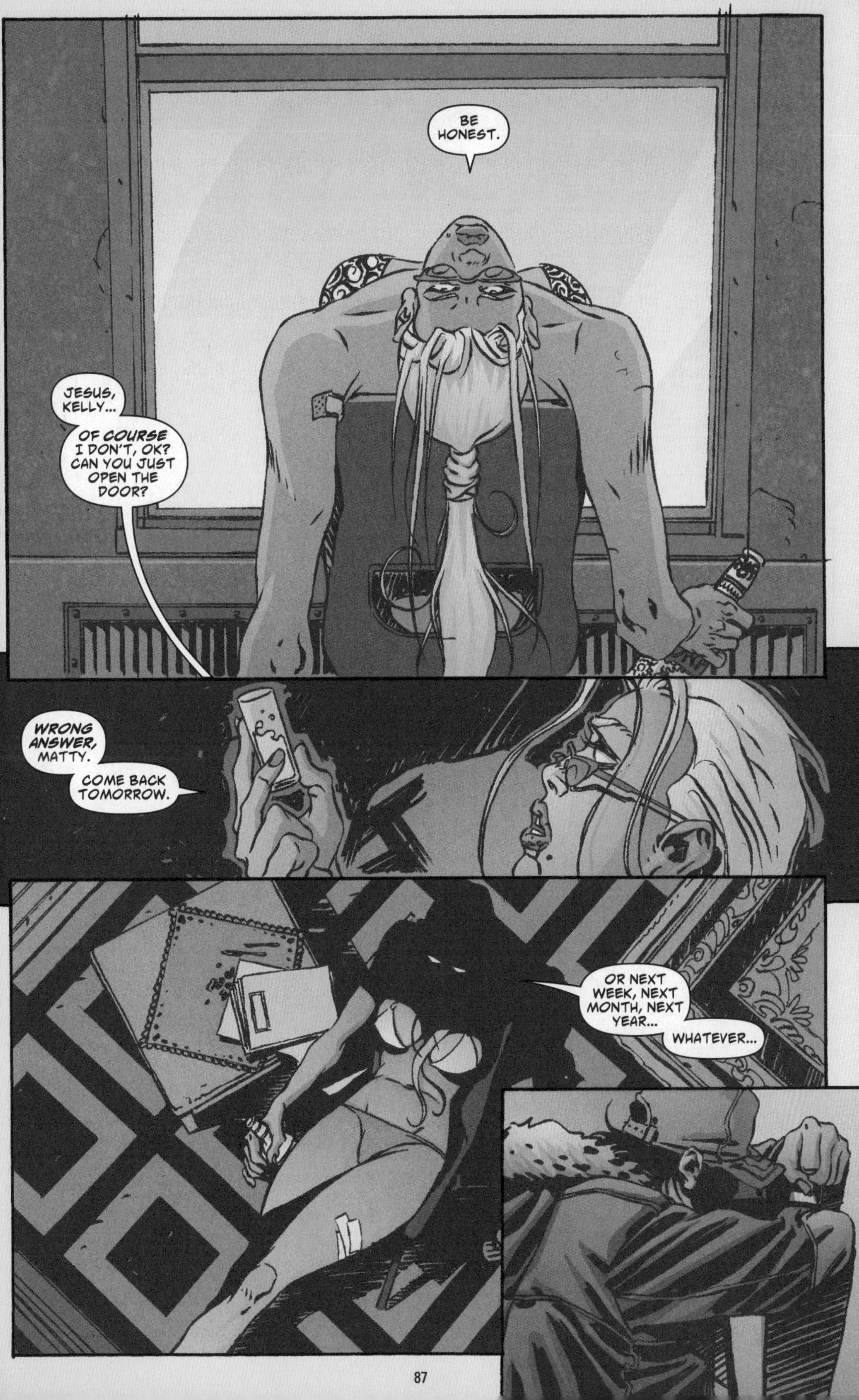
BE HONEST.
JESUS, KELLY...
OF COURSE I DON'T, OK? CAN YOU JUST OPEN THE DOOR?
WRONG ANSWER, MATTY.
COME BACK TOMORROW.
OR NEXT WEEK, NEXT MONTH, NEXT YEAR...
WHATEVER...

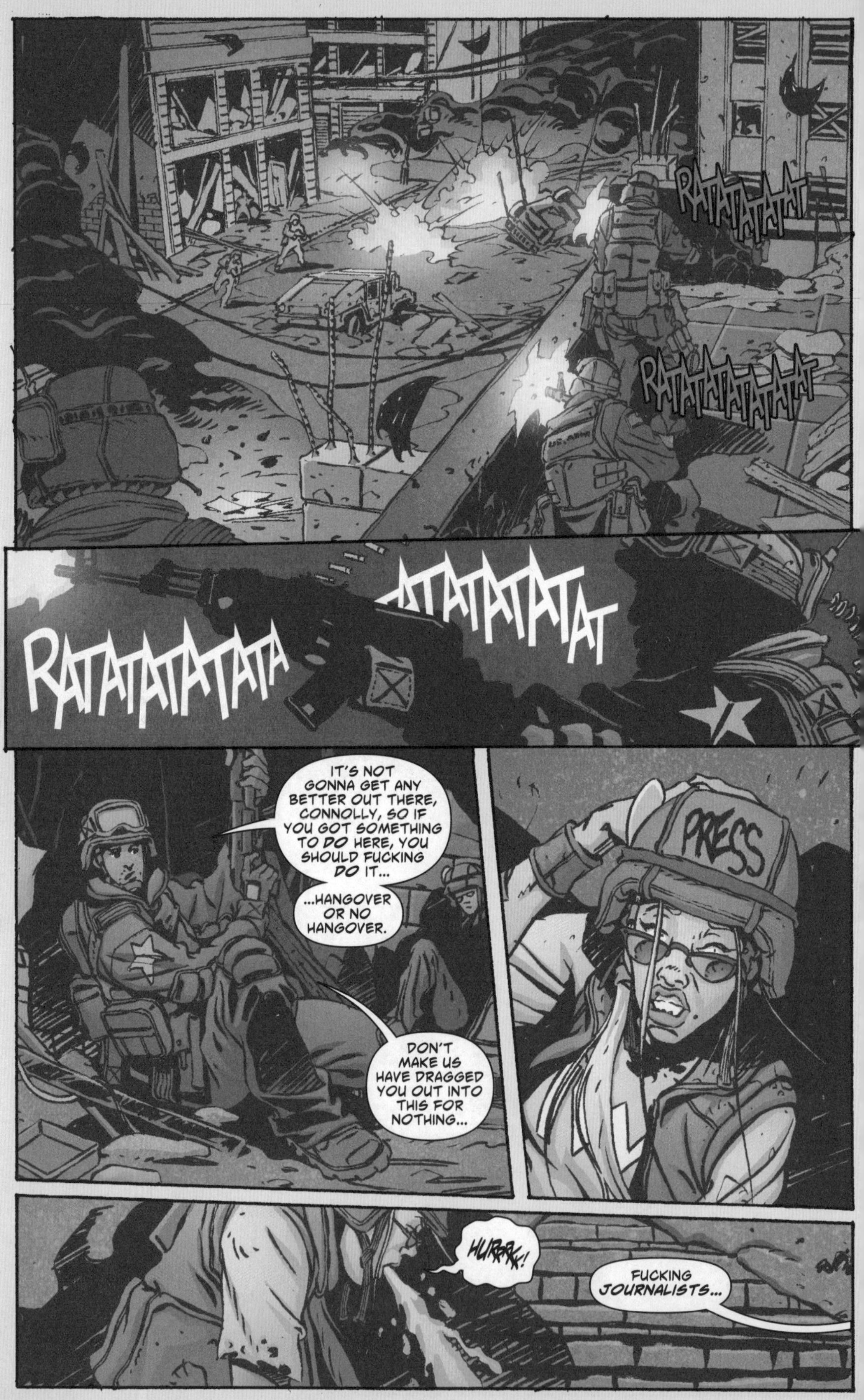

RATATATATAT
RATATATATATATAT
RATATATATATA
TATATATATAT
IT'S NOT GONNA GET ANY BETTER OUT THERE, CONNOLLY, SO IF YOU GOT SOMETHING TO *DO* HERE, YOU SHOULD FUCKING *DO* IT...
...HANGOVER OR NO HANGOVER.
DON'T MAKE US HAVE DRAGGED YOU OUT INTO THIS FOR NOTHING...
PRESS
HURRRK!
FUCKING JOURNALISTS...

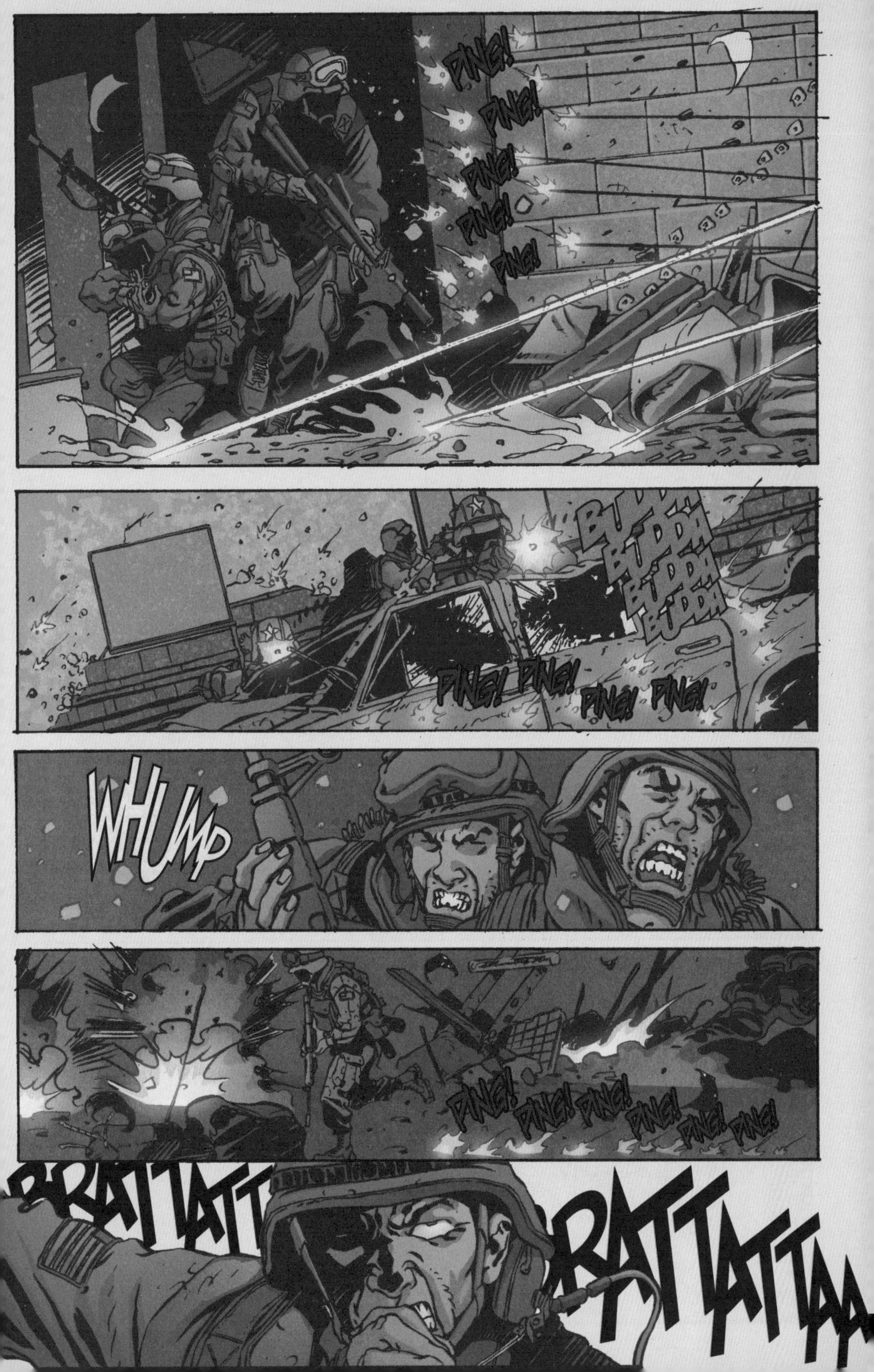
PING!
PING!
PING!
PING!
PING!
BUDDA
BUDDA
BUDDA
BUDDA
PING! PING!
PING! PING!
WHUMP
PING!
PING! PING!
PING!
PING! PING!
BRATTATT
BRATTATTAA

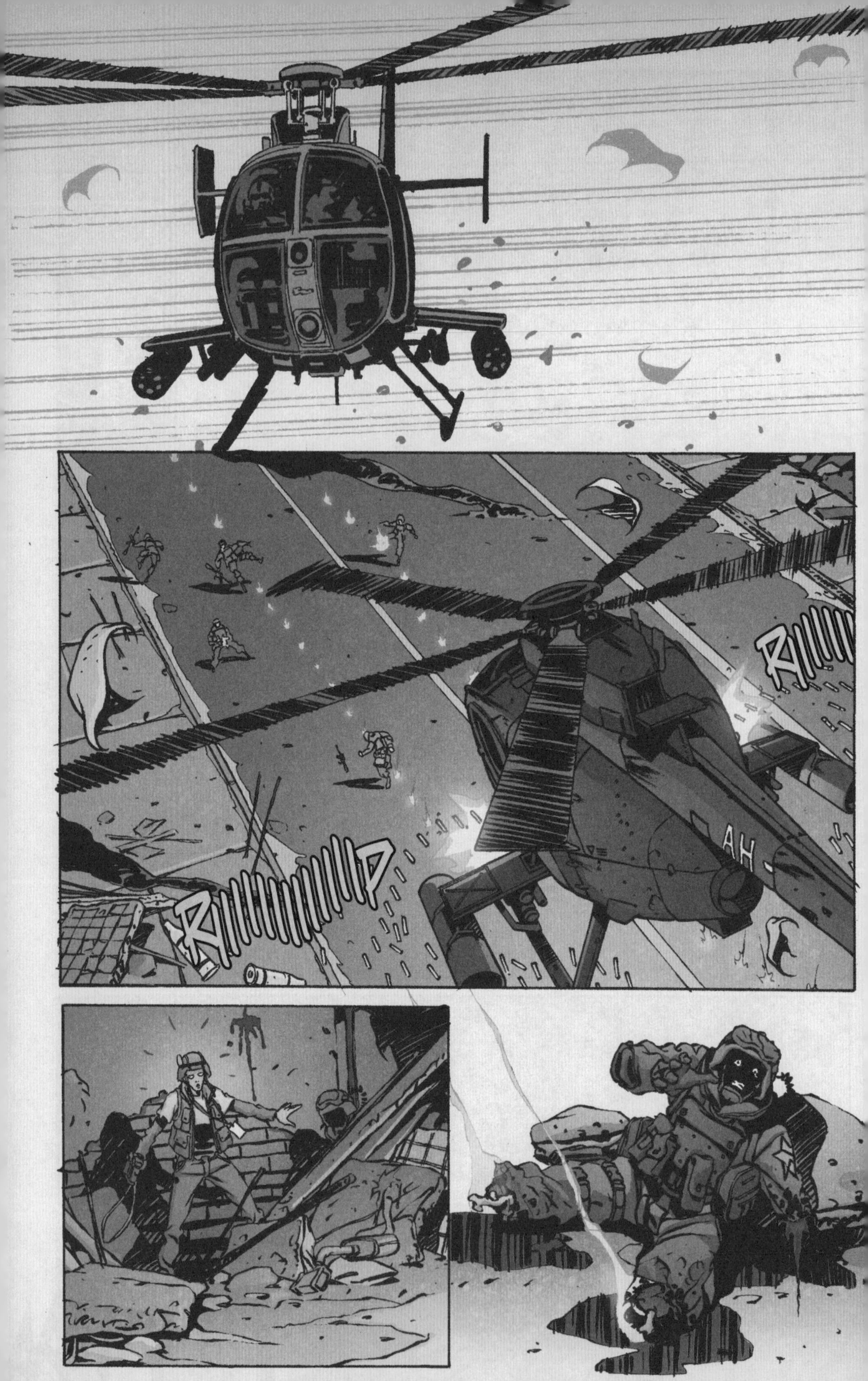
RIIIII
AH-
RIIIIIIIIIIIIIP

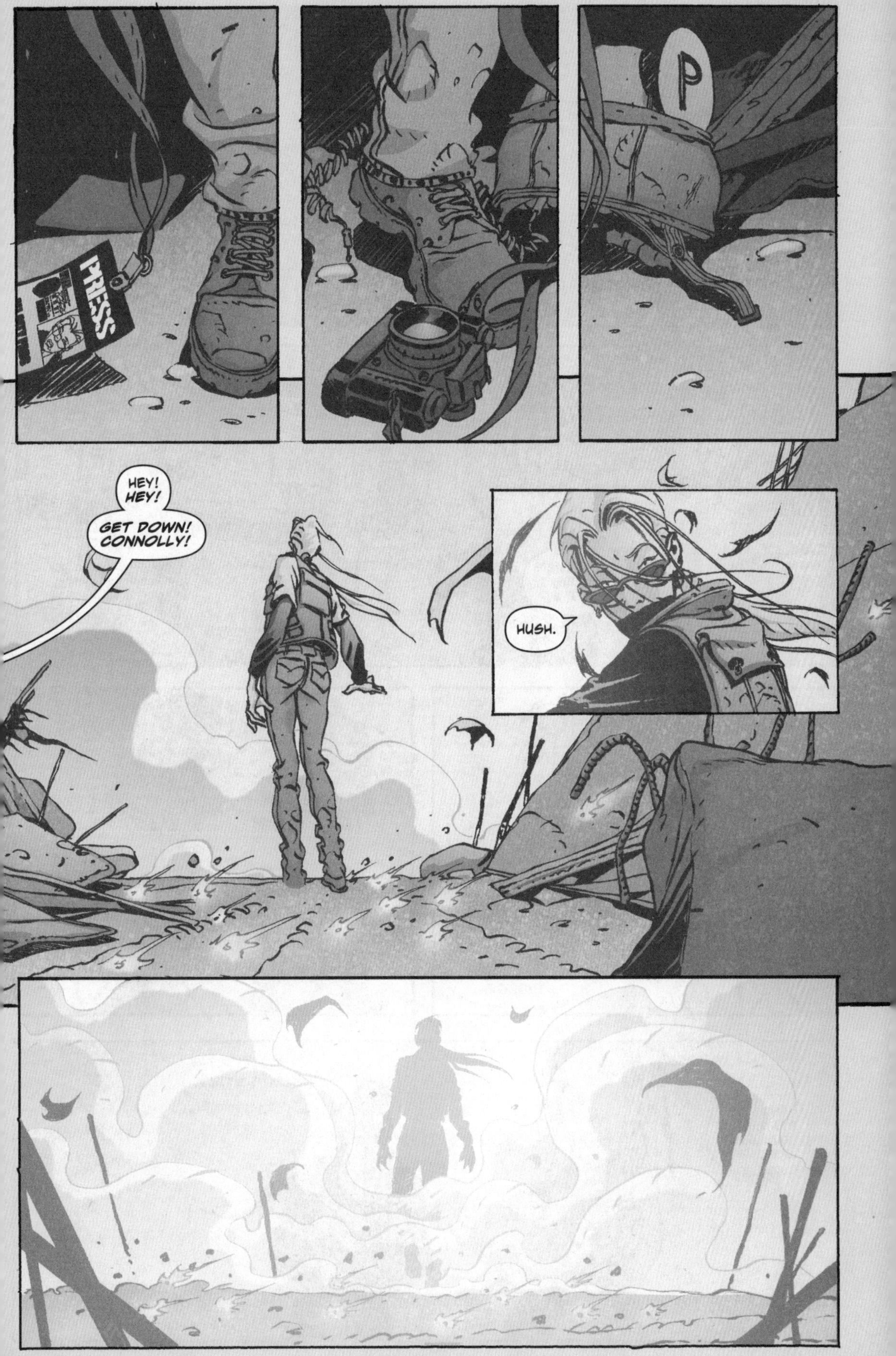
PRESS
HEY! HEY!
GET DOWN! CONNOLLY!
HUSH.

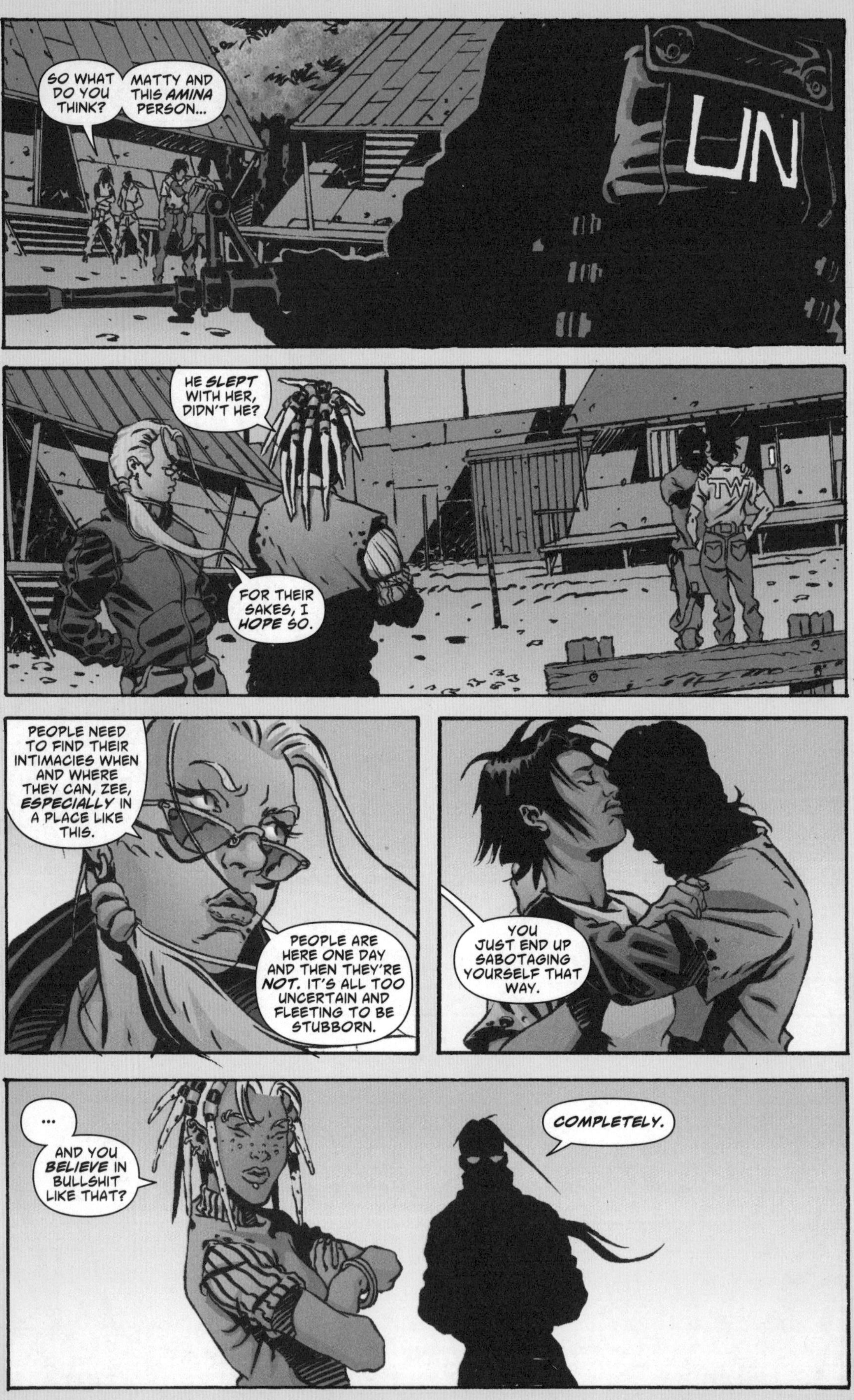

SO WHAT DO YOU THINK?
MATTY AND THIS AMINA PERSON...
UN
HE SLEPT WITH HER, DIDN'T HE?
FOR THEIR SAKES, I HOPE SO.
PEOPLE NEED TO FIND THEIR INTIMACIES WHEN AND WHERE THEY CAN, ZEE, ESPECIALLY IN A PLACE LIKE THIS.
PEOPLE ARE HERE ONE DAY AND THEN THEY'RE NOT. IT'S ALL TOO UNCERTAIN AND FLEETING TO BE STUBBORN.
YOU JUST END UP SABOTAGING YOURSELF THAT WAY.
...
AND YOU BELIEVE IN BULLSHIT LIKE THAT?
COMPLETELY.

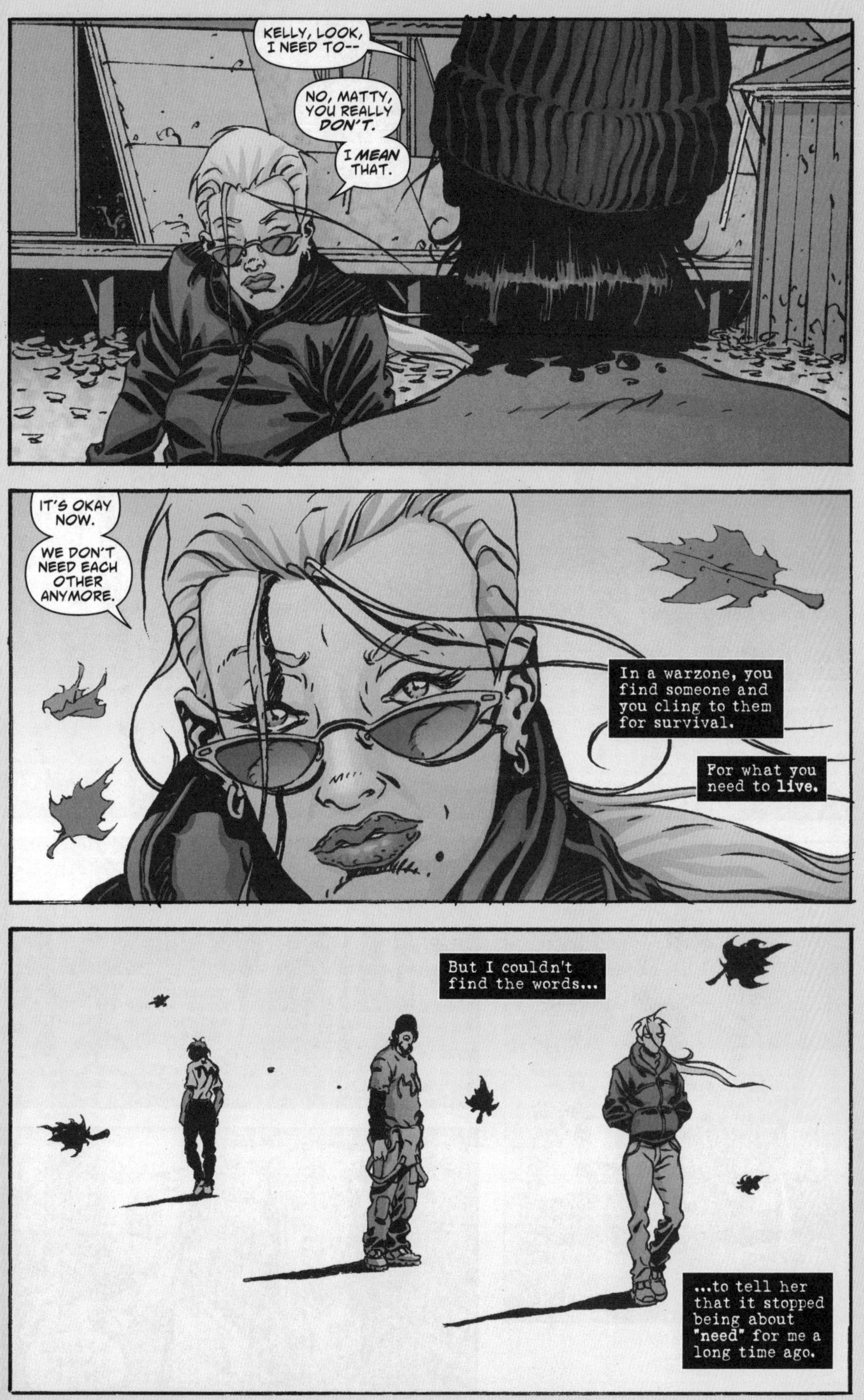
KELLY, LOOK, I NEED TO--
NO, MATTY, YOU REALLY DON'T.
I MEAN THAT.
IT'S OKAY NOW.
WE DON'T NEED EACH OTHER ANYMORE.
In a warzone, you find someone and you cling to them for survival.
For what you need to live.
But I couldn't find the words...
...to tell her that it stopped being about "need" for me a long time ago.

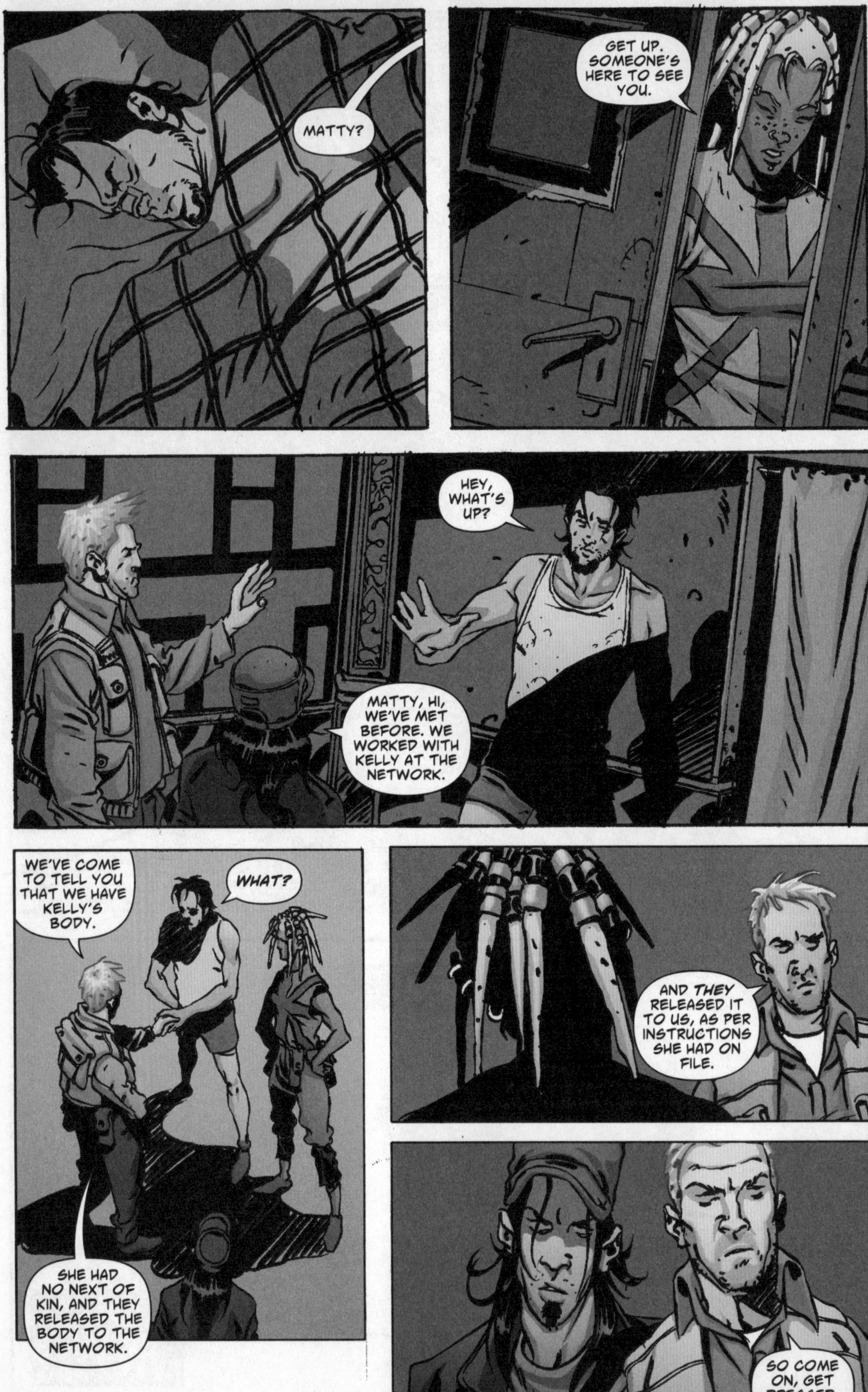
MATTY?
GET UP. SOMEONE'S HERE TO SEE YOU.
HEY, WHAT'S UP?
MATTY, HI, WE'VE MET BEFORE. WE WORKED WITH KELLY AT THE NETWORK.
WE'VE COME TO TELL YOU THAT WE HAVE KELLY'S BODY.
WHAT?
SHE HAD NO NEXT OF KIN, AND THEY RELEASED THE BODY TO THE NETWORK.
AND THEY RELEASED IT TO US, AS PER INSTRUCTIONS SHE HAD ON FILE.
SO COME ON, GET DRESSED.

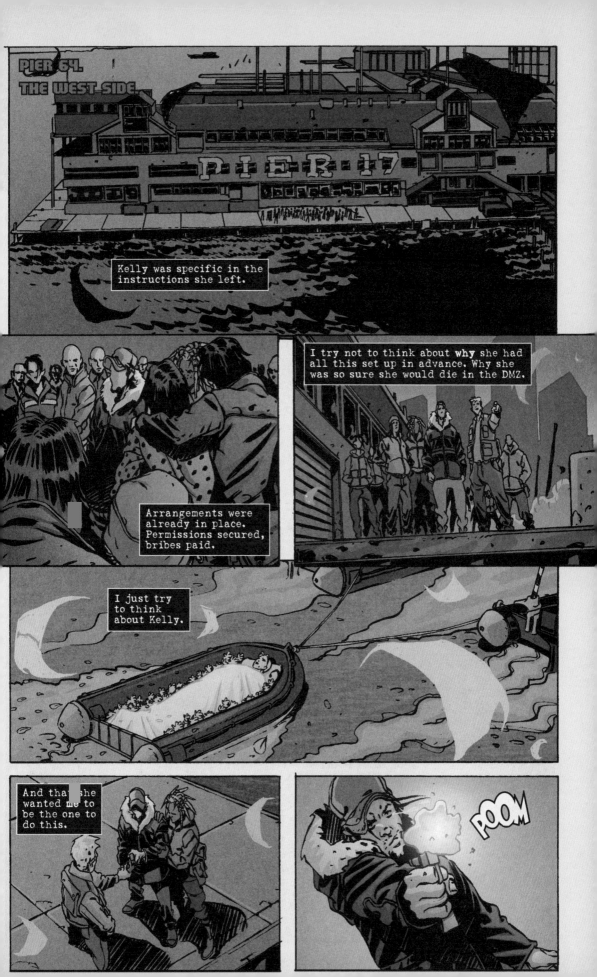

PIER 64.
THE WEST SIDE.

PIER·17

Kelly was specific in the instructions she left.

I try not to think about **why** she had all this set up in advance. Why she was so sure she would die in the DMZ.

Arrangements were already in place. Permissions secured, bribes paid.

I just try to think about Kelly.

And that she wanted me to be the one to do this.

POOM

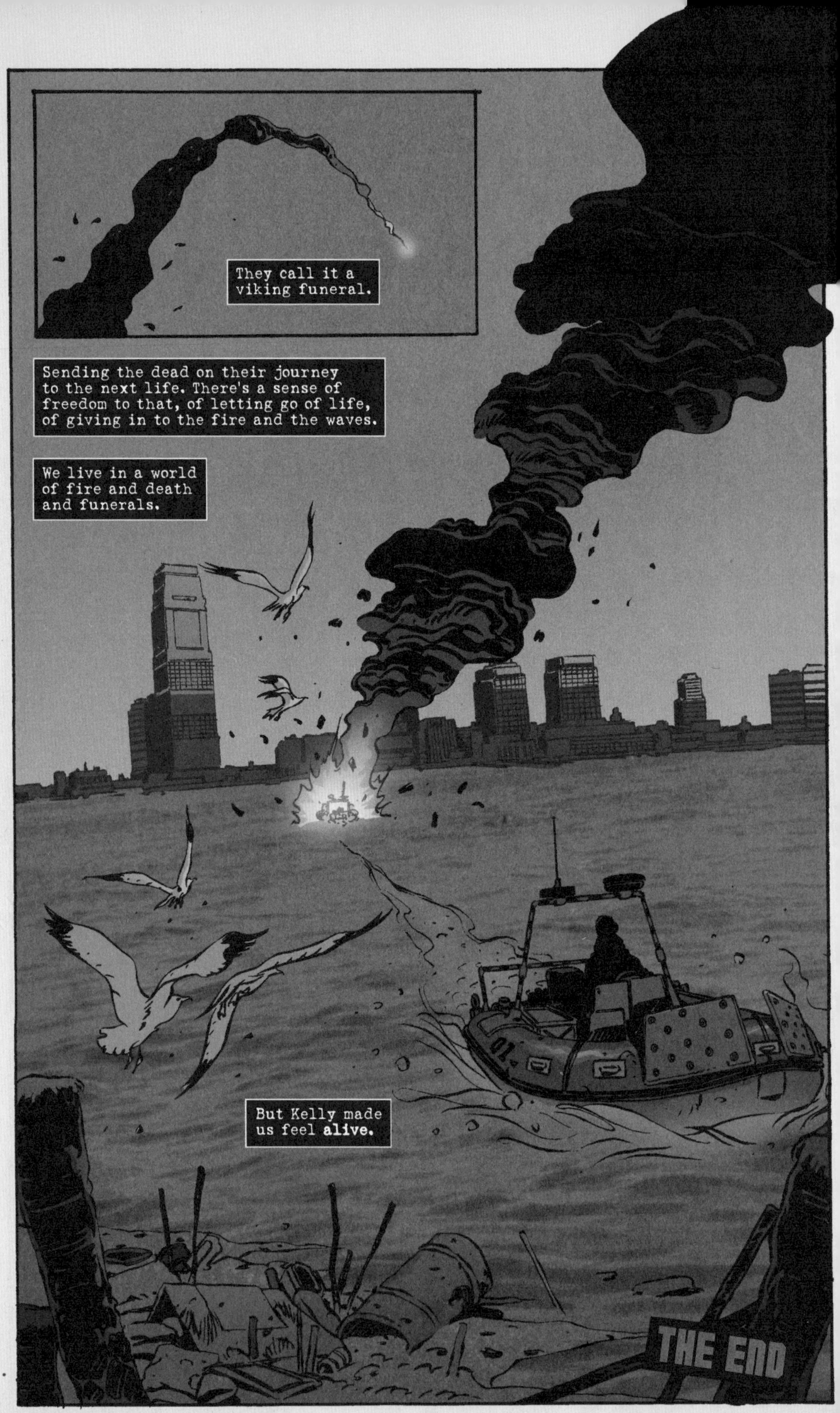
They call it a viking funeral.
Sending the dead on their journey to the next life. There's a sense of freedom to that, of letting go of life, of giving in to the fire and the waves.
We live in a world of fire and death and funerals.
But Kelly made us feel alive.
10
THE END

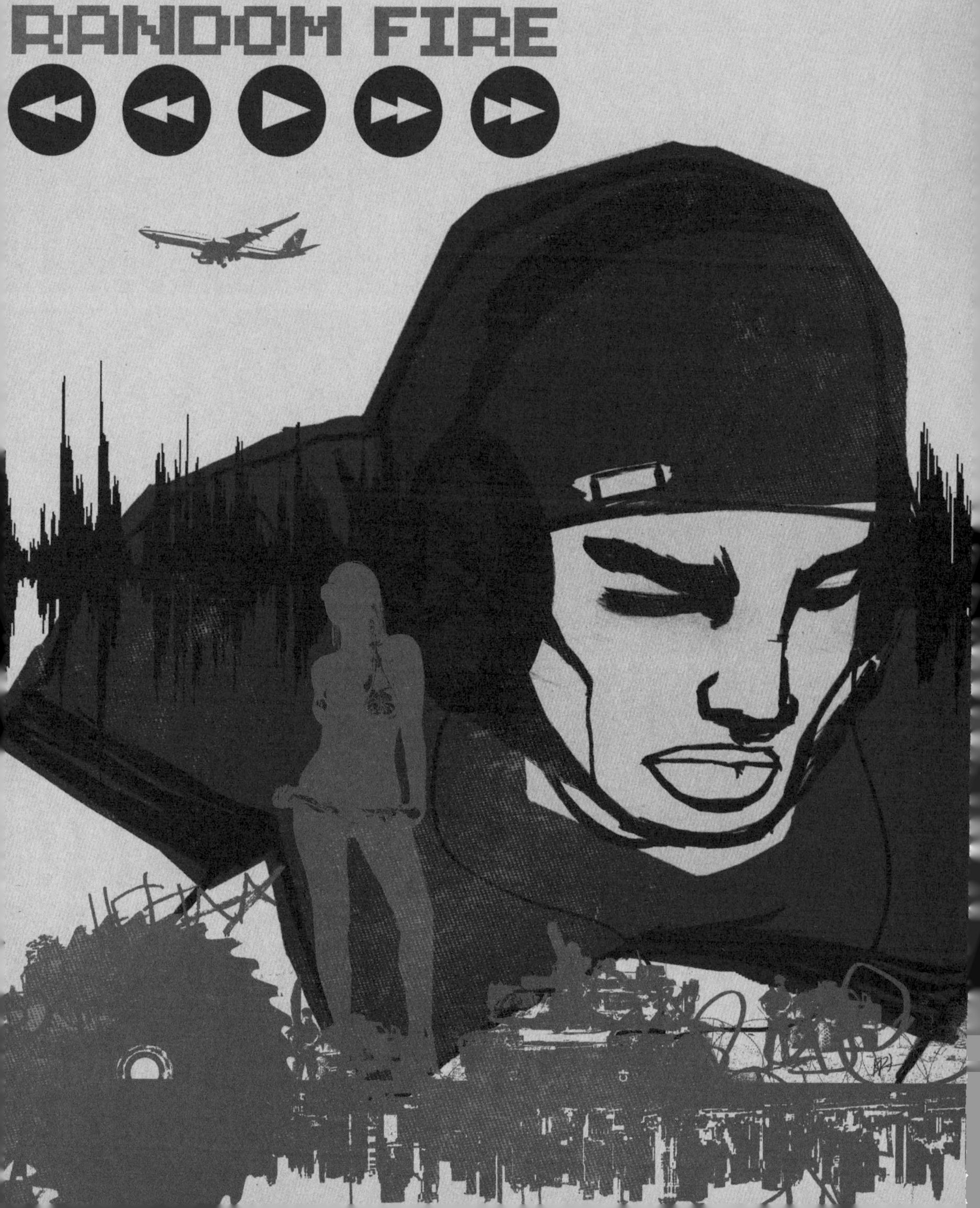
RANDOM FIRE

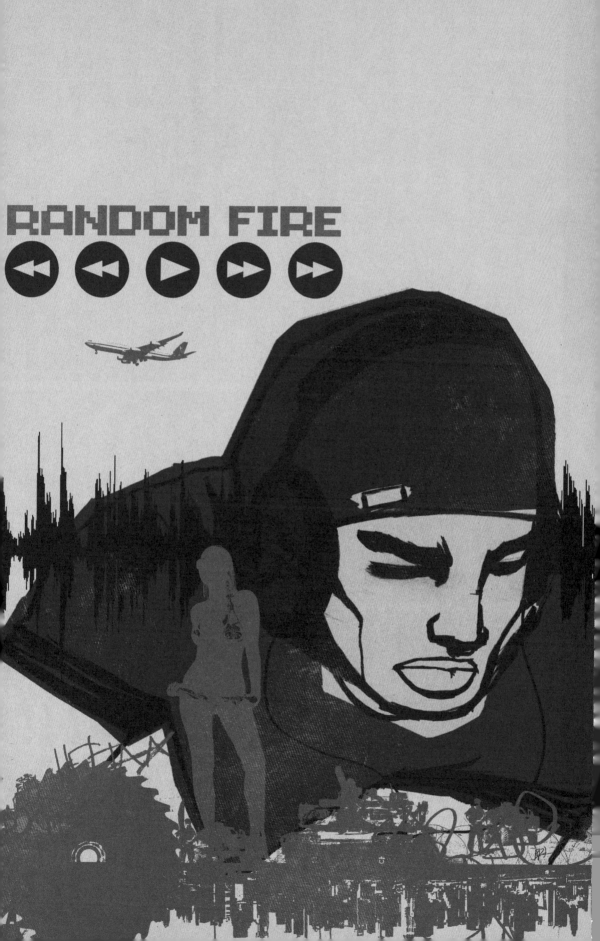

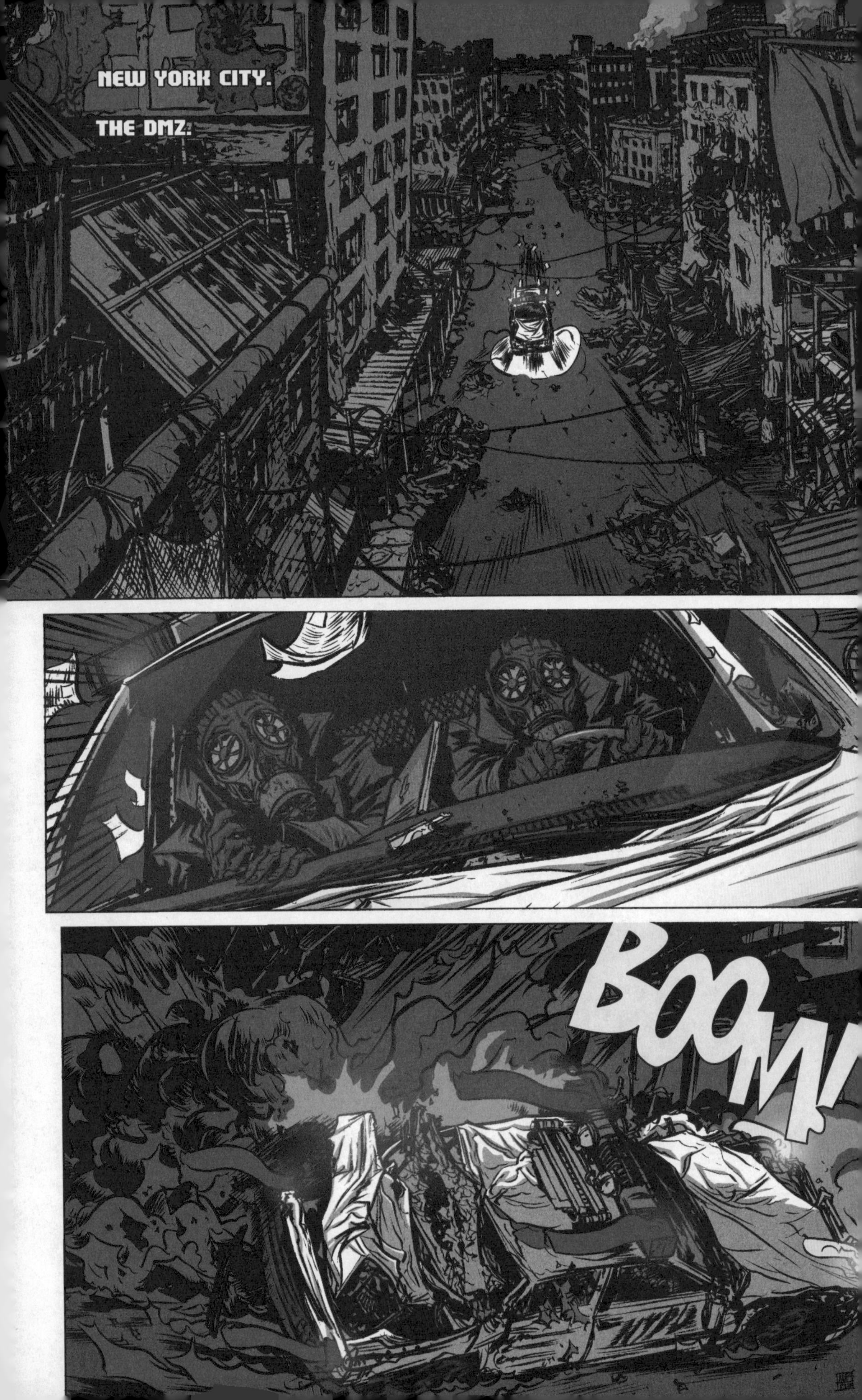
NEW YORK CITY.
THE DMZ.
BOOM!

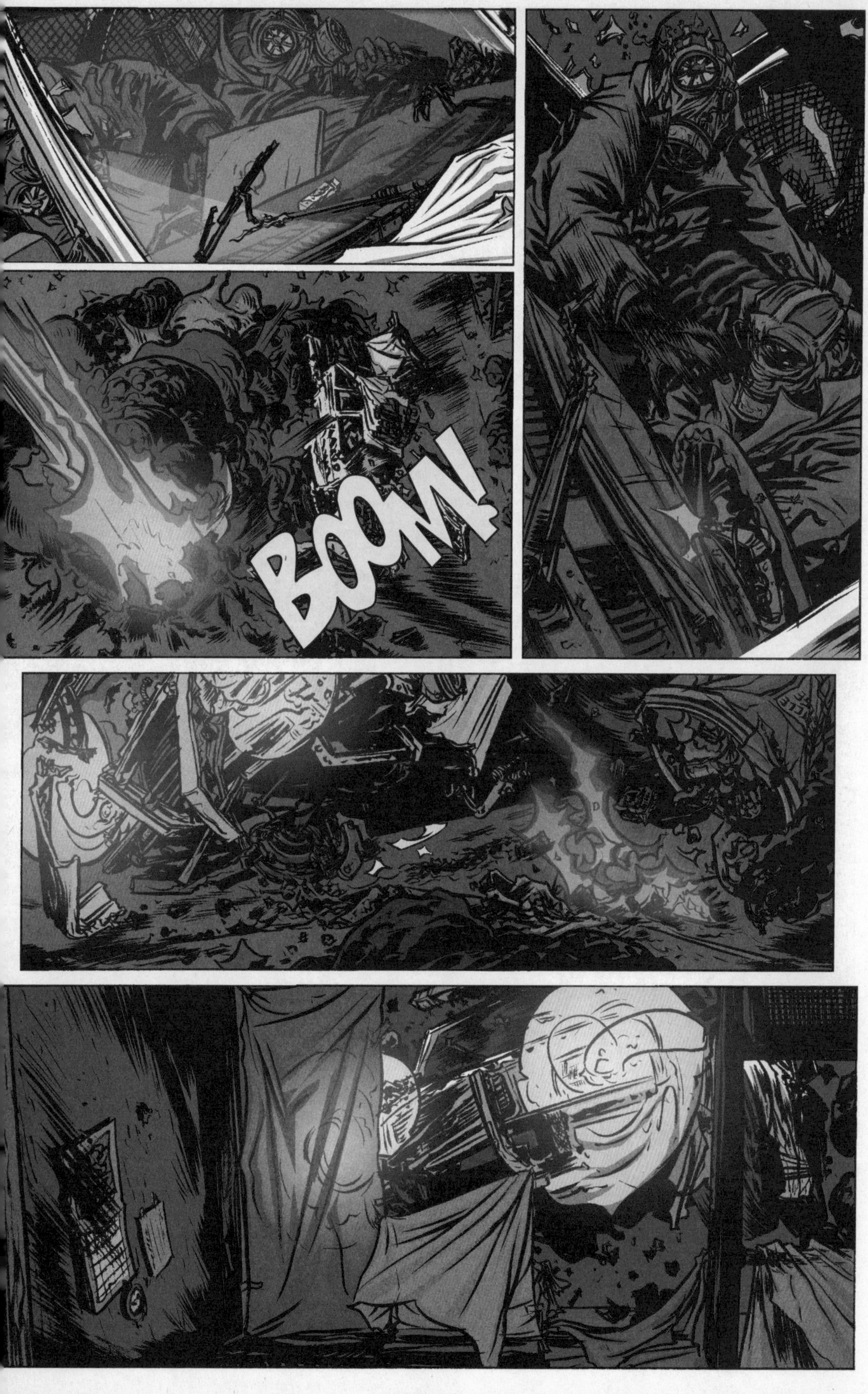
BOOM!

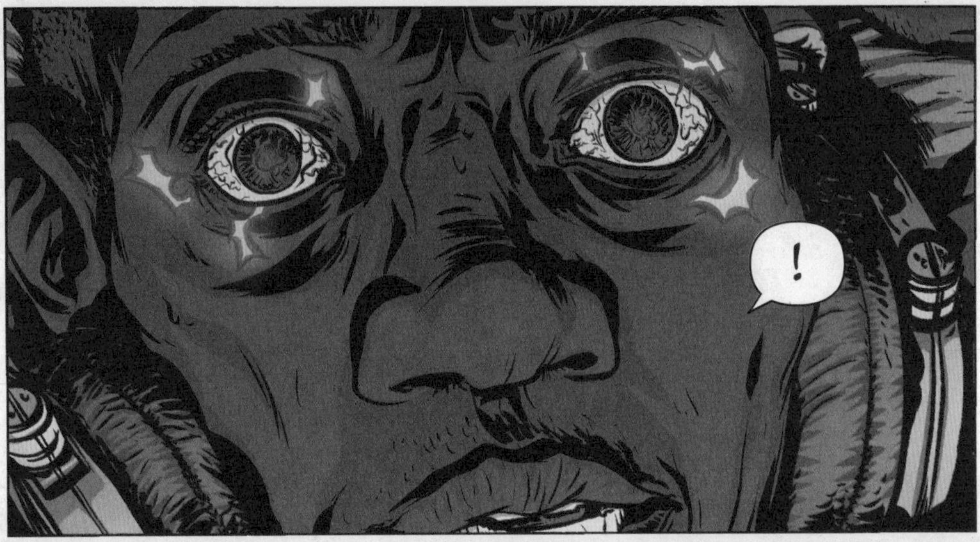
!

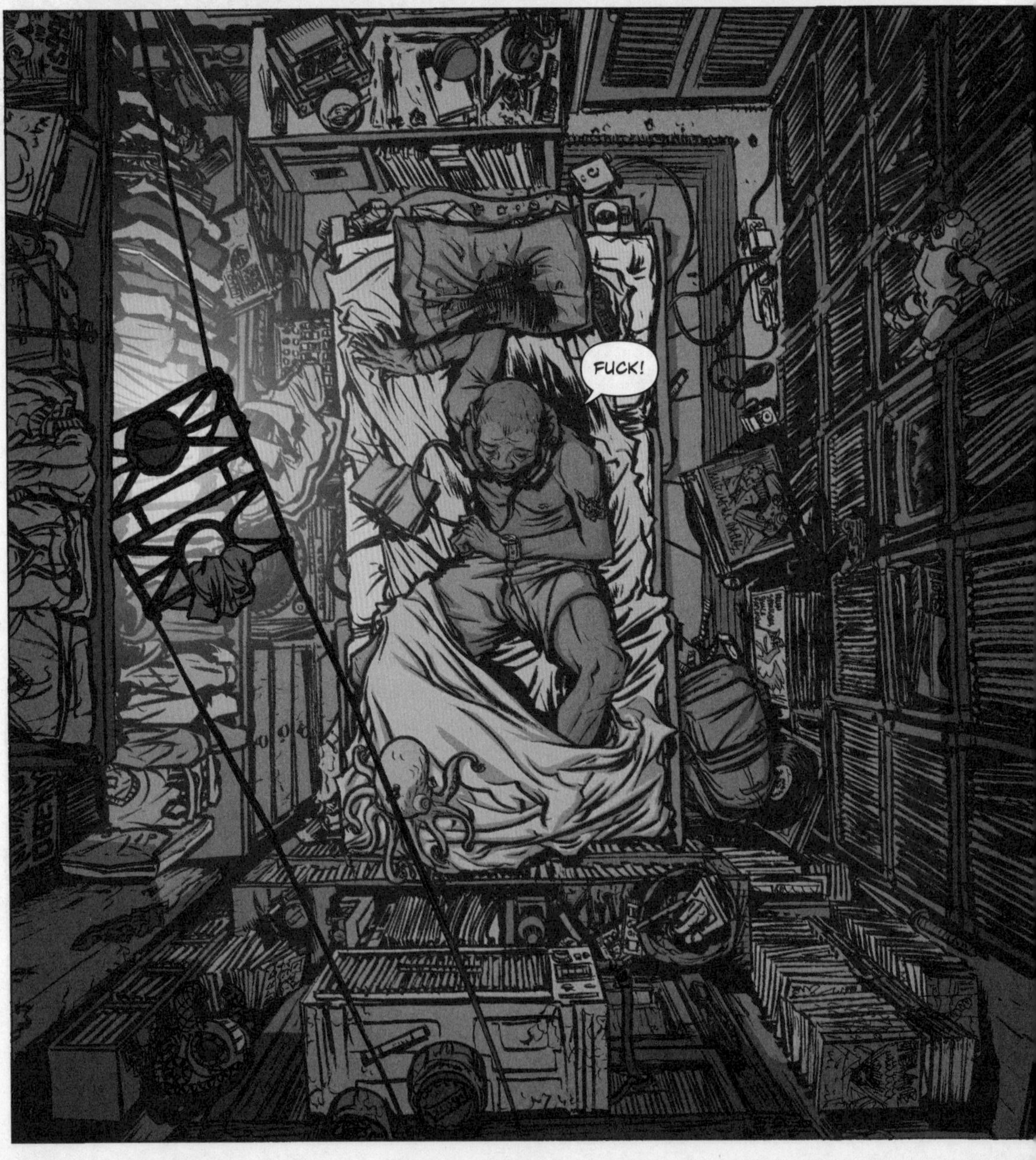
FUCK!

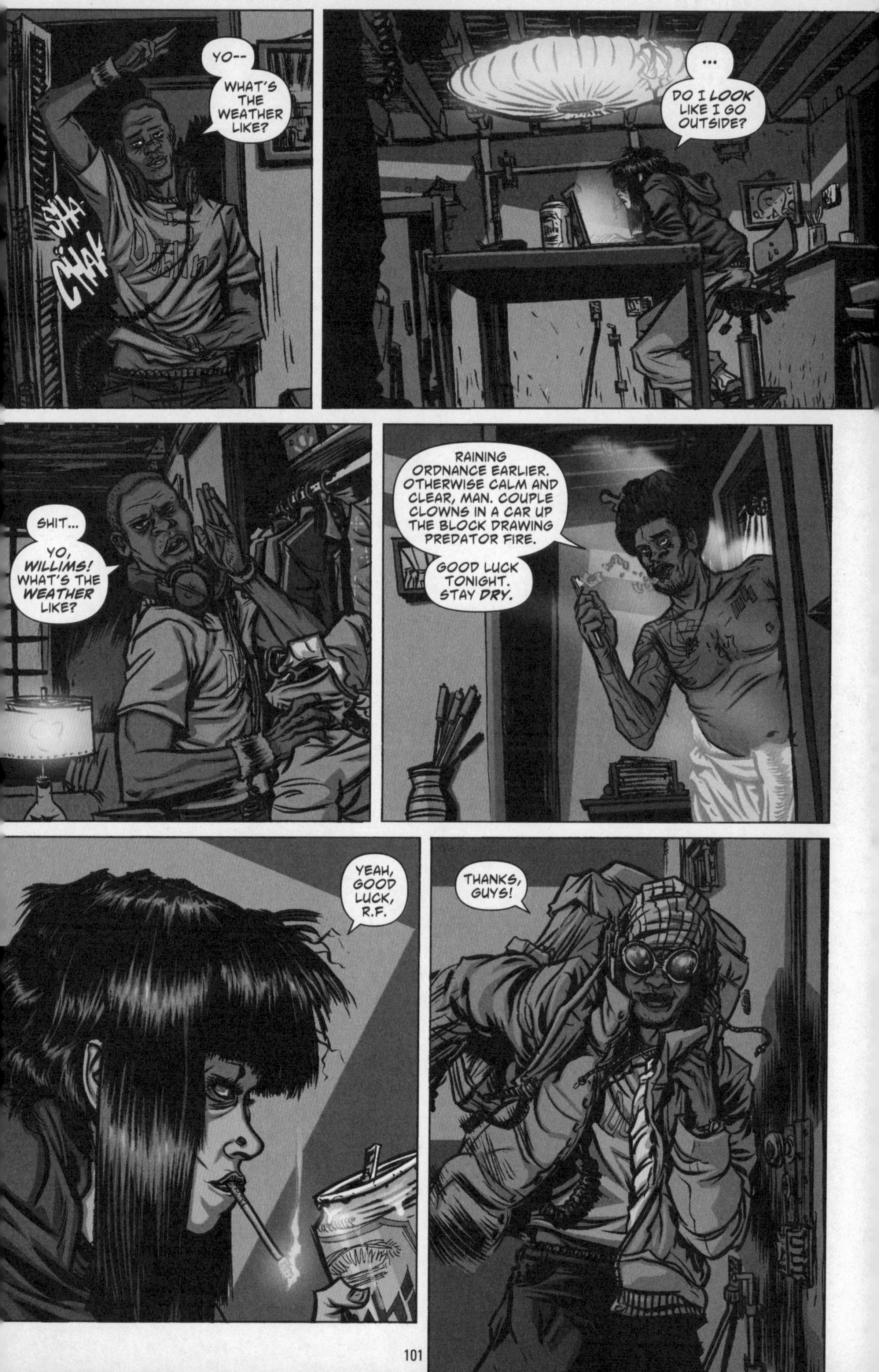
YO--
WHAT'S THE WEATHER LIKE?
SHA-CHAK
...
DO I LOOK LIKE I GO OUTSIDE?
SHIT...
YO, WILLIMS! WHAT'S THE WEATHER LIKE?
RAINING ORDNANCE EARLIER. OTHERWISE CALM AND CLEAR, MAN. COUPLE CLOWNS IN A CAR UP THE BLOCK DRAWING PREDATOR FIRE.
GOOD LUCK TONIGHT. STAY DRY.
YEAH, GOOD LUCK, R.F.
THANKS, GUYS!

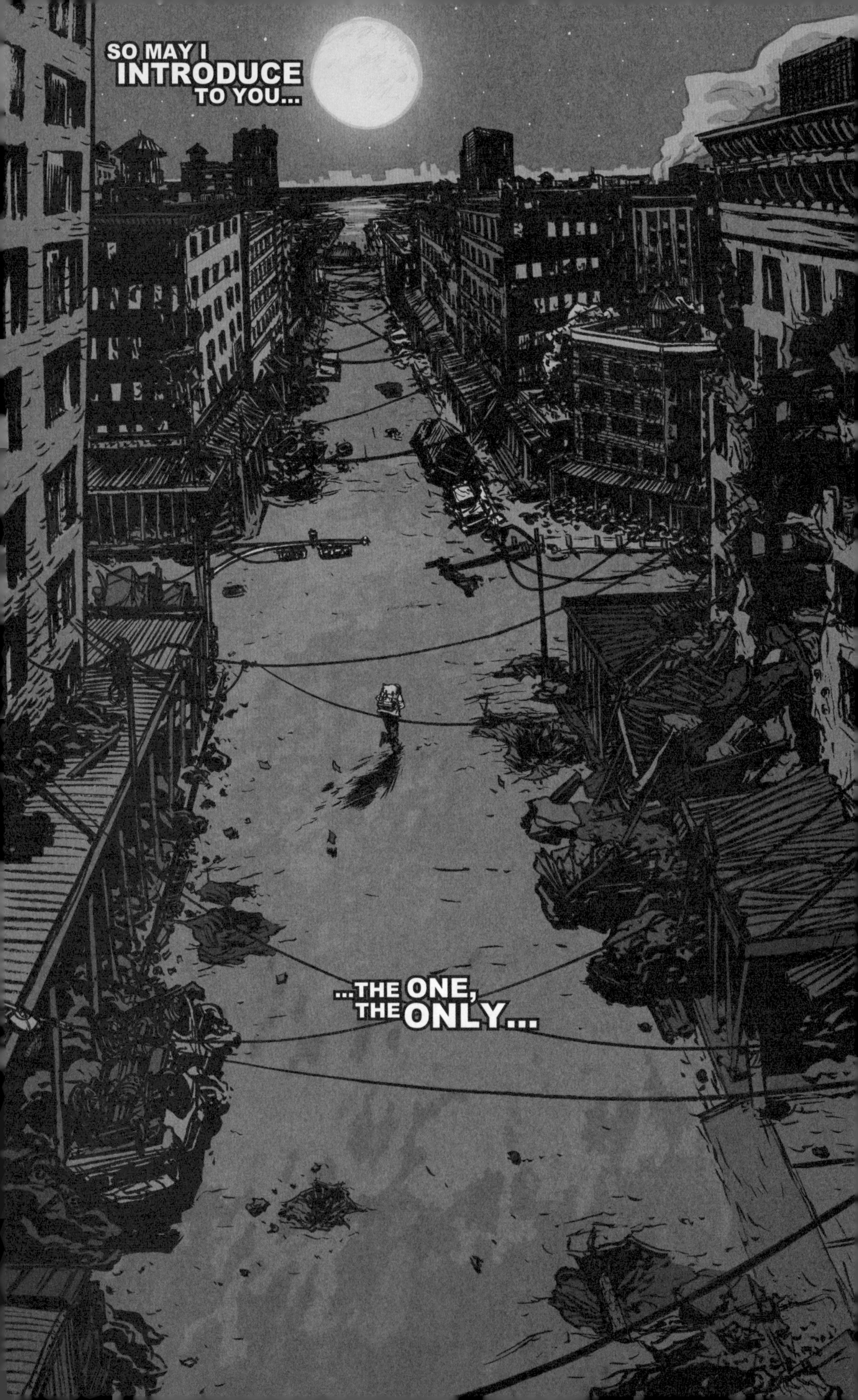
SO MAY I INTRODUCE TO YOU...
...THE ONE, THE ONLY...

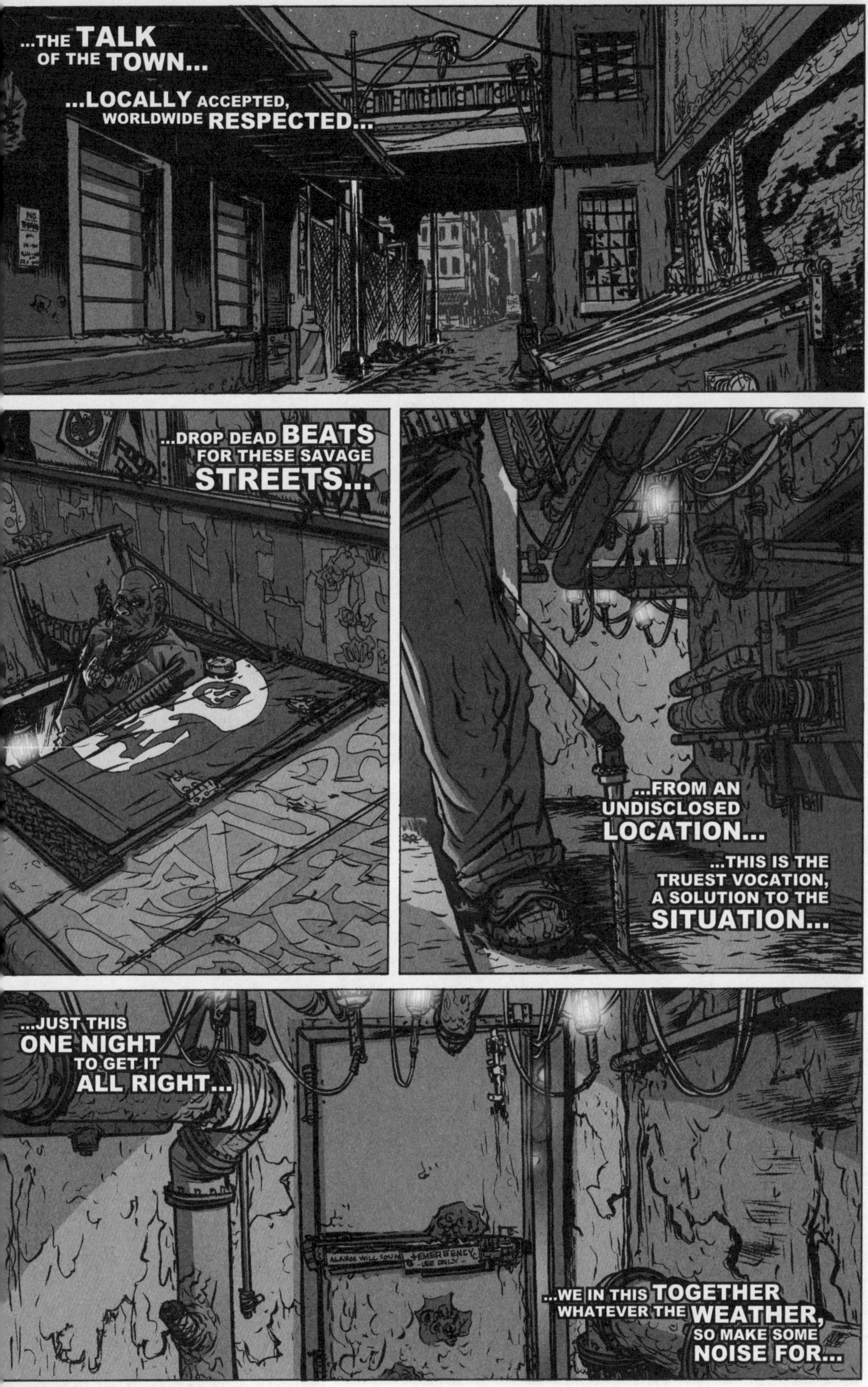
...THE TALK OF THE TOWN...
...LOCALLY ACCEPTED, WORLDWIDE RESPECTED...
...DROP DEAD BEATS FOR THESE SAVAGE STREETS...
...FROM AN UNDISCLOSED LOCATION...
...THIS IS THE TRUEST VOCATION, A SOLUTION TO THE SITUATION...
...JUST THIS ONE NIGHT TO GET IT ALL RIGHT...
...WE IN THIS TOGETHER WHATEVER THE WEATHER, SO MAKE SOME NOISE FOR...

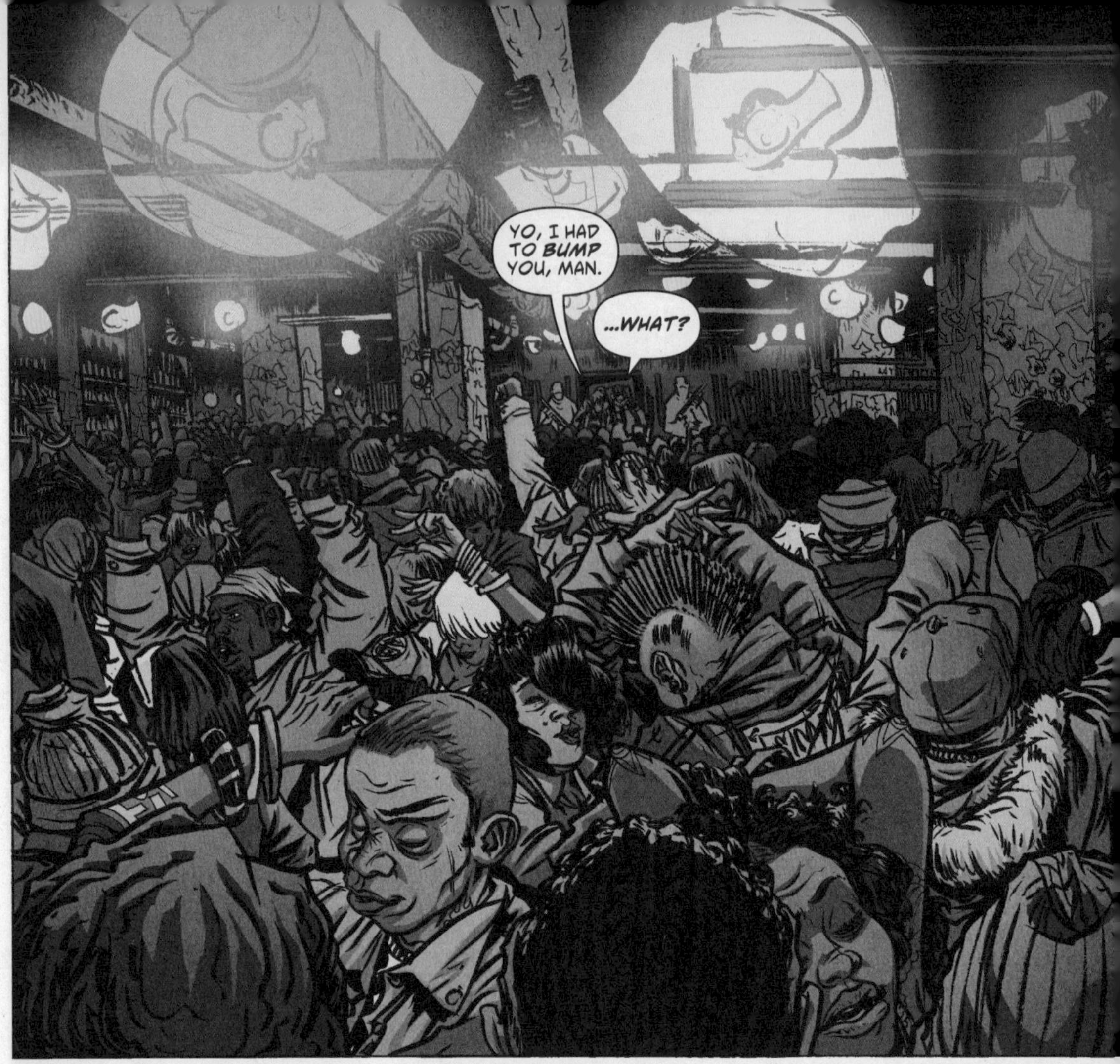
YO, I HAD TO BUMP YOU, MAN.
...WHAT?

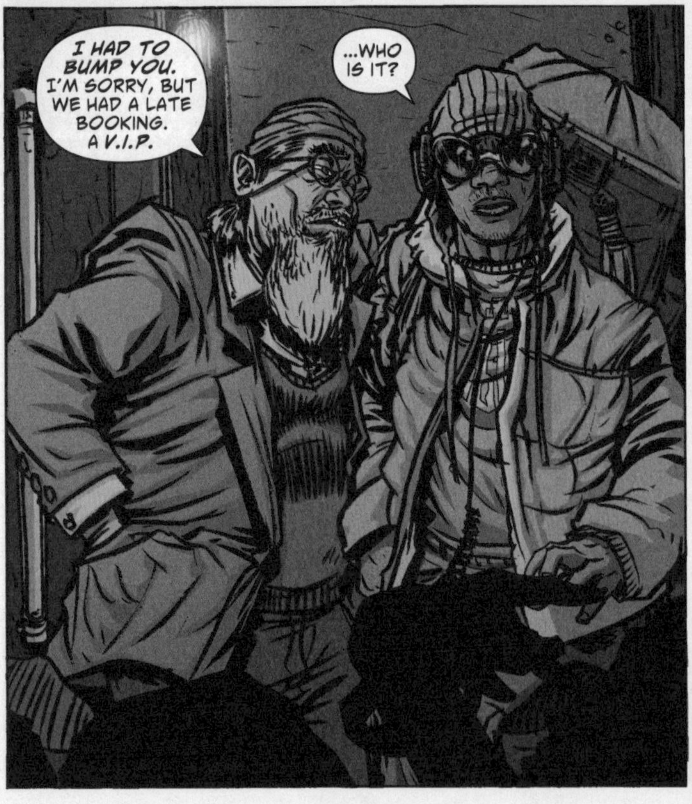
I HAD TO BUMP YOU. I'M SORRY, BUT WE HAD A LATE BOOKING. A V.I.P.
...WHO IS IT?

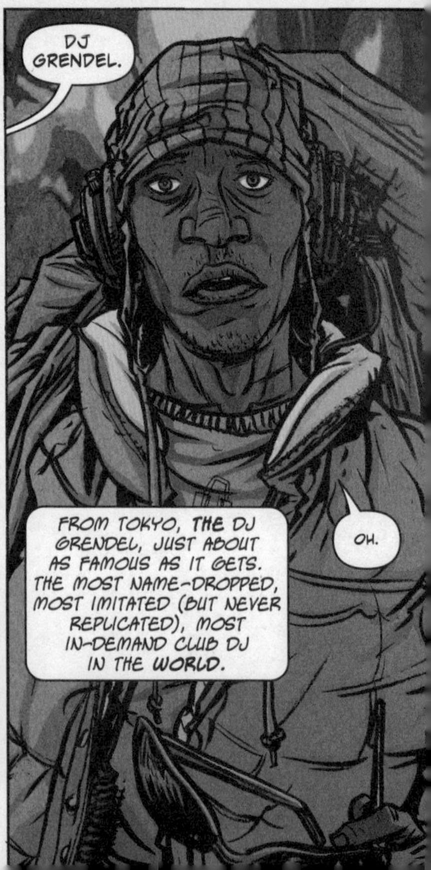
DJ GRENDEL.
FROM TOKYO, THE DJ GRENDEL, JUST ABOUT AS FAMOUS AS IT GETS. THE MOST NAME-DROPPED, MOST IMITATED (BUT NEVER REPLICATED), MOST IN-DEMAND CLUB DJ IN THE WORLD.
OH.

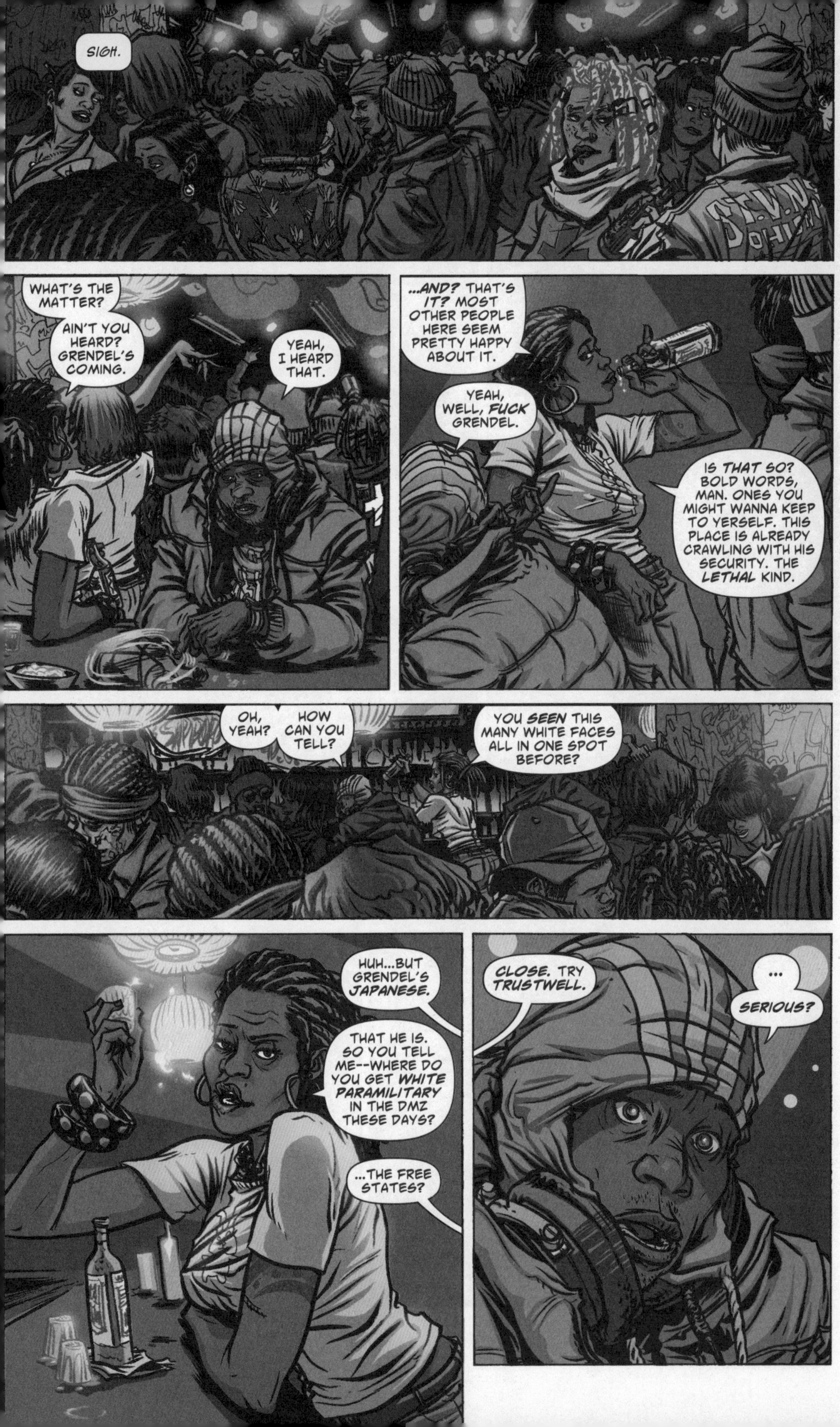
SIGH.
WHAT'S THE MATTER?
AIN'T YOU HEARD? GRENDEL'S COMING.
YEAH, I HEARD THAT.
...AND? THAT'S IT? MOST OTHER PEOPLE HERE SEEM PRETTY HAPPY ABOUT IT.
YEAH, WELL, FUCK GRENDEL.
IS THAT SO? BOLD WORDS, MAN. ONES YOU MIGHT WANNA KEEP TO YERSELF. THIS PLACE IS ALREADY CRAWLING WITH HIS SECURITY. THE LETHAL KIND.
OH, YEAH?
HOW CAN YOU TELL?
YOU SEEN THIS MANY WHITE FACES ALL IN ONE SPOT BEFORE?
HUH...BUT GRENDEL'S JAPANESE.
THAT HE IS. SO YOU TELL ME--WHERE DO YOU GET WHITE PARAMILITARY IN THE DMZ THESE DAYS?
...THE FREE STATES?
CLOSE. TRY TRUSTWELL.
...
SERIOUS?

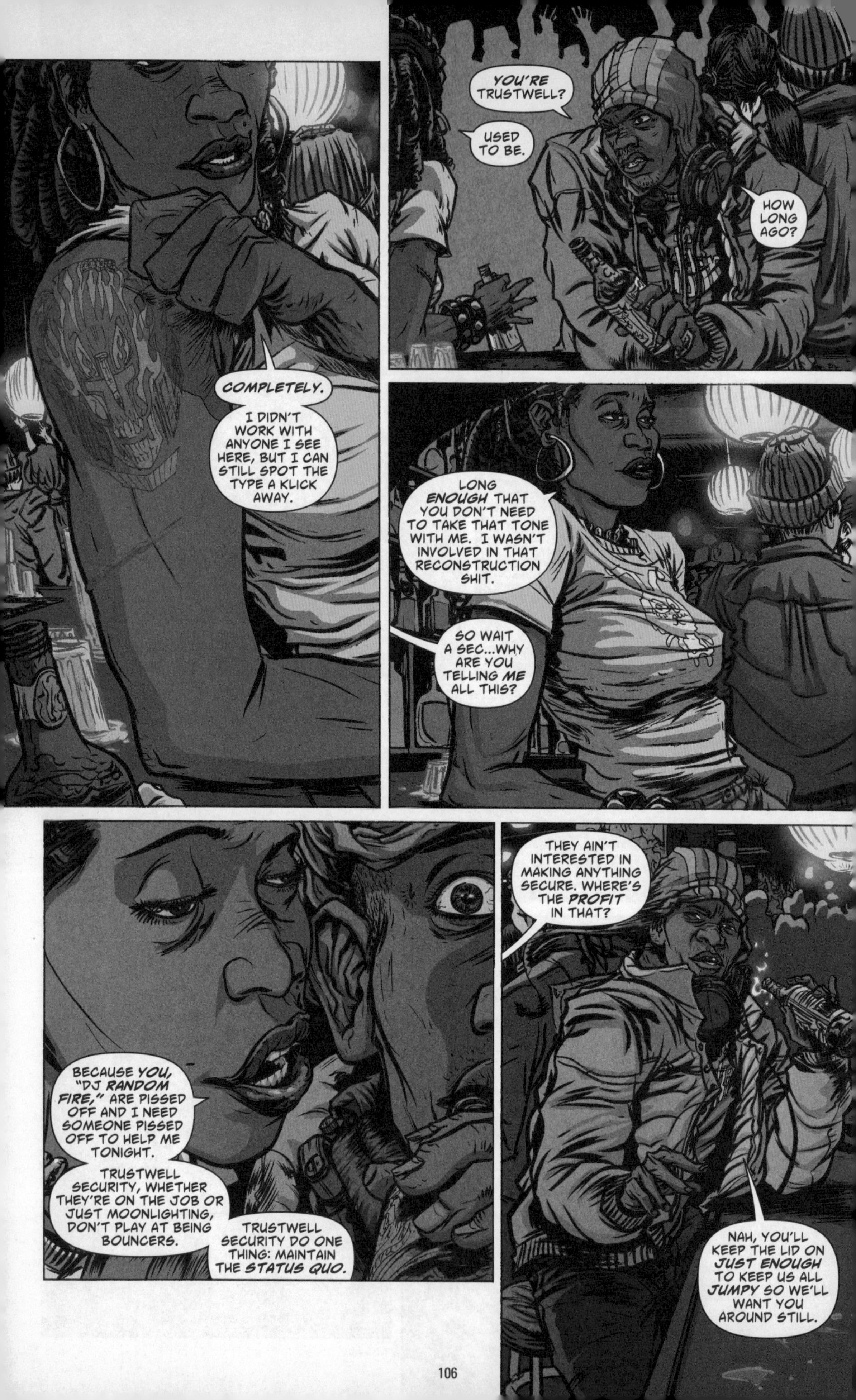
COMPLETELY.
I DIDN'T WORK WITH ANYONE I SEE HERE, BUT I CAN STILL SPOT THE TYPE A KLICK AWAY.
YOU'RE TRUSTWELL?
USED TO BE.
HOW LONG AGO?
LONG ENOUGH THAT YOU DON'T NEED TO TAKE THAT TONE WITH ME. I WASN'T INVOLVED IN THAT RECONSTRUCTION SHIT.
SO WAIT A SEC...WHY ARE YOU TELLING ME ALL THIS?
BECAUSE YOU, "DJ RANDOM FIRE," ARE PISSED OFF AND I NEED SOMEONE PISSED OFF TO HELP ME TONIGHT.
TRUSTWELL SECURITY, WHETHER THEY'RE ON THE JOB OR JUST MOONLIGHTING, DON'T PLAY AT BEING BOUNCERS.
TRUSTWELL SECURITY DO ONE THING: MAINTAIN THE STATUS QUO.
THEY AIN'T INTERESTED IN MAKING ANYTHING SECURE. WHERE'S THE PROFIT IN THAT?
NAH, YOU'LL KEEP THE LID ON JUST ENOUGH TO KEEP US ALL JUMPY SO WE'LL WANT YOU AROUND STILL.

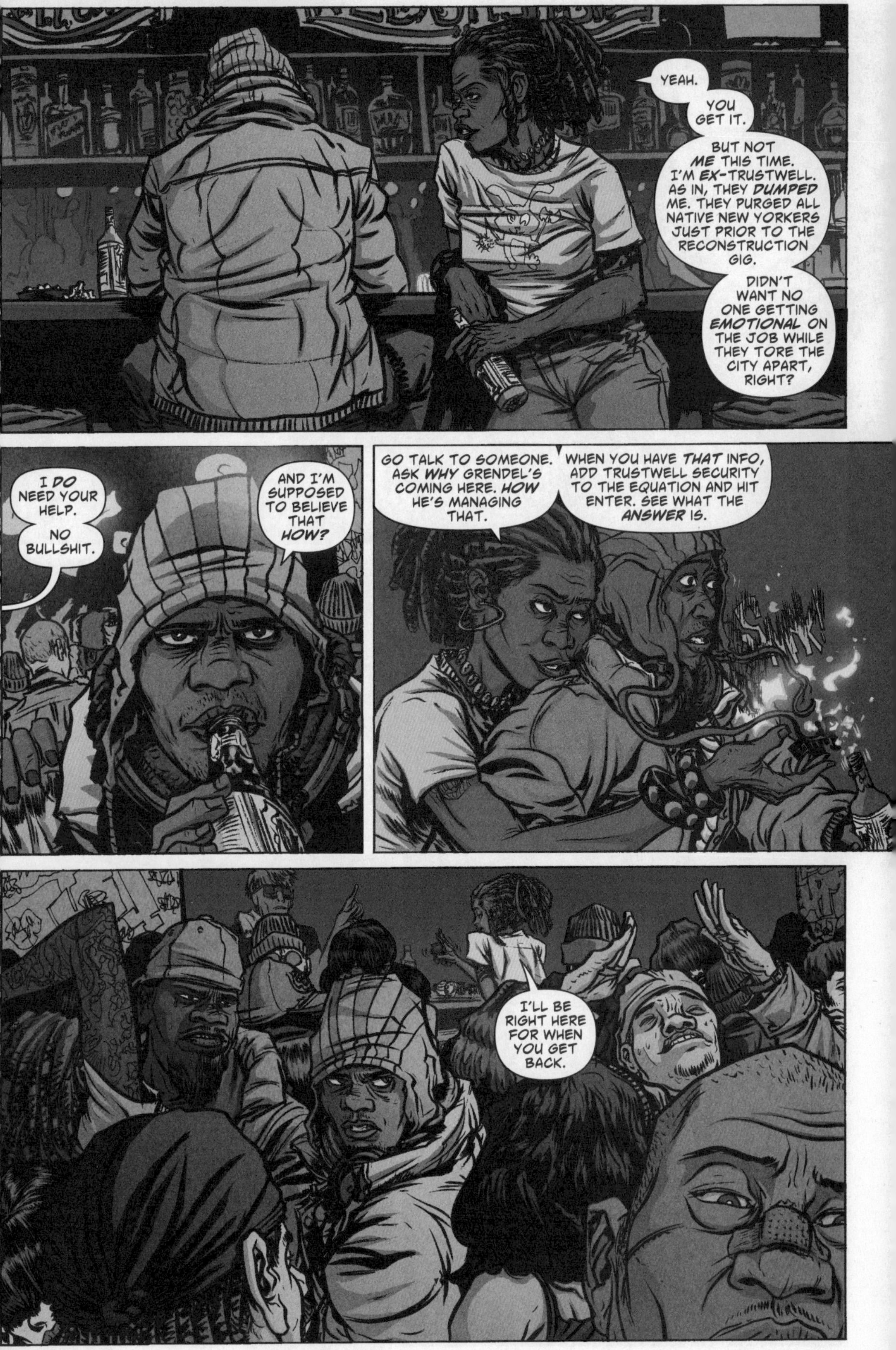
YEAH.
YOU GET IT.
BUT NOT ME THIS TIME. I'M EX-TRUSTWELL. AS IN, THEY DUMPED ME. THEY PURGED ALL NATIVE NEW YORKERS JUST PRIOR TO THE RECONSTRUCTION GIG.
DIDN'T WANT NO ONE GETTING EMOTIONAL ON THE JOB WHILE THEY TORE THE CITY APART, RIGHT?
I DO NEED YOUR HELP.
NO BULLSHIT.
AND I'M SUPPOSED TO BELIEVE THAT HOW?
GO TALK TO SOMEONE. ASK WHY GRENDEL'S COMING HERE. HOW HE'S MANAGING THAT.
WHEN YOU HAVE THAT INFO, ADD TRUSTWELL SECURITY TO THE EQUATION AND HIT ENTER. SEE WHAT THE ANSWER IS.
I'LL BE RIGHT HERE FOR WHEN YOU GET BACK.

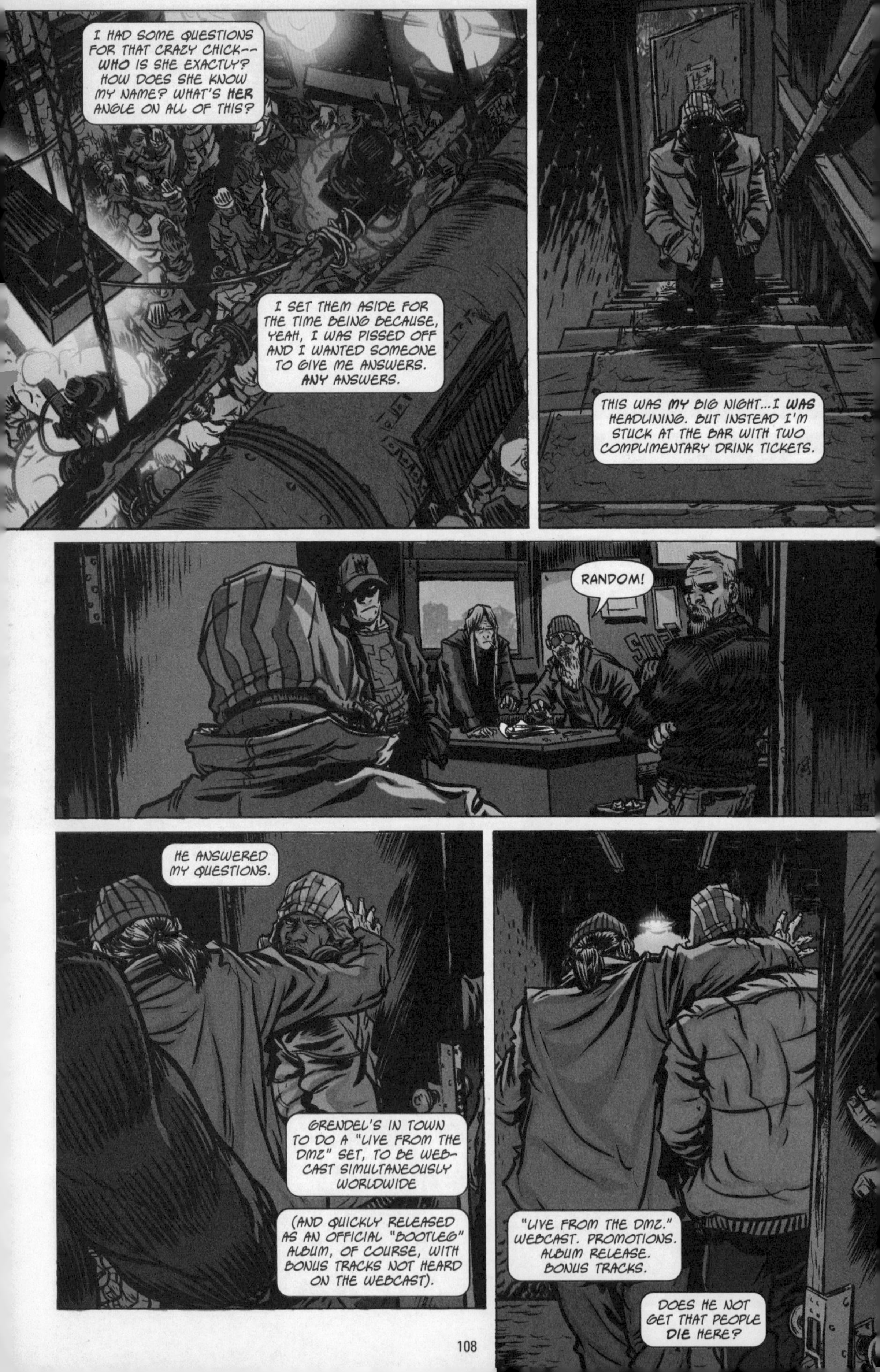
I HAD SOME QUESTIONS FOR THAT CRAZY CHICK-- WHO IS SHE EXACTLY? HOW DOES SHE KNOW MY NAME? WHAT'S HER ANGLE ON ALL OF THIS?
I SET THEM ASIDE FOR THE TIME BEING BECAUSE, YEAH, I WAS PISSED OFF AND I WANTED SOMEONE TO GIVE ME ANSWERS. ANY ANSWERS.
THIS WAS MY BIG NIGHT...I WAS HEADLINING. BUT INSTEAD I'M STUCK AT THE BAR WITH TWO COMPLIMENTARY DRINK TICKETS.
RANDOM!
HE ANSWERED MY QUESTIONS.
GRENDEL'S IN TOWN TO DO A "LIVE FROM THE DMZ" SET, TO BE WEB-CAST SIMULTANEOUSLY WORLDWIDE
(AND QUICKLY RELEASED AS AN OFFICIAL "BOOTLEG" ALBUM, OF COURSE, WITH BONUS TRACKS NOT HEARD ON THE WEBCAST).
"LIVE FROM THE DMZ." WEBCAST. PROMOTIONS. ALBUM RELEASE. BONUS TRACKS.
DOES HE NOT GET THAT PEOPLE DIE HERE?

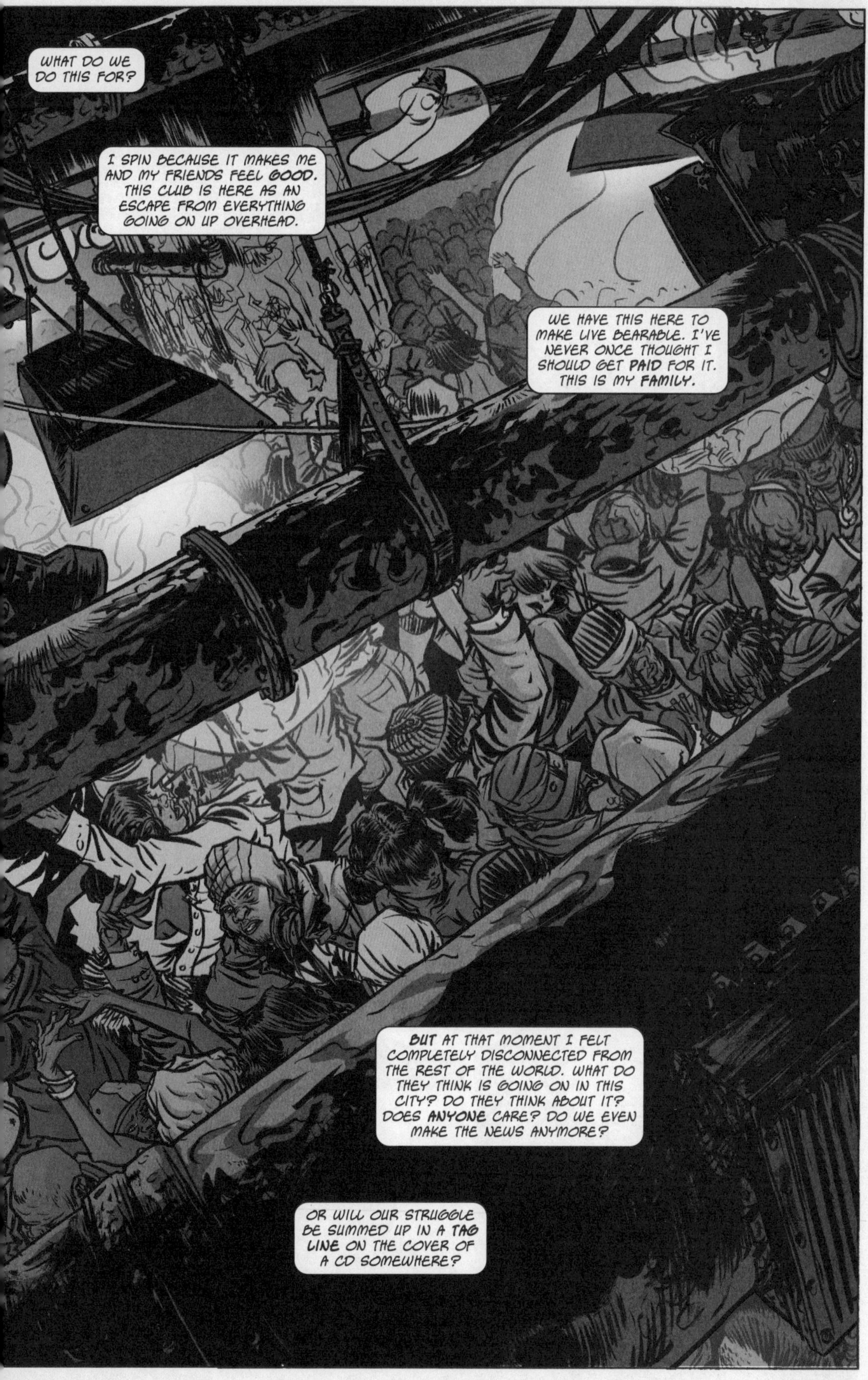
WHAT DO WE DO THIS FOR?
I SPIN BECAUSE IT MAKES ME AND MY FRIENDS FEEL **GOOD**. THIS CLUB IS HERE AS AN ESCAPE FROM EVERYTHING GOING ON UP OVERHEAD.
WE HAVE THIS HERE TO MAKE LIVE BEARABLE. I'VE NEVER ONCE THOUGHT I SHOULD GET **PAID** FOR IT. THIS IS MY **FAMILY**.
BUT AT THAT MOMENT I FELT COMPLETELY DISCONNECTED FROM THE REST OF THE WORLD. WHAT DO THEY THINK IS GOING ON IN THIS CITY? DO THEY THINK ABOUT IT? DOES **ANYONE** CARE? DO WE EVEN MAKE THE NEWS ANYMORE?
OR WILL OUR STRUGGLE BE SUMMED UP IN A **TAG LINE** ON THE COVER OF A CD SOMEWHERE?

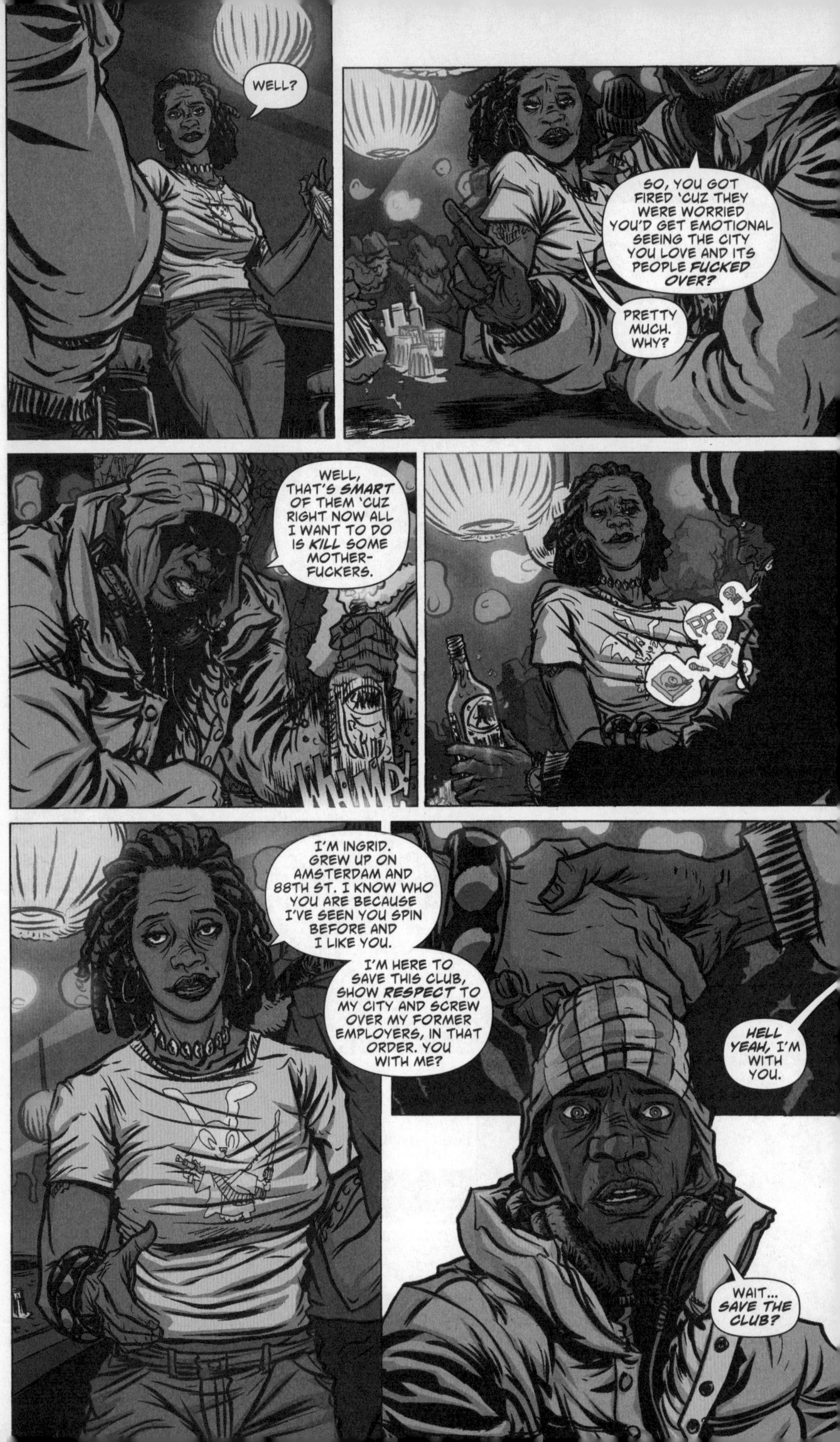
WELL?
SO, YOU GOT FIRED 'CUZ THEY WERE WORRIED YOU'D GET EMOTIONAL SEEING THE CITY YOU LOVE AND ITS PEOPLE FUCKED OVER?
PRETTY MUCH. WHY?
WELL, THAT'S SMART OF THEM 'CUZ RIGHT NOW ALL I WANT TO DO IS KILL SOME MOTHER-FUCKERS.
WHAMP!
I'M INGRID. GREW UP ON AMSTERDAM AND 88TH ST. I KNOW WHO YOU ARE BECAUSE I'VE SEEN YOU SPIN BEFORE AND I LIKE YOU.
I'M HERE TO SAVE THIS CLUB, SHOW RESPECT TO MY CITY AND SCREW OVER MY FORMER EMPLOYERS, IN THAT ORDER. YOU WITH ME?
HELL YEAH, I'M WITH YOU.
WAIT... SAVE THE CLUB?

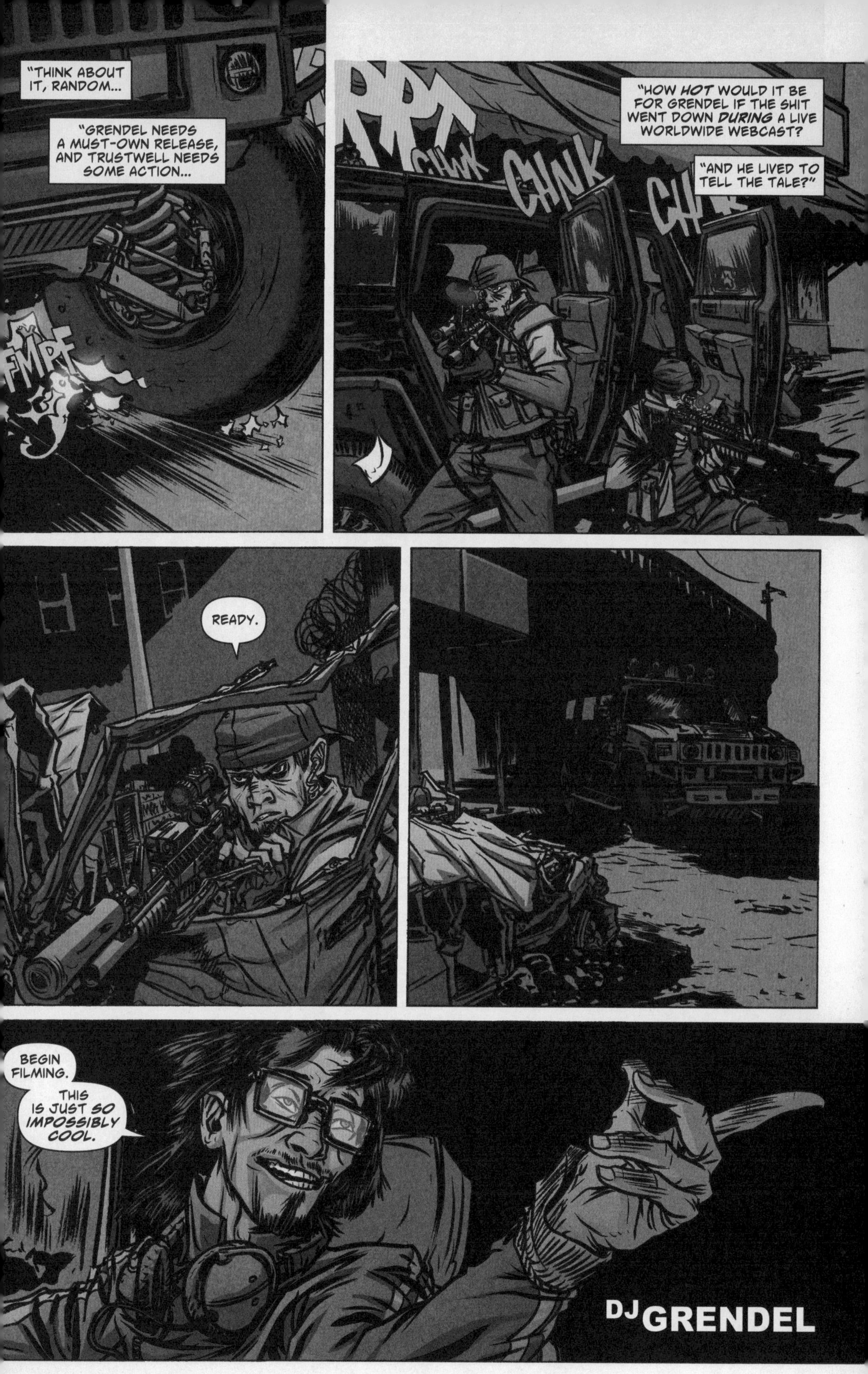
"THINK ABOUT IT, RANDOM...
"GRENDEL NEEDS A MUST-OWN RELEASE, AND TRUSTWELL NEEDS SOME ACTION...
FMPF
RPPT
CHNK
CHNK
"HOW HOT WOULD IT BE FOR GRENDEL IF THE SHIT WENT DOWN DURING A LIVE WORLDWIDE WEBCAST?
"AND HE LIVED TO TELL THE TALE?"
READY.
BEGIN FILMING.
THIS IS JUST SO IMPOSSIBLY COOL.
DJ GRENDEL

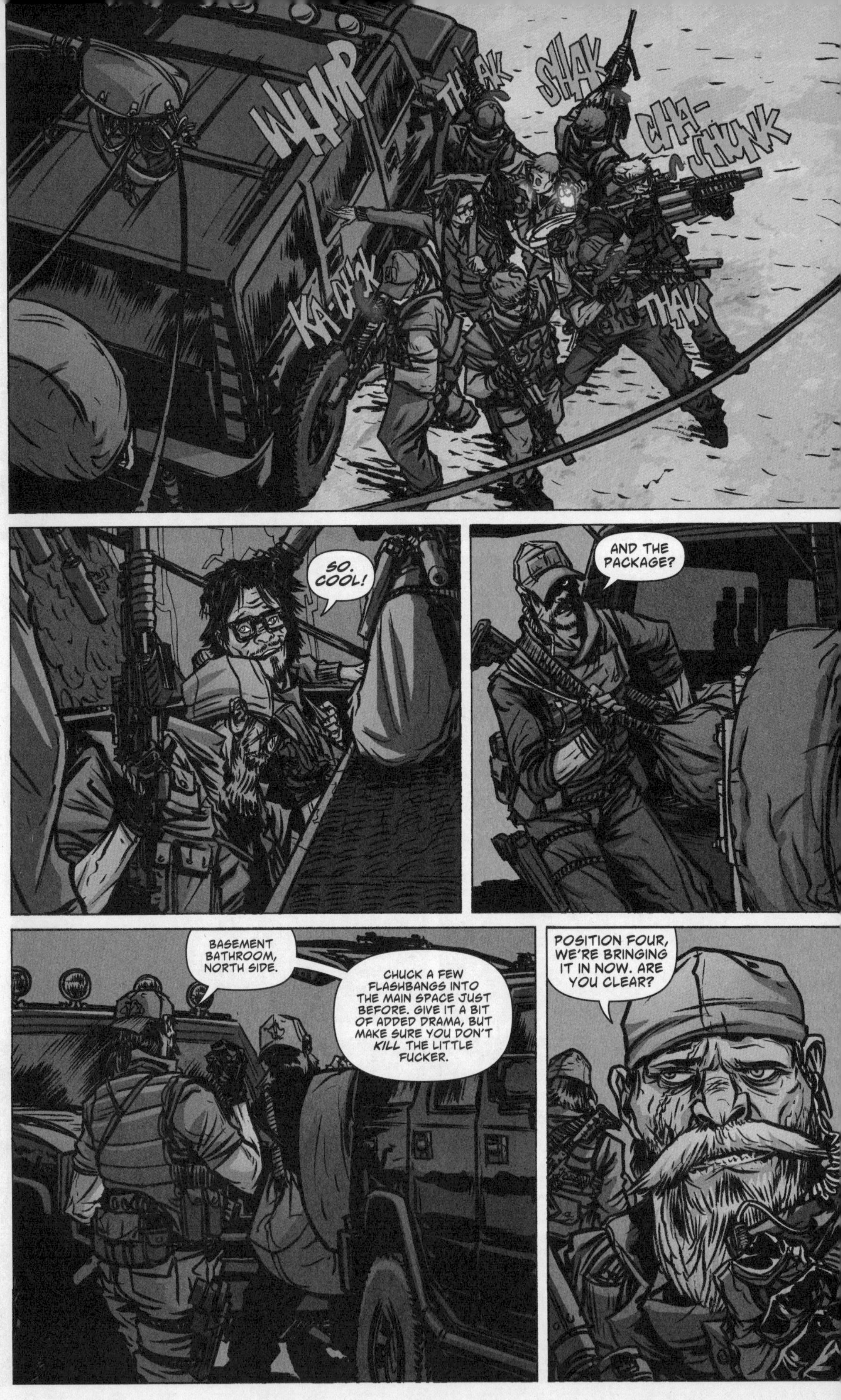
WHMP
THAK
SHAK
CHA-SHUNK
KA-CHUCK
THAK
SO. COOL!
AND THE PACKAGE?
BASEMENT BATHROOM, NORTH SIDE.
CHUCK A FEW FLASHBANGS INTO THE MAIN SPACE JUST BEFORE. GIVE IT A BIT OF ADDED DRAMA, BUT MAKE SURE YOU DON'T KILL THE LITTLE FUCKER.
POSITION FOUR, WE'RE BRINGING IT IN NOW. ARE YOU CLEAR?

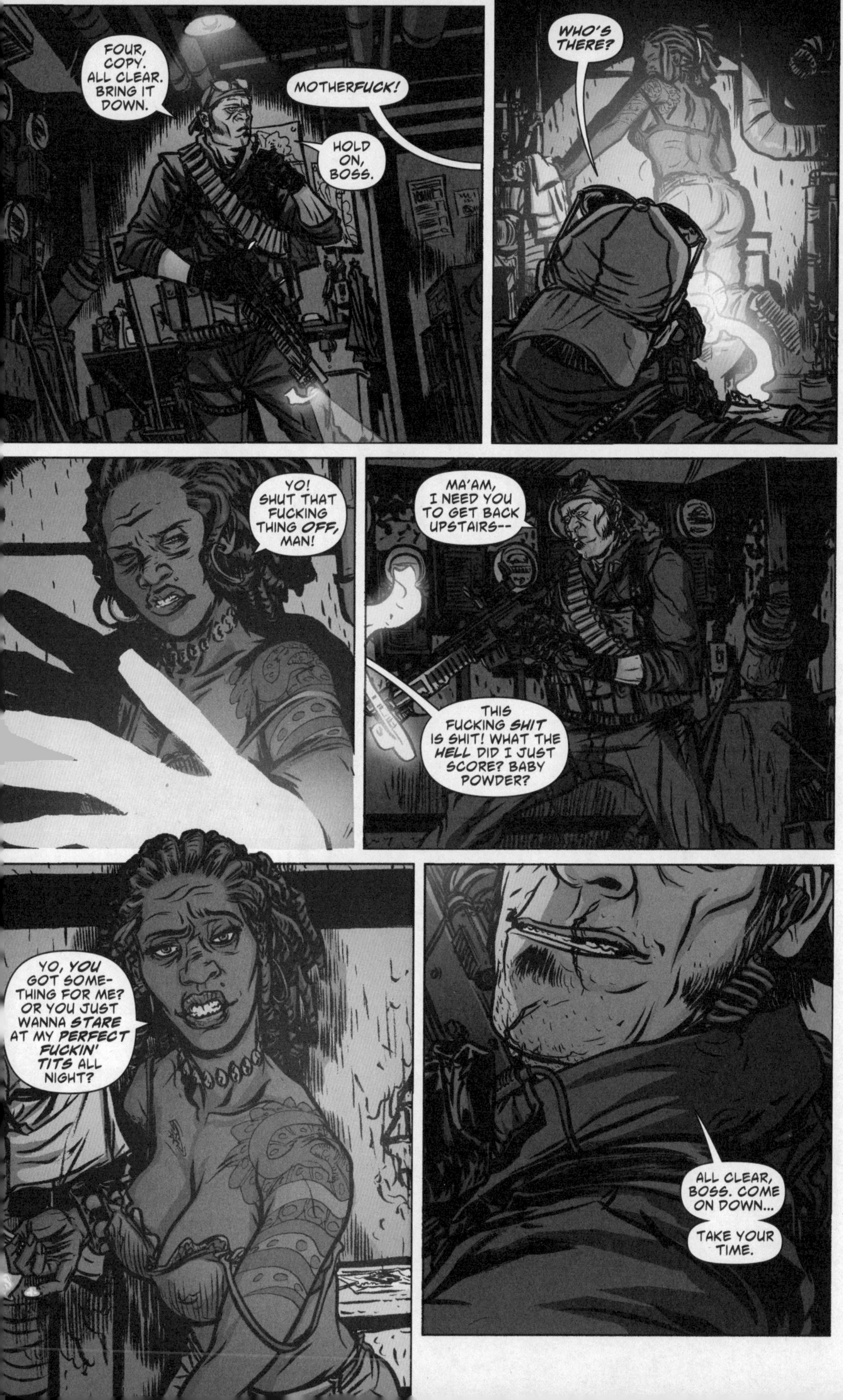
FOUR, COPY. ALL CLEAR. BRING IT DOWN.
MOTHERFUCK!
HOLD ON, BOSS.
WHO'S THERE?
YO! SHUT THAT FUCKING THING OFF, MAN!
MA'AM, I NEED YOU TO GET BACK UPSTAIRS--
THIS FUCKING SHIT IS SHIT! WHAT THE HELL DID I JUST SCORE? BABY POWDER?
YO, YOU GOT SOME-THING FOR ME? OR YOU JUST WANNA STARE AT MY PERFECT FUCKIN' TITS ALL NIGHT?
ALL CLEAR, BOSS. COME ON DOWN...
TAKE YOUR TIME.

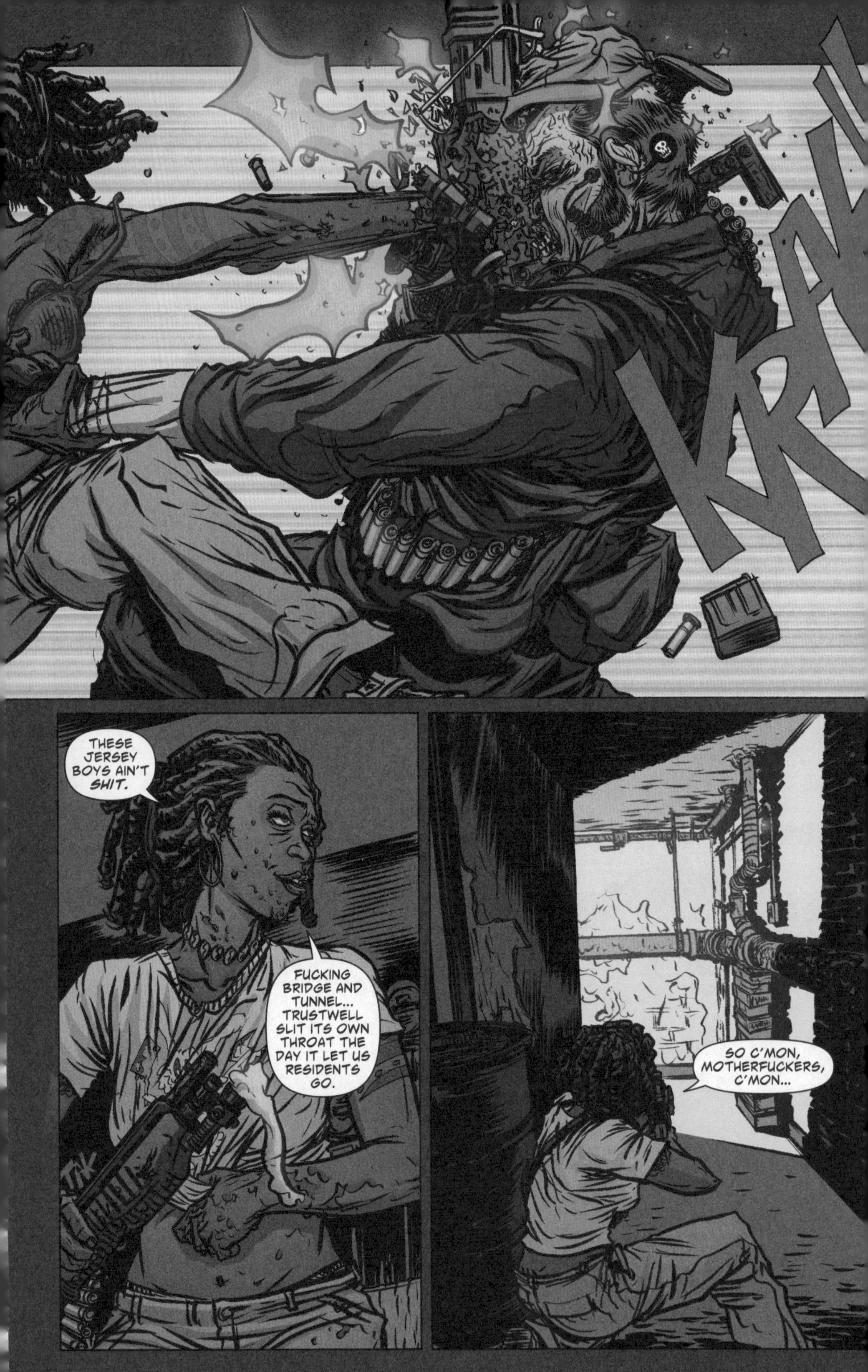
KRAK
THESE JERSEY BOYS AIN'T SHIT.
FUCKING BRIDGE AND TUNNEL... TRUSTWELL SLIT ITS OWN THROAT THE DAY IT LET US RESIDENTS GO.
SO C'MON, MOTHERFUCKERS, C'MON...

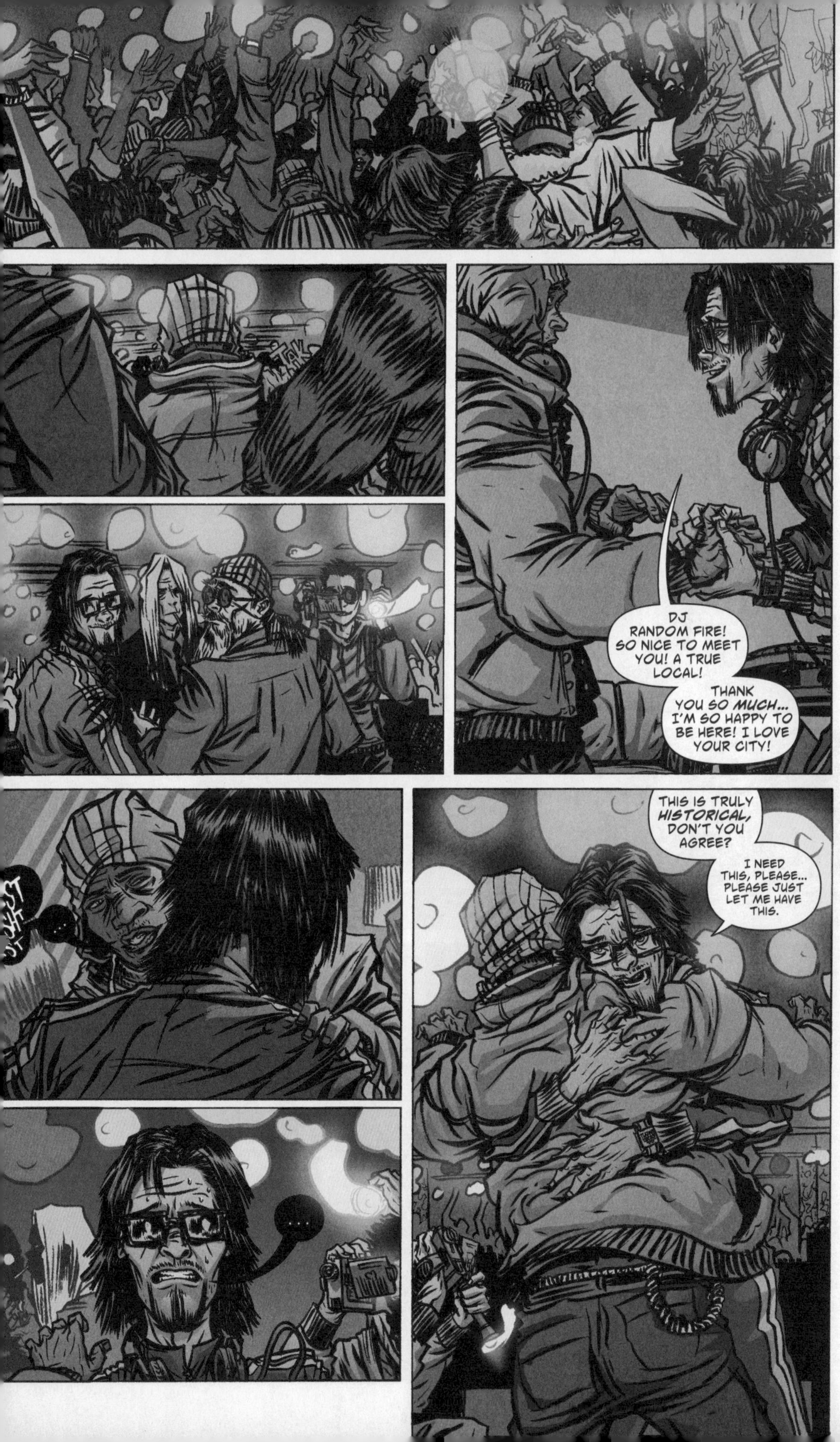
DJ RANDOM FIRE! SO NICE TO MEET YOU! A TRUE LOCAL!
THANK YOU SO *MUCH*... I'M SO HAPPY TO BE HERE! I LOVE YOUR CITY!
THIS IS TRULY *HISTORICAL*, DON'T YOU AGREE?
I NEED THIS, PLEASE... PLEASE JUST LET ME HAVE THIS.

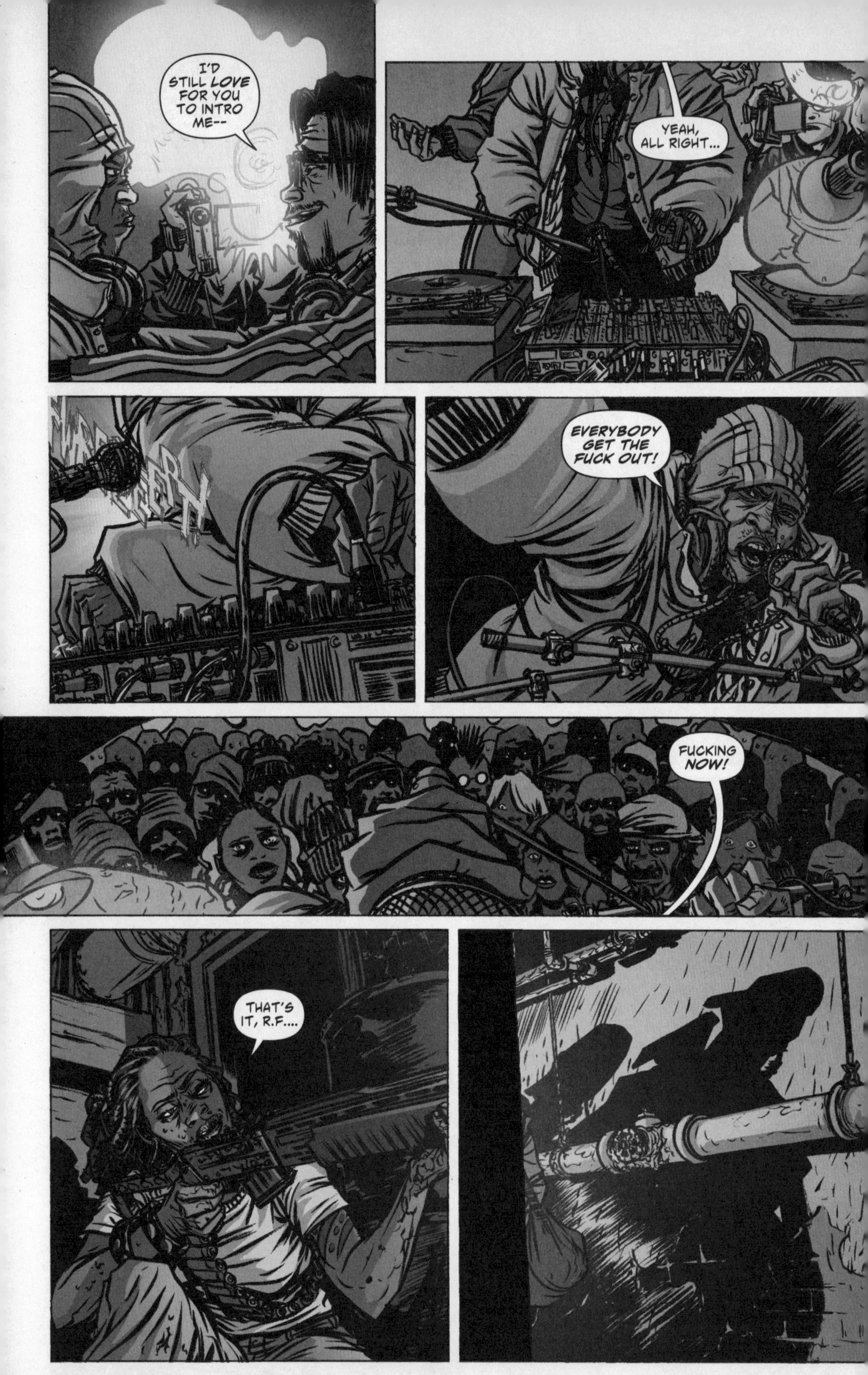
I'D STILL *LOVE* FOR YOU TO INTRO ME--
YEAH, ALL RIGHT...
EVERYBODY GET THE FUCK OUT!
FUCKING *NOW!*
THAT'S IT, R.F....

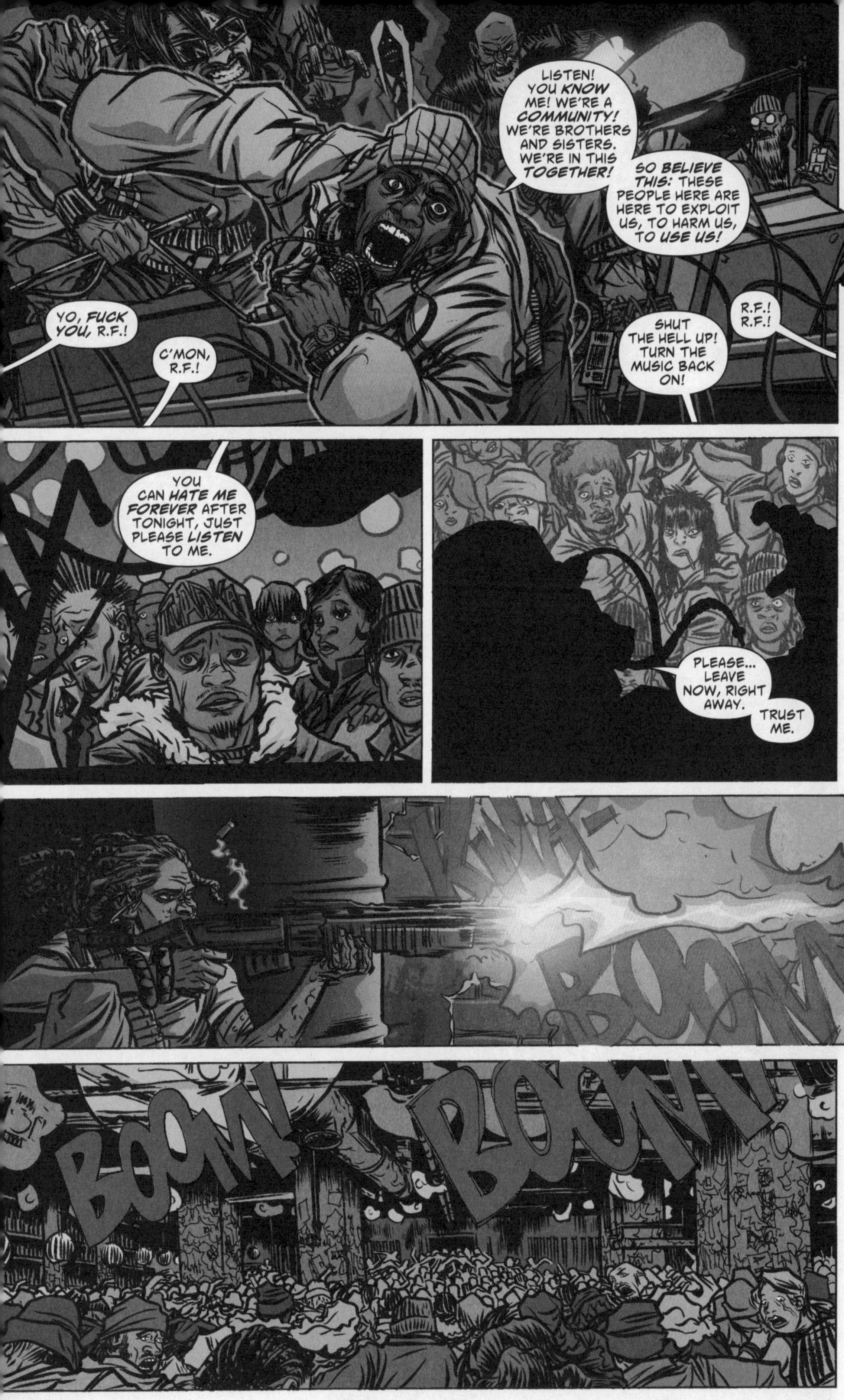
LISTEN! YOU KNOW ME! WE'RE A COMMUNITY! WE'RE BROTHERS AND SISTERS. WE'RE IN THIS TOGETHER!
SO BELIEVE THIS: THESE PEOPLE HERE ARE HERE TO EXPLOIT US, TO HARM US, TO USE US!
YO, FUCK YOU, R.F.!
C'MON, R.F.!
SHUT THE HELL UP! TURN THE MUSIC BACK ON!
R.F.! R.F.!
YOU CAN HATE ME FOREVER AFTER TONIGHT, JUST PLEASE LISTEN TO ME.
PLEASE... LEAVE NOW, RIGHT AWAY.
TRUST ME.
BOOM!
BOOM!

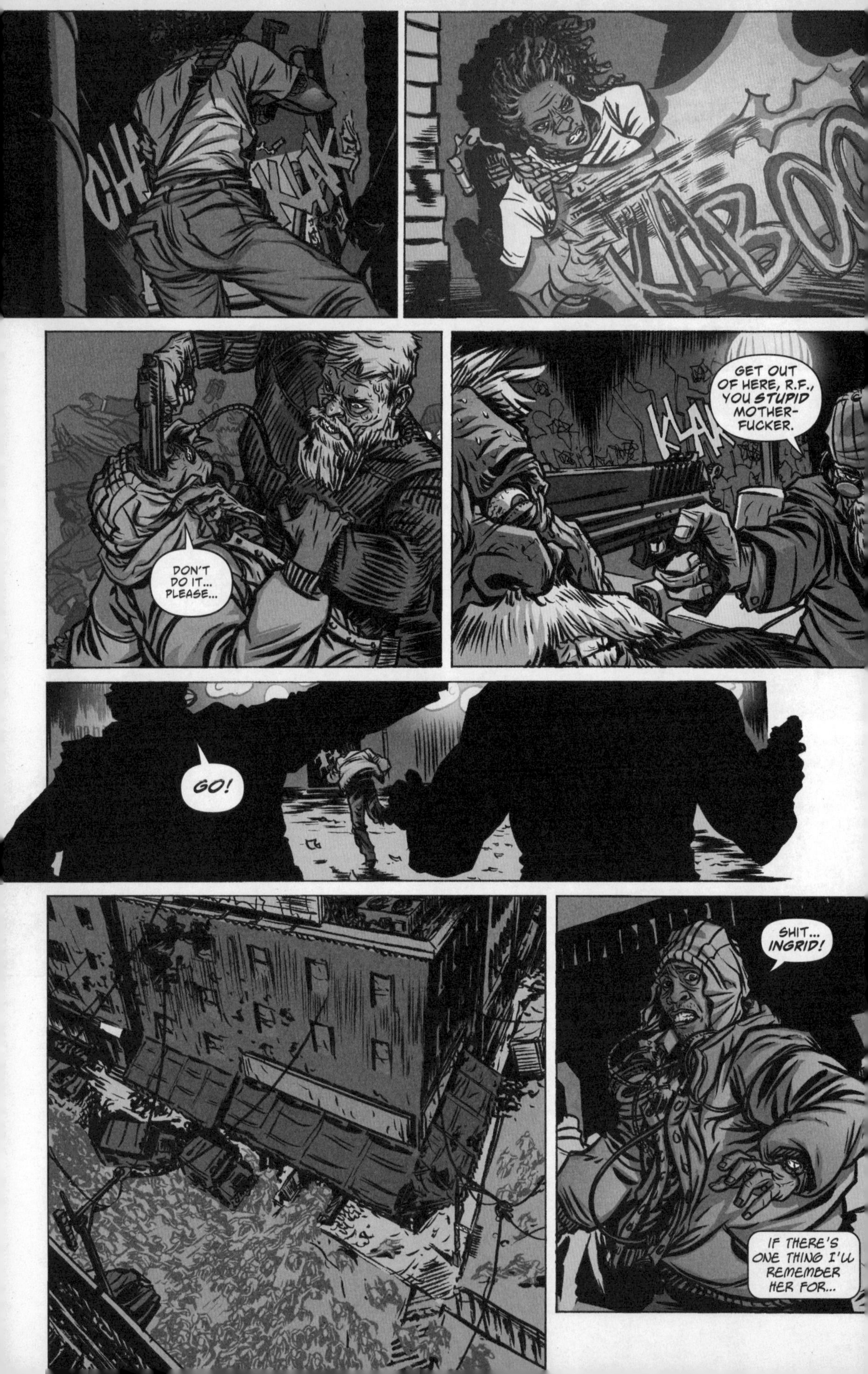
CHA
KLAK
KABOO
DON'T DO IT... PLEASE...
KLAK
GET OUT OF HERE, R.F., YOU STUPID MOTHER-FUCKER.
GO!
SHIT... INGRID!
IF THERE'S ONE THING I'LL REMEMBER HER FOR...

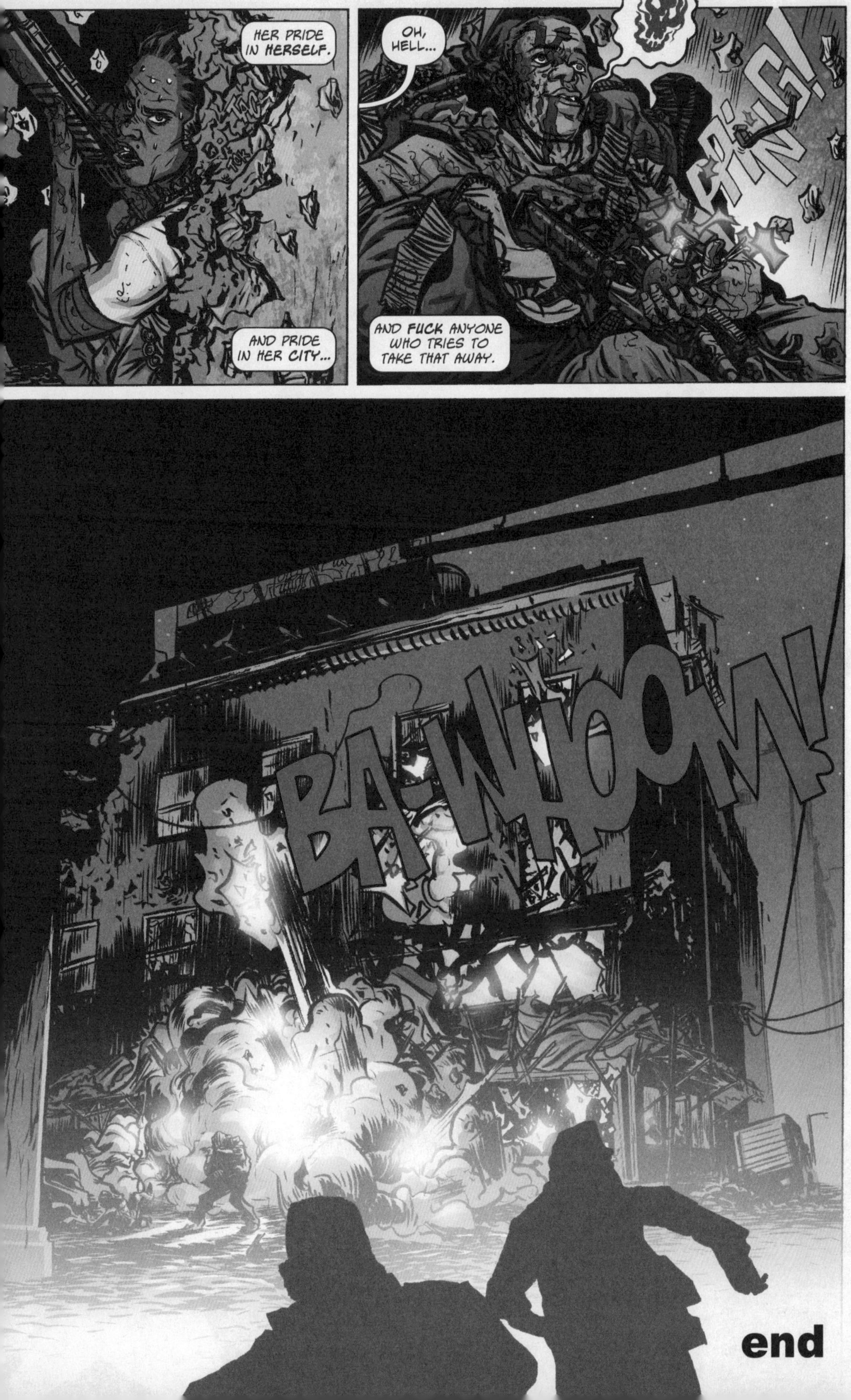
HER PRIDE IN HERSELF.
AND PRIDE IN HER CITY...
OH, HELL...
AND FUCK ANYONE WHO TRIES TO TAKE THAT AWAY.
PTING!
BA-WHOOM!
end

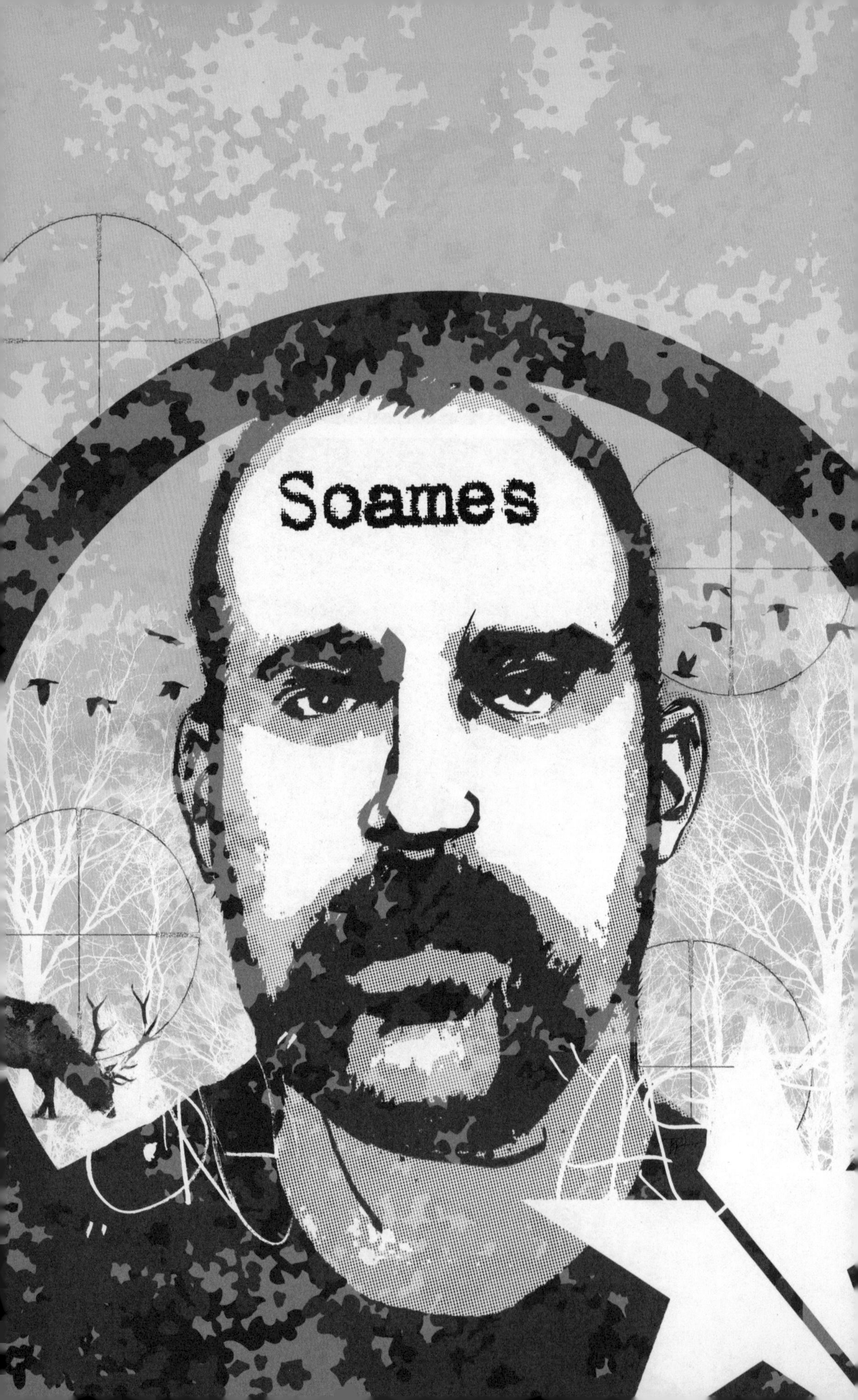
Soames

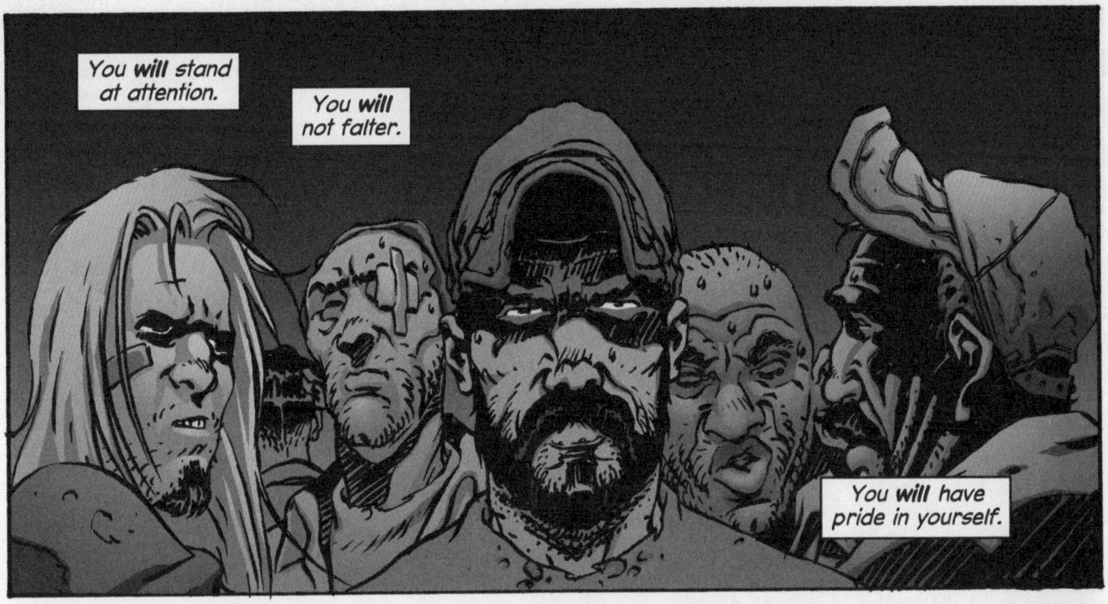
You **will** stand at attention.
You **will** not falter.
You **will** have pride in yourself.

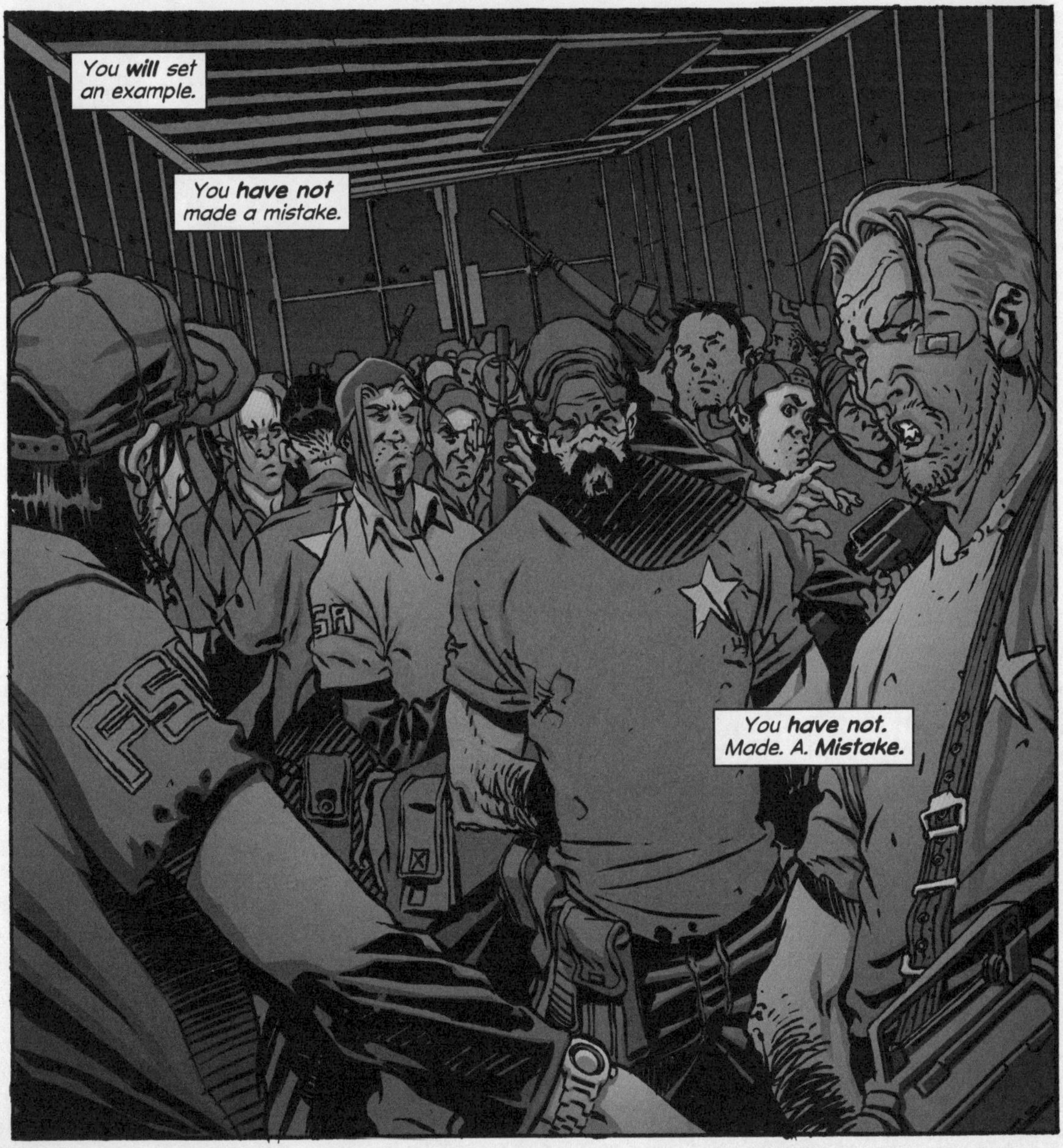
You **will** set an example.
You **have not** made a mistake.
You **have not.** Made. A. **Mistake.**

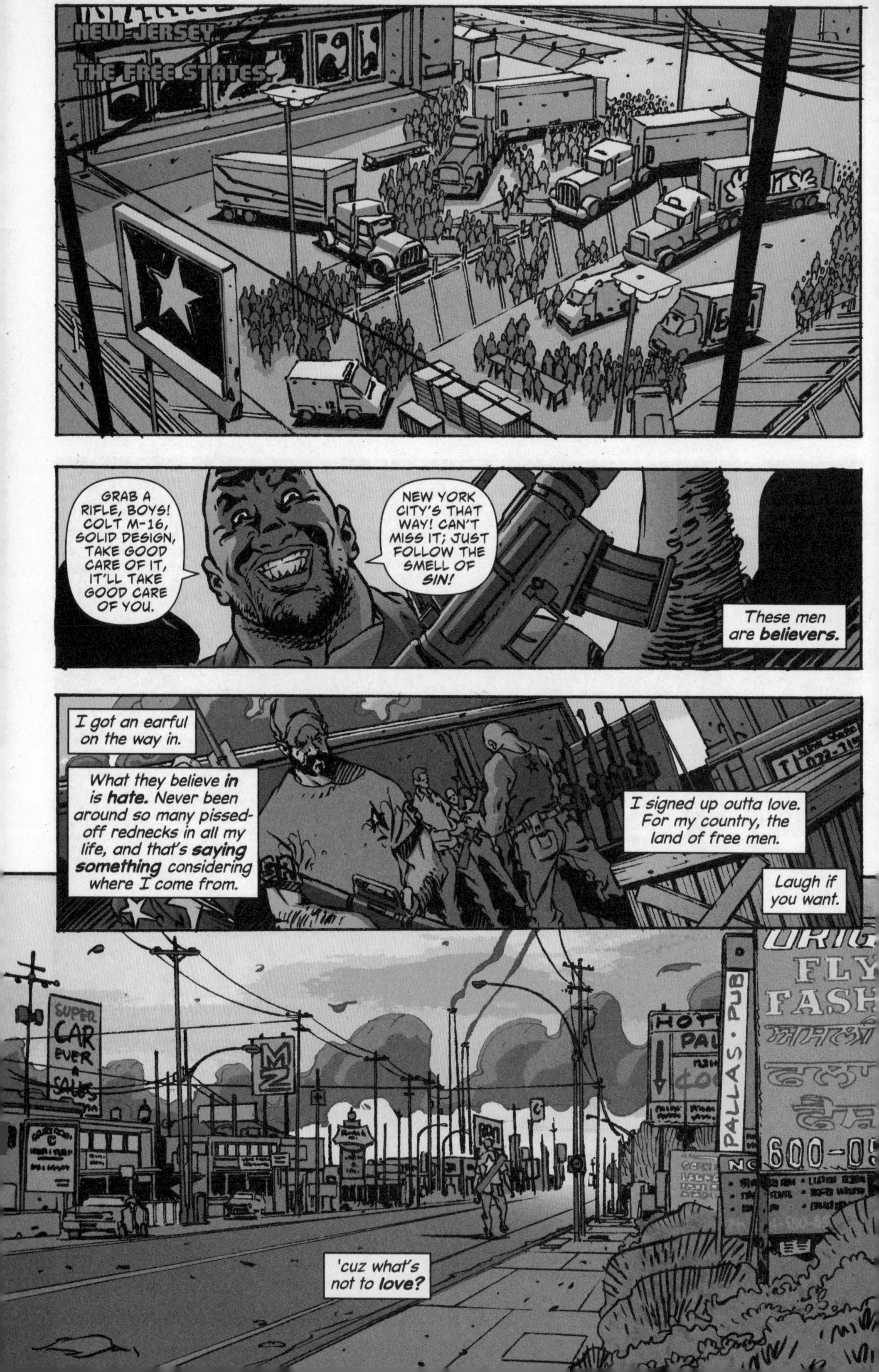
NEW JERSEY.
THE FREE STATES.
GRAB A RIFLE, BOYS! COLT M-16, SOLID DESIGN, TAKE GOOD CARE OF IT, IT'LL TAKE GOOD CARE OF YOU.
NEW YORK CITY'S THAT WAY! CAN'T MISS IT; JUST FOLLOW THE SMELL OF SIN!
These men are believers.
I got an earful on the way in.
What they believe in is hate. Never been around so many pissed-off rednecks in all my life, and that's saying something considering where I come from.
I signed up outta love. For my country, the land of free men.
Laugh if you want.
SUPER CAR
HOT
PALLAS · PUB
FLY
FASH
600-05
'cuz what's not to love?

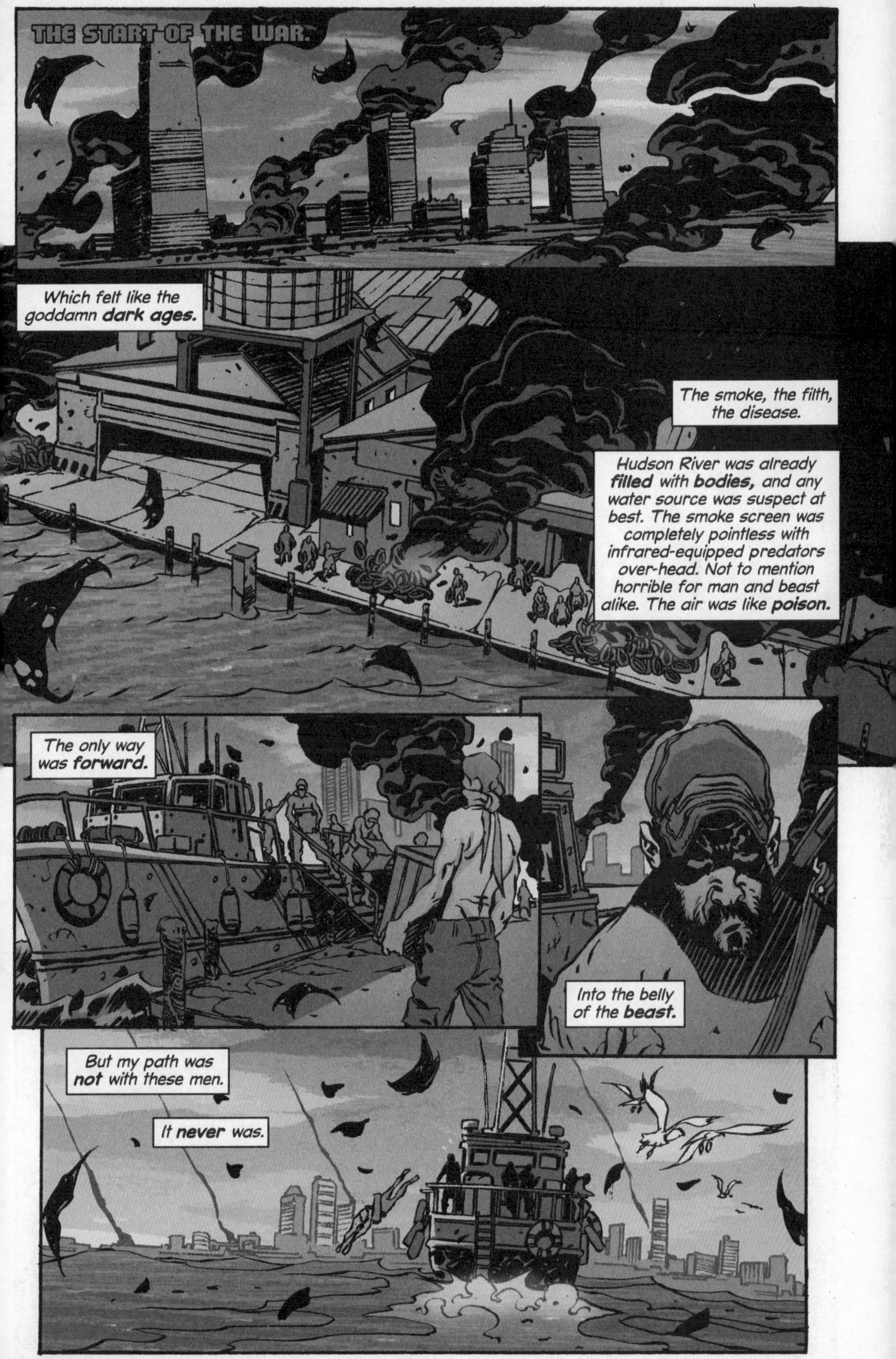
THE START OF THE WAR.
Which felt like the goddamn **dark ages.**
The smoke, the filth, the disease.
Hudson River was already **filled** with **bodies,** and any water source was suspect at best. The smoke screen was completely pointless with infrared-equipped predators over-head. Not to mention horrible for man and beast alike. The air was like **poison.**
The only way was **forward.**
Into the belly of the **beast.**
But my path was **not** with these men.
It **never** was.

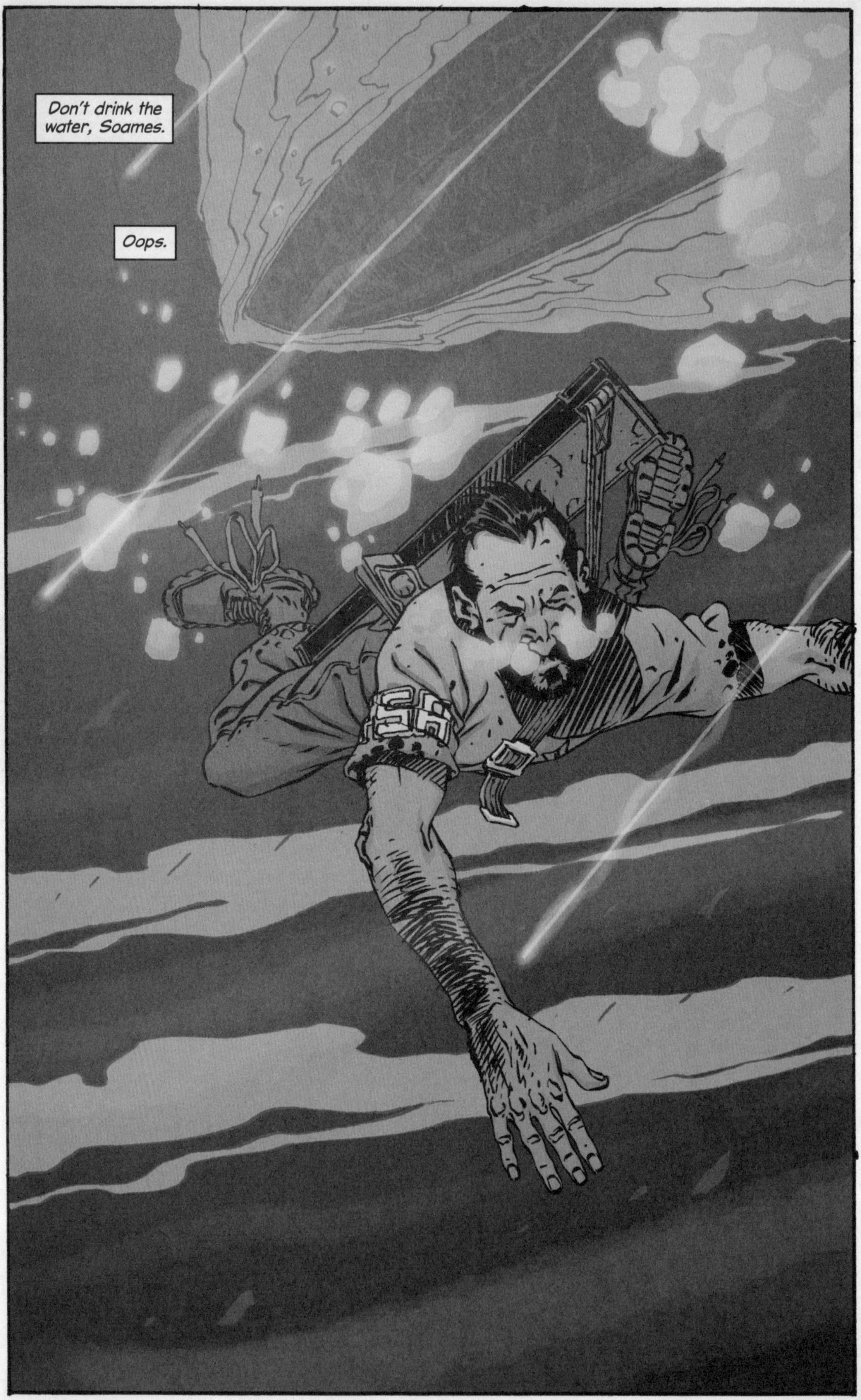
Don't drink the water, Soames.
Oops.

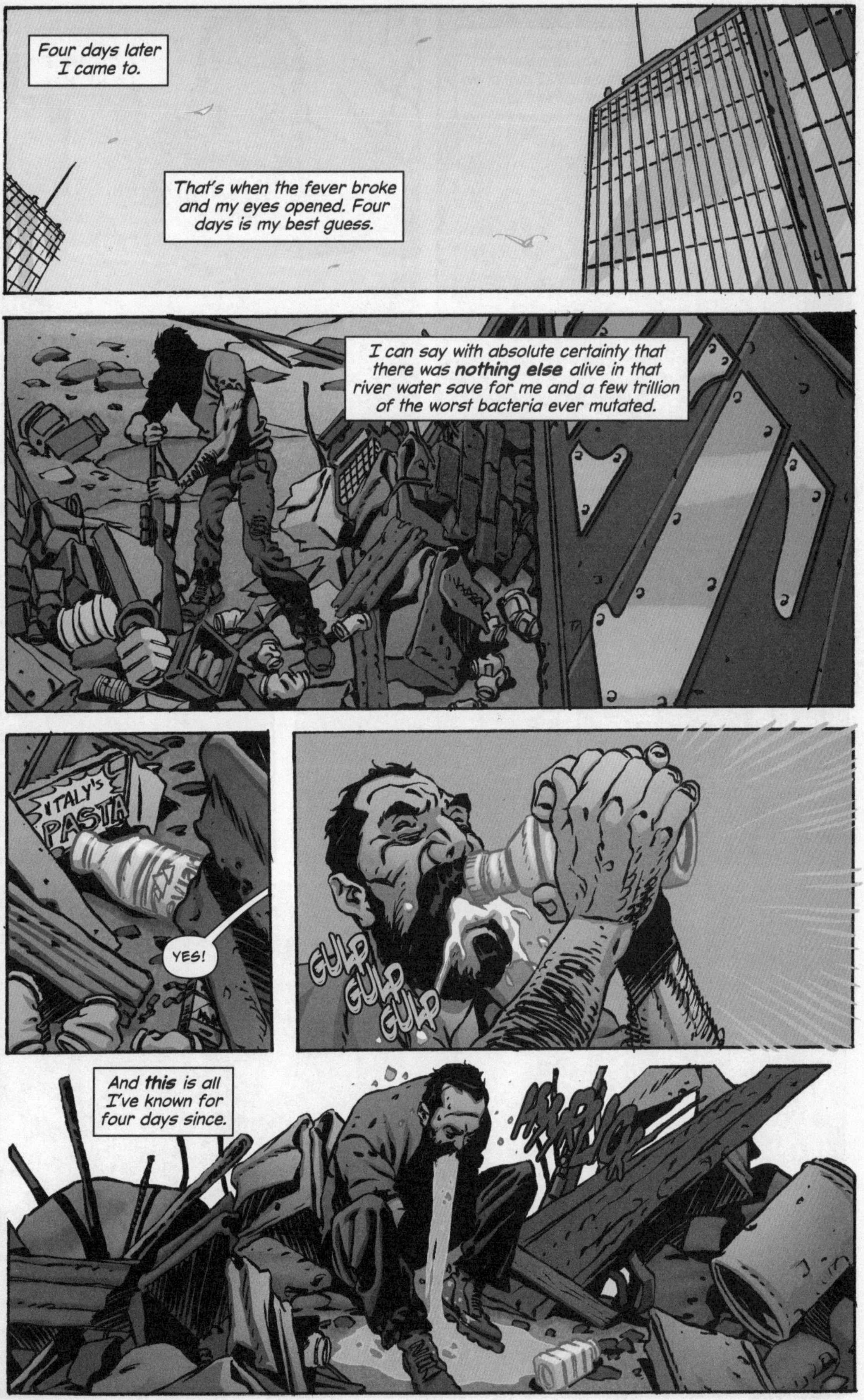

Four days later I came to.
That's when the fever broke and my eyes opened. Four days is my best guess.
I can say with absolute certainty that there was **nothing else** alive in that river water save for me and a few trillion of the worst bacteria ever mutated.
ITALY'S PASTA
YES!
GULP GULP GULP
And **this** is all I've known for four days since.

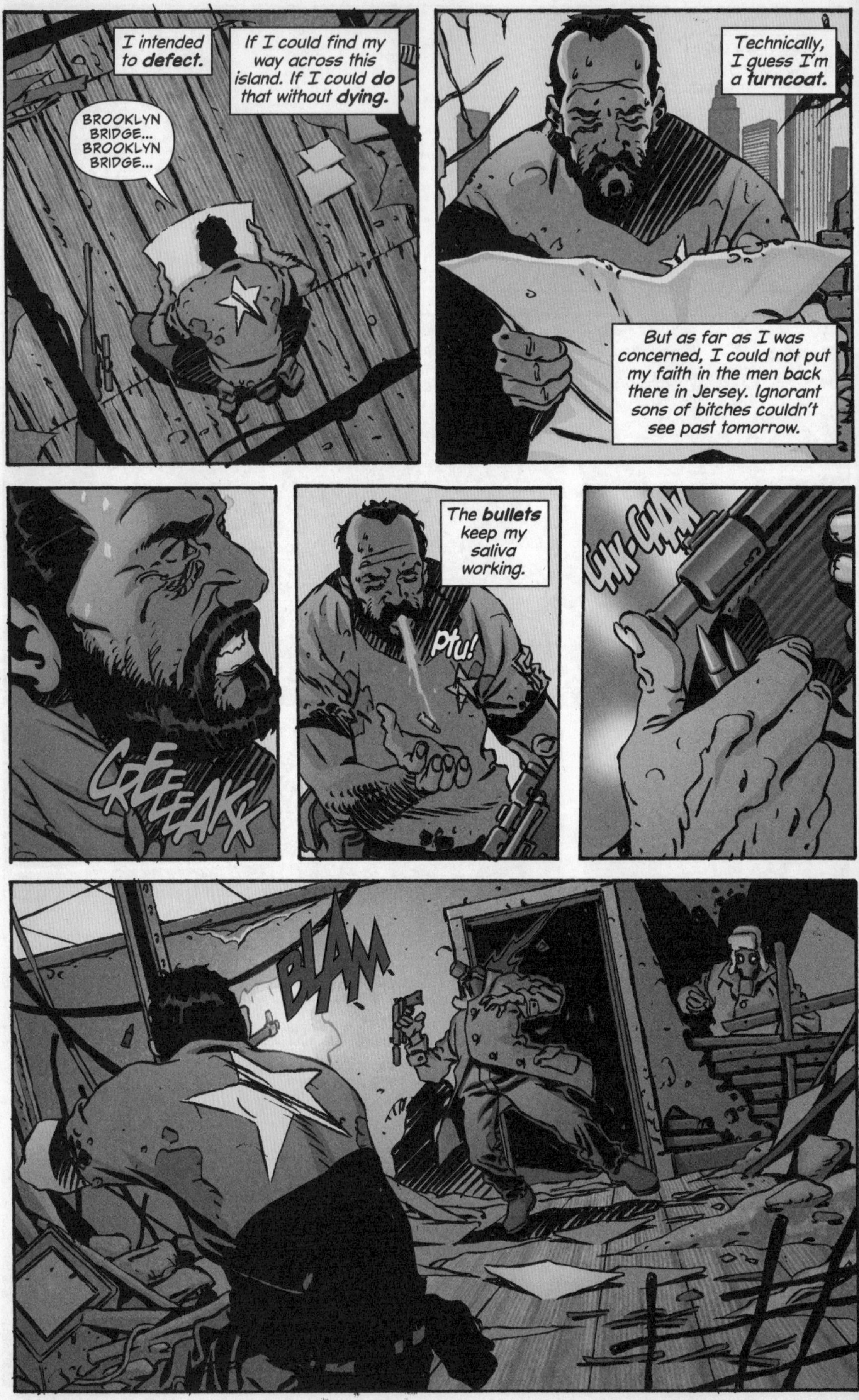
I intended to **defect.**
If I could find my way across this island. If I could **do** that without **dying.**
BROOKLYN BRIDGE... BROOKLYN BRIDGE...
Technically, I guess I'm a **turncoat.**
But as far as I was concerned, I could not put my faith in the men back there in Jersey. Ignorant sons of bitches couldn't see past tomorrow.
The **bullets** keep my saliva working.
Ptu!
CHK-CHAK
BLAM

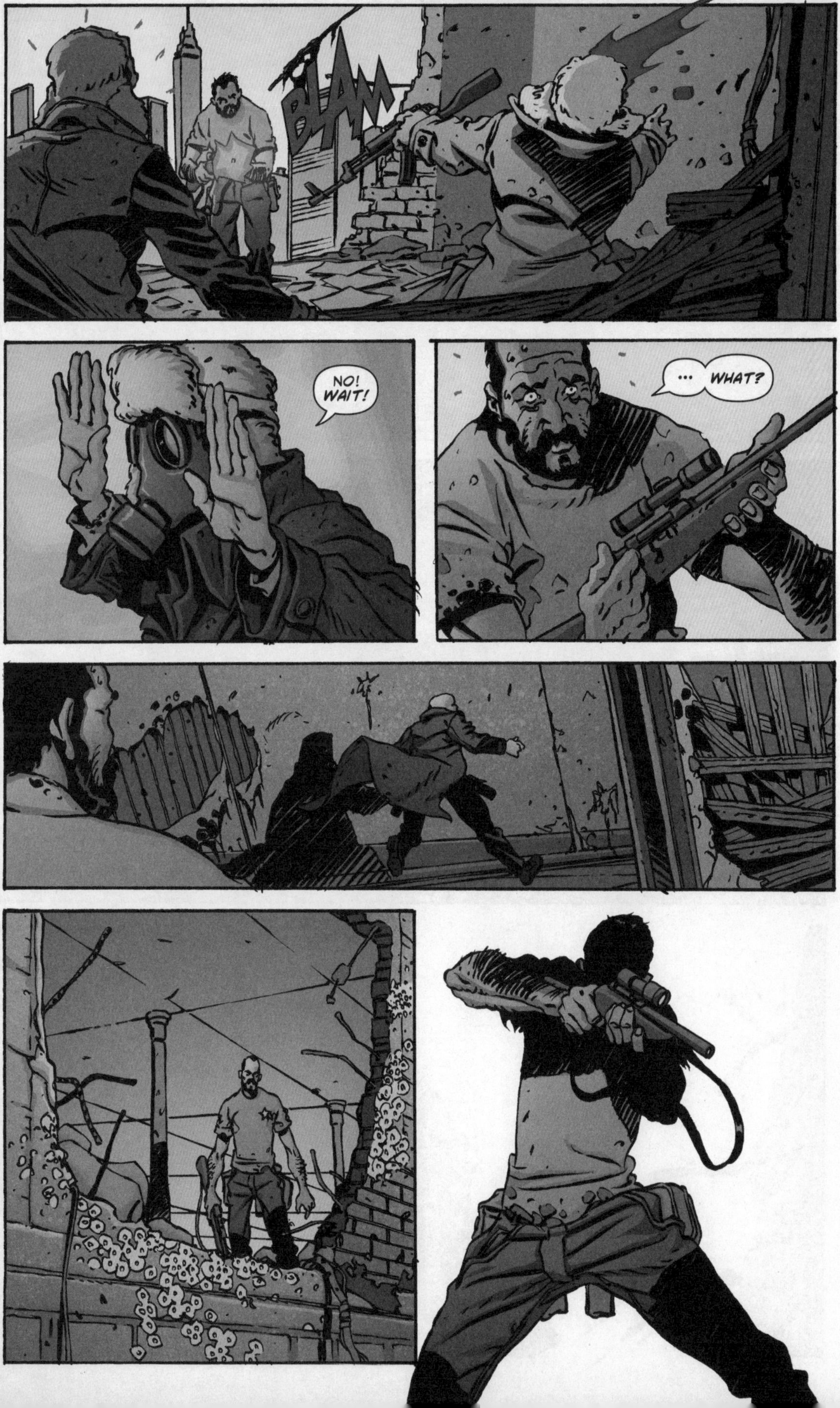
BLAM
NO! WAIT!
... WHAT?

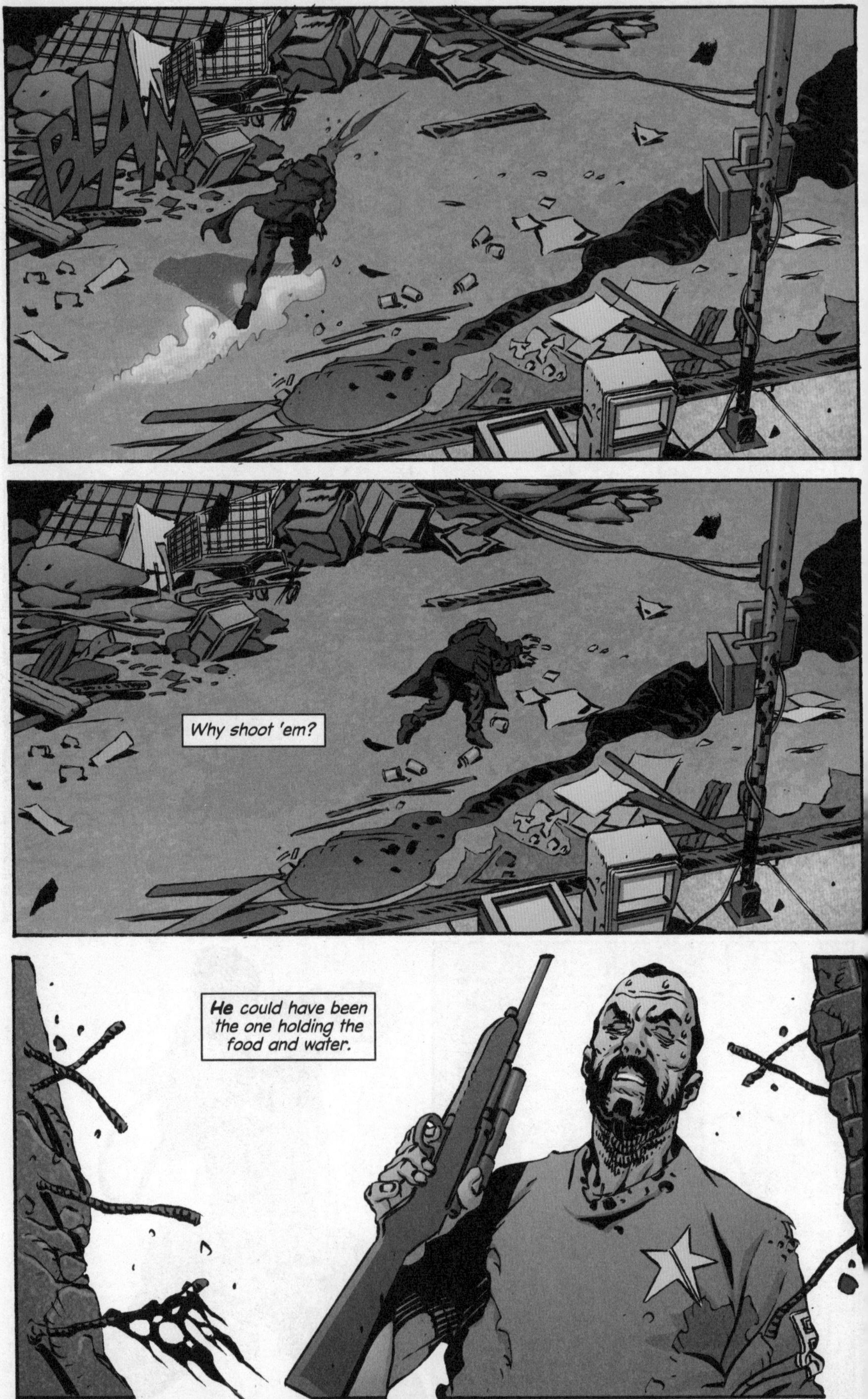
BLAM
Why shoot 'em?
He could have been the one holding the food and water.

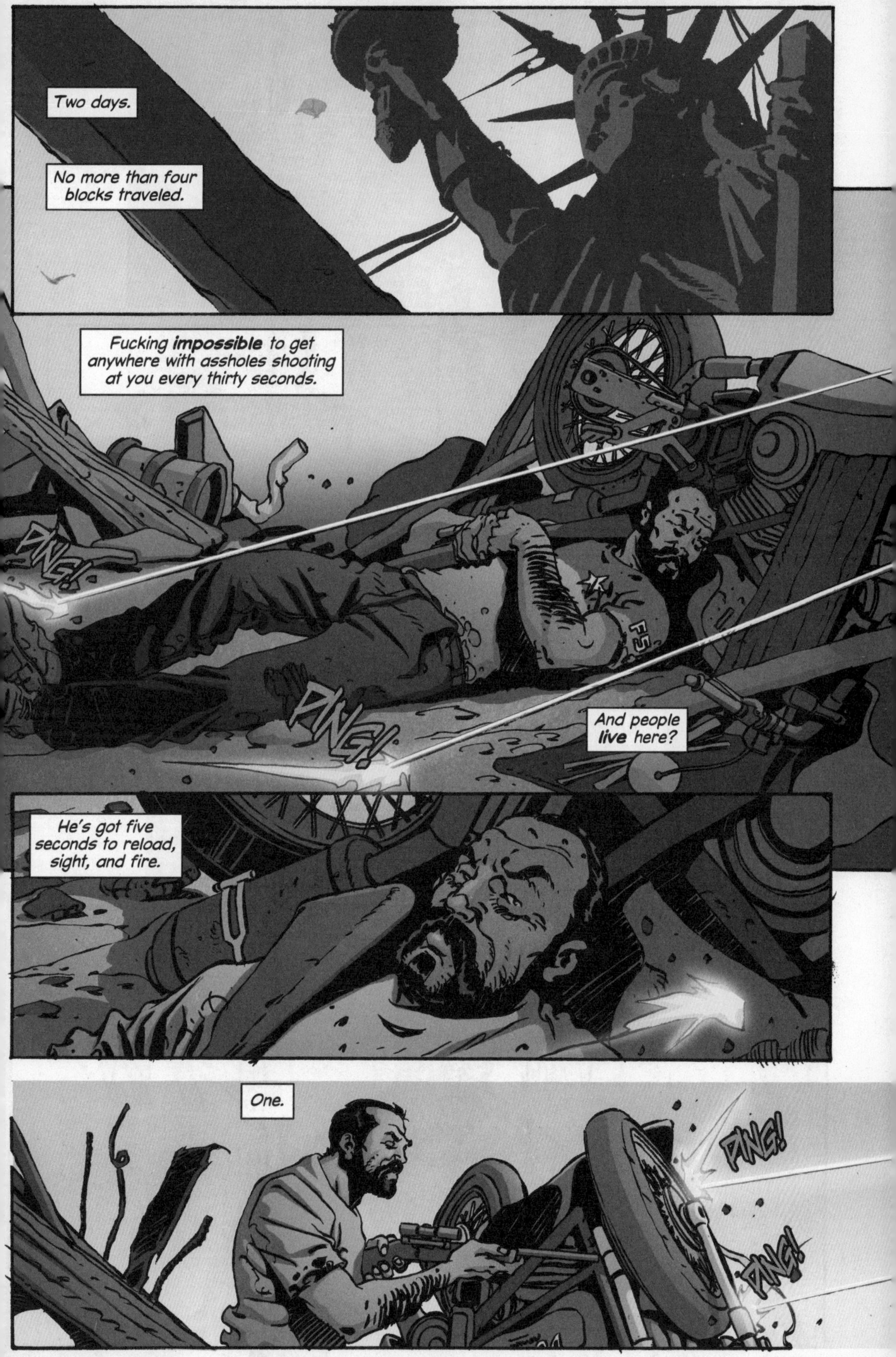

Two days.
No more than four blocks traveled.
Fucking **impossible** to get anywhere with assholes shooting at you every thirty seconds.
PING!
PING!
And people **live** here?
He's got five seconds to reload, sight, and fire.
One.
PING!
PING!

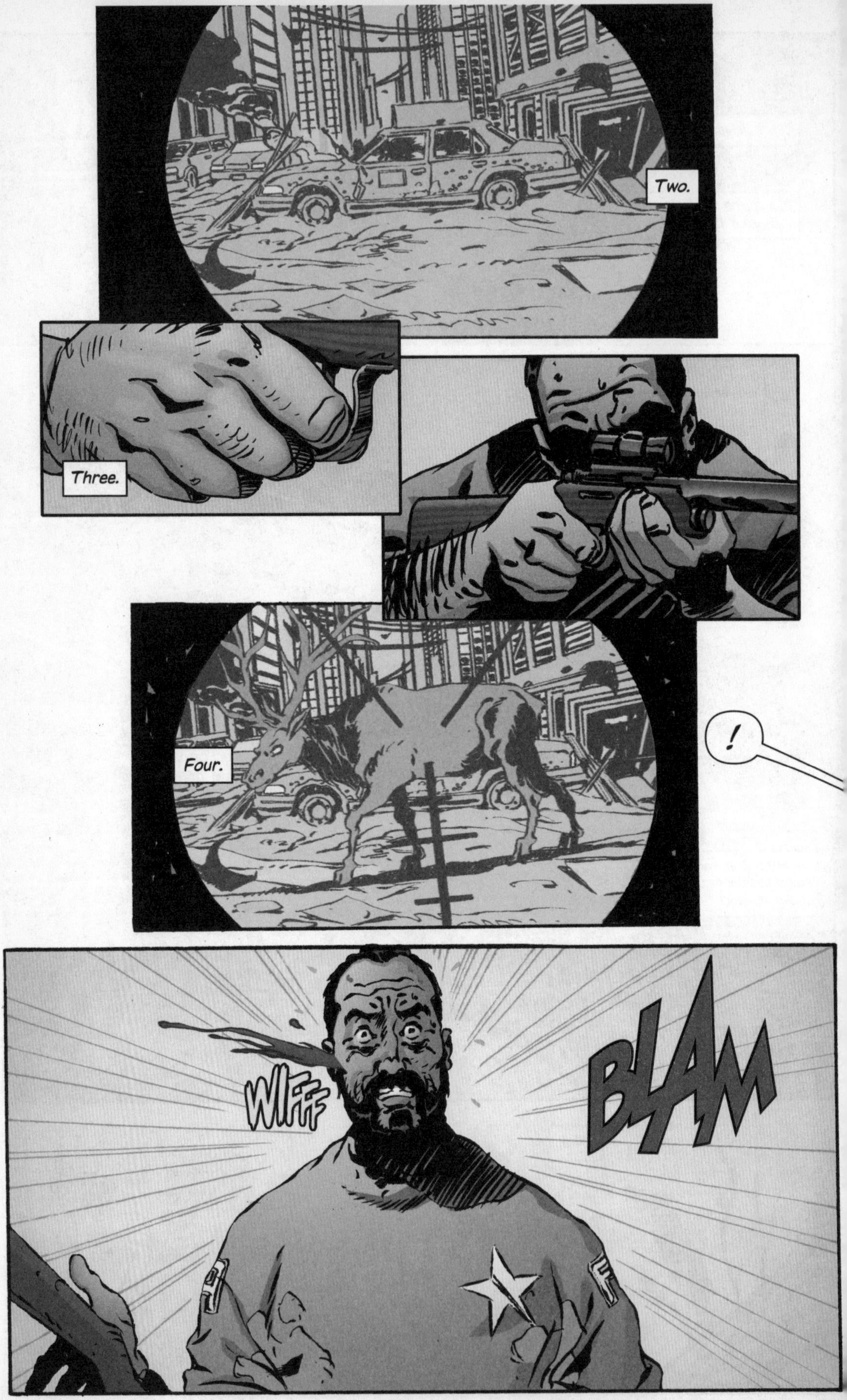
Two.
Three.
Four.
!
WIFFF
BLAM

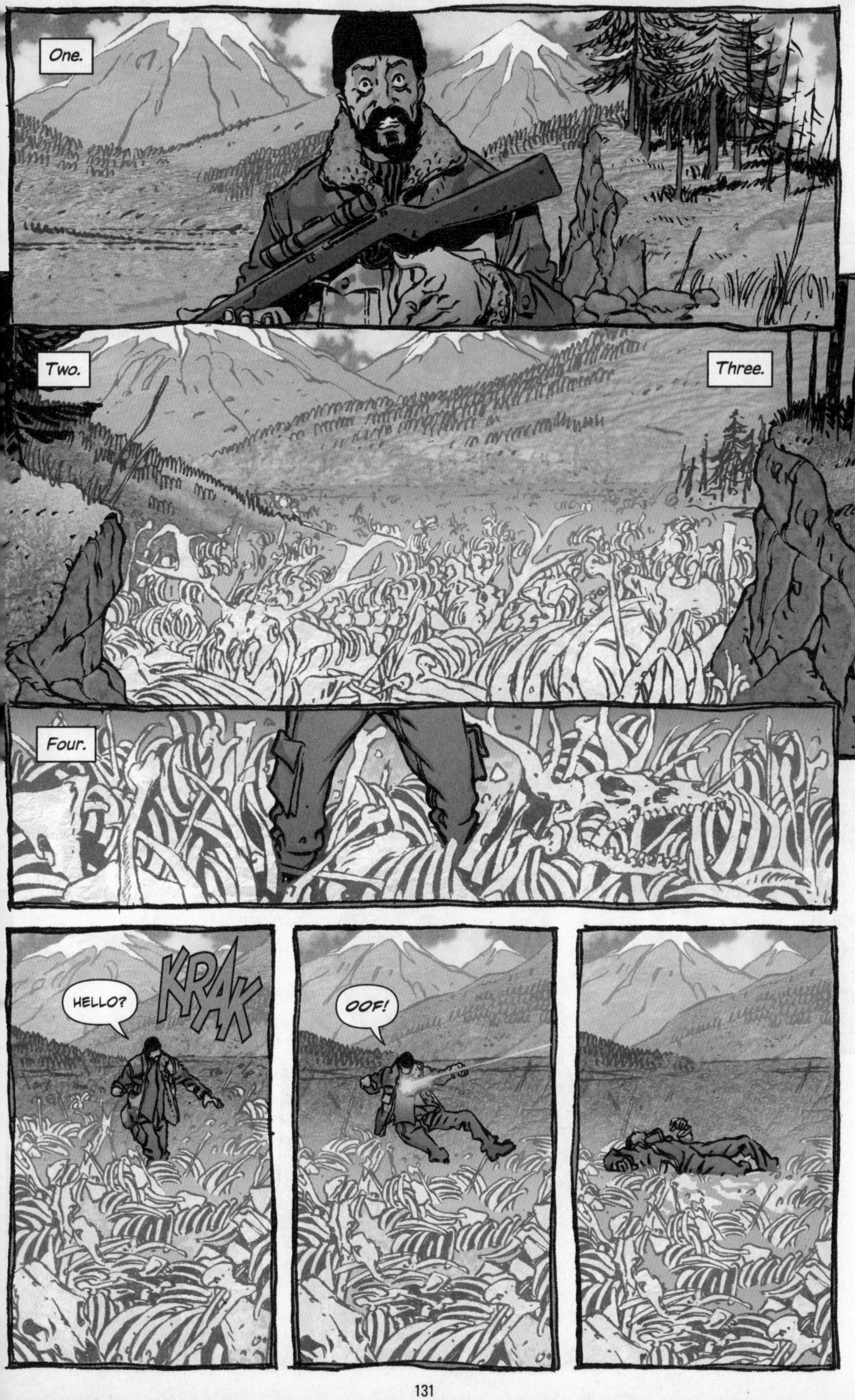
One.
Two.
Three.
Four.
HELLO?
KRAK
OOF!

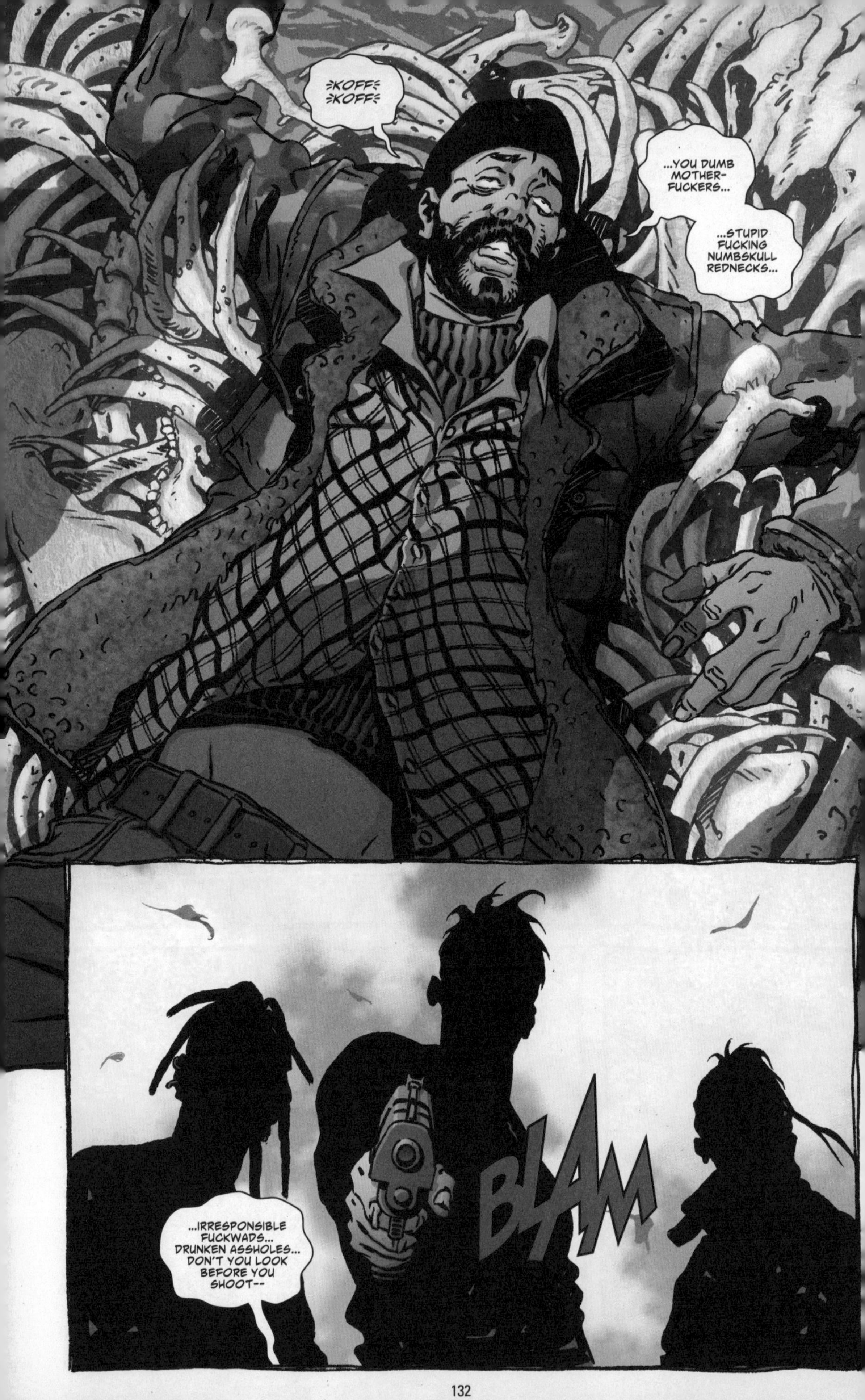
KOFF KOFF
...YOU DUMB MOTHER-FUCKERS...
...STUPID FUCKING NUMBSKULL REDNECKS...
...IRRESPONSIBLE FUCKWADS... DRUNKEN ASSHOLES... DON'T YOU LOOK BEFORE YOU SHOOT--
BLAM

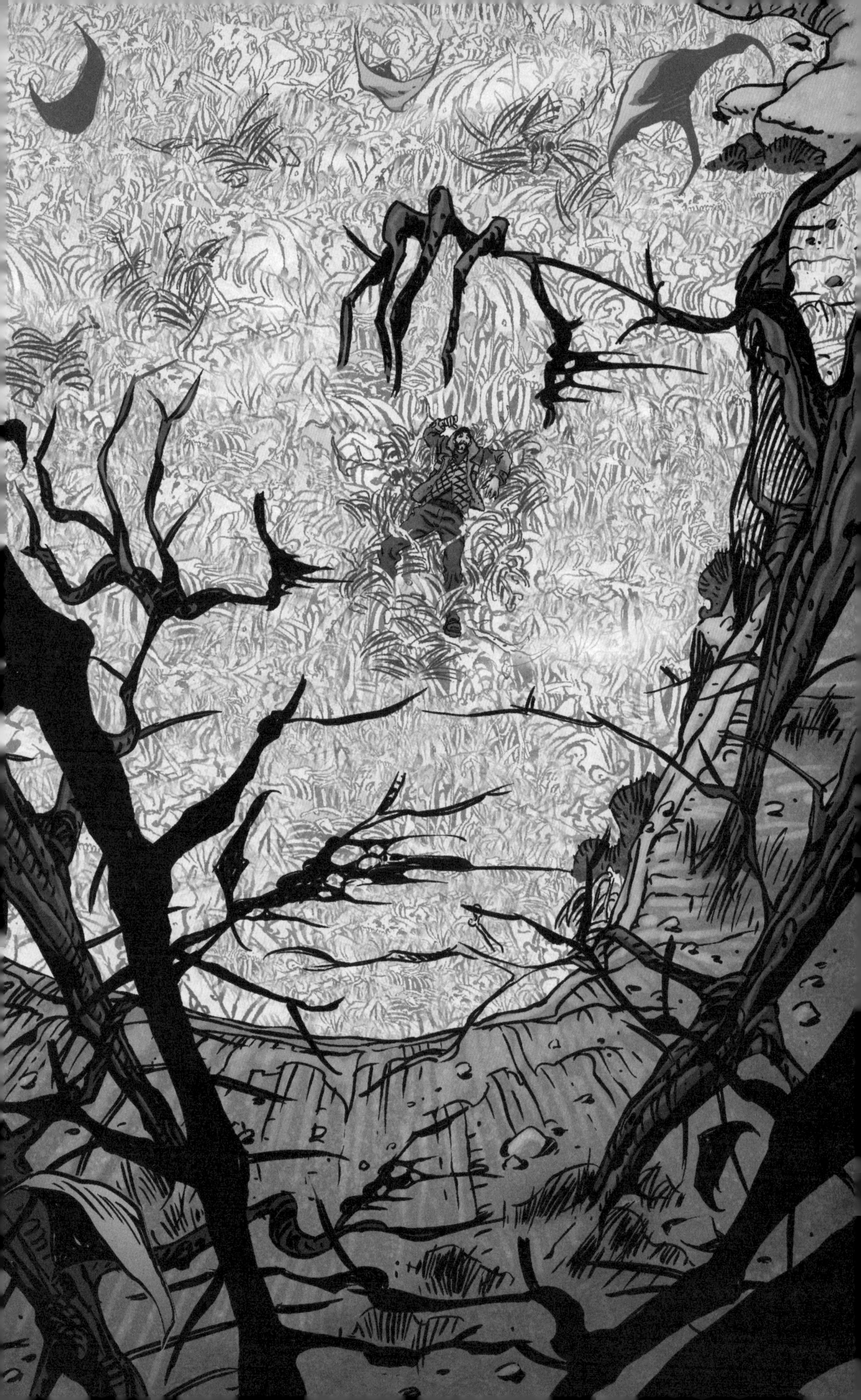

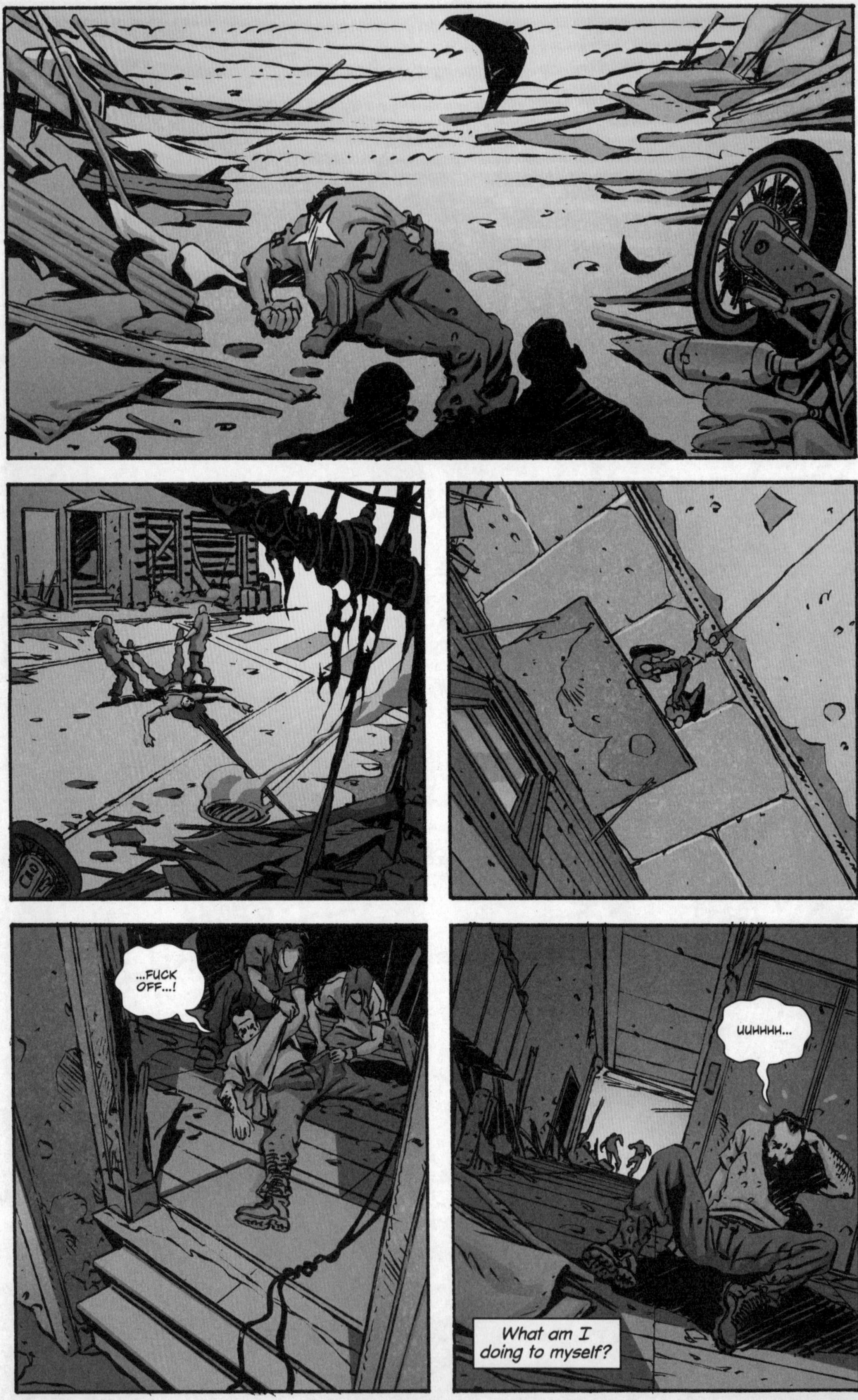
...FUCK OFF...!
UUHHHH...
What am I doing to myself?

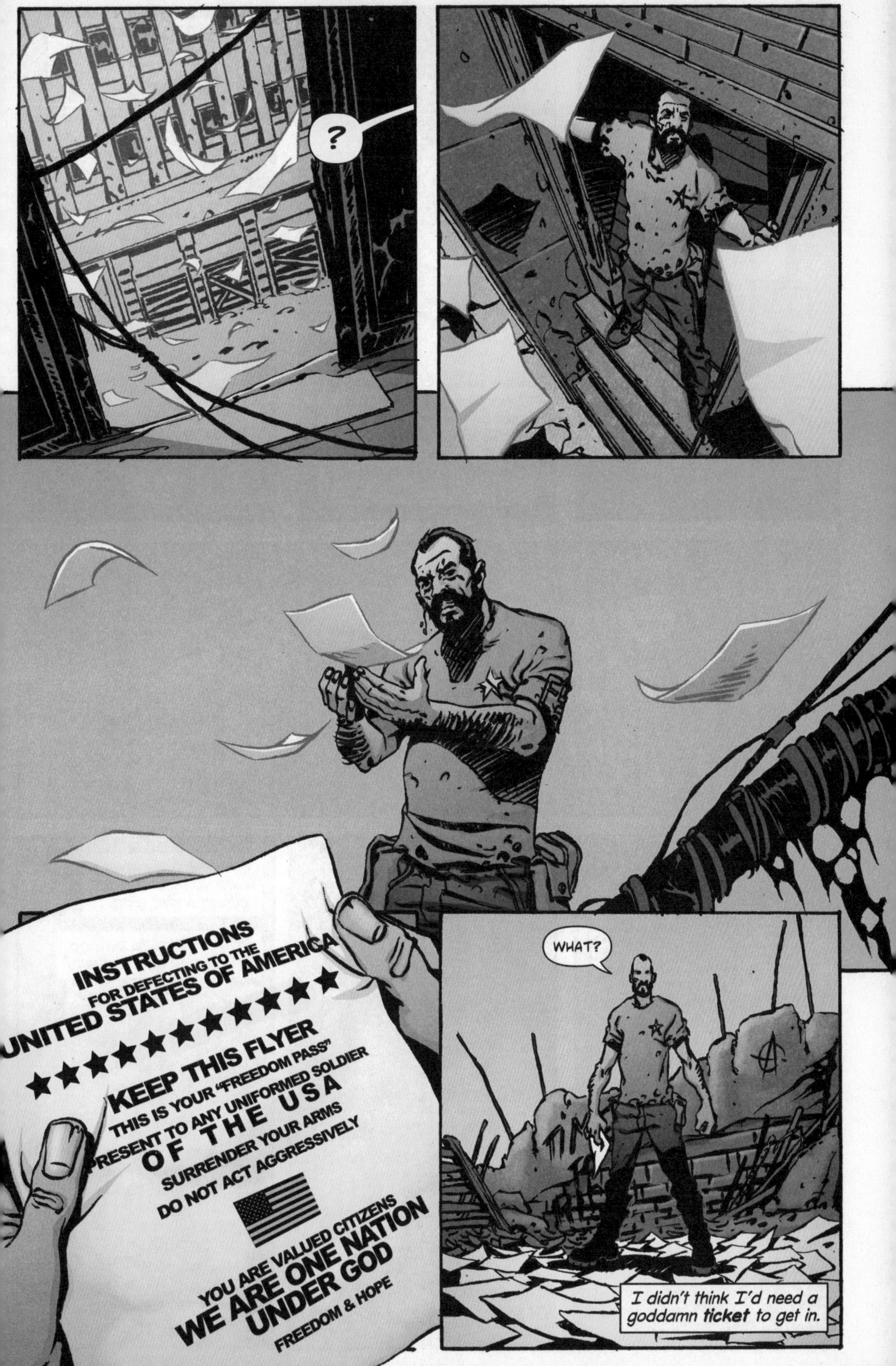
?
WHAT?
INSTRUCTIONS
FOR DEFECTING TO THE
UNITED STATES OF AMERICA
KEEP THIS FLYER
THIS IS YOUR "FREEDOM PASS"
PRESENT TO ANY UNIFORMED SOLDIER
OF THE USA
SURRENDER YOUR ARMS
DO NOT ACT AGGRESSIVELY
YOU ARE VALUED CITIZENS
WE ARE ONE NATION
UNDER GOD
FREEDOM & HOPE
I didn't think I'd need a goddamn **ticket** to get in.

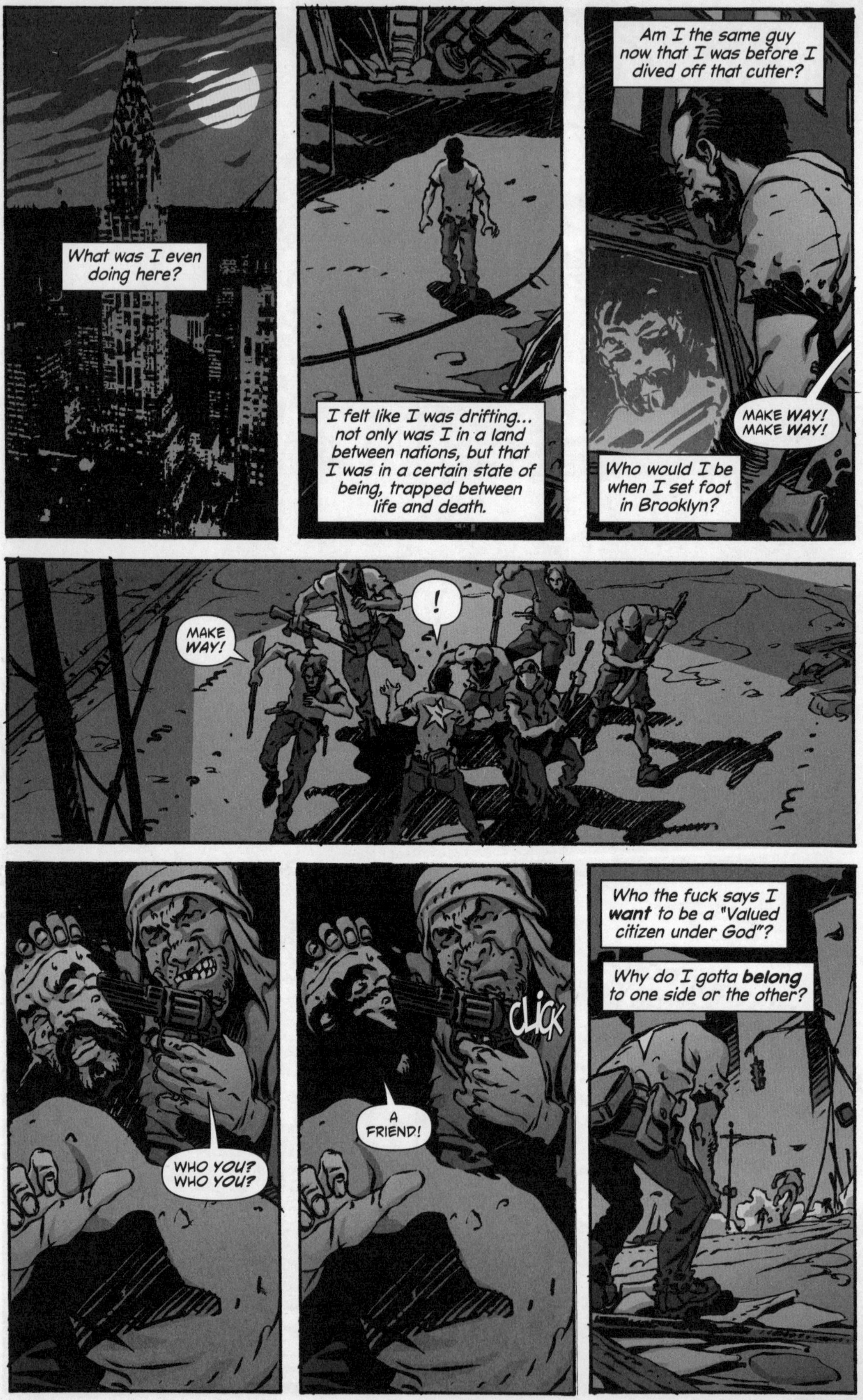
What was I even doing here?
I felt like I was drifting... not only was I in a land between nations, but that I was in a certain state of being, trapped between life and death.
Am I the same guy now that I was before I dived off that cutter?
MAKE WAY! MAKE WAY!
Who would I be when I set foot in Brooklyn?
MAKE WAY!
!
WHO YOU? WHO YOU?
CLICK
A FRIEND!
Who the fuck says I want to be a "Valued citizen under God"?
Why do I gotta belong to one side or the other?

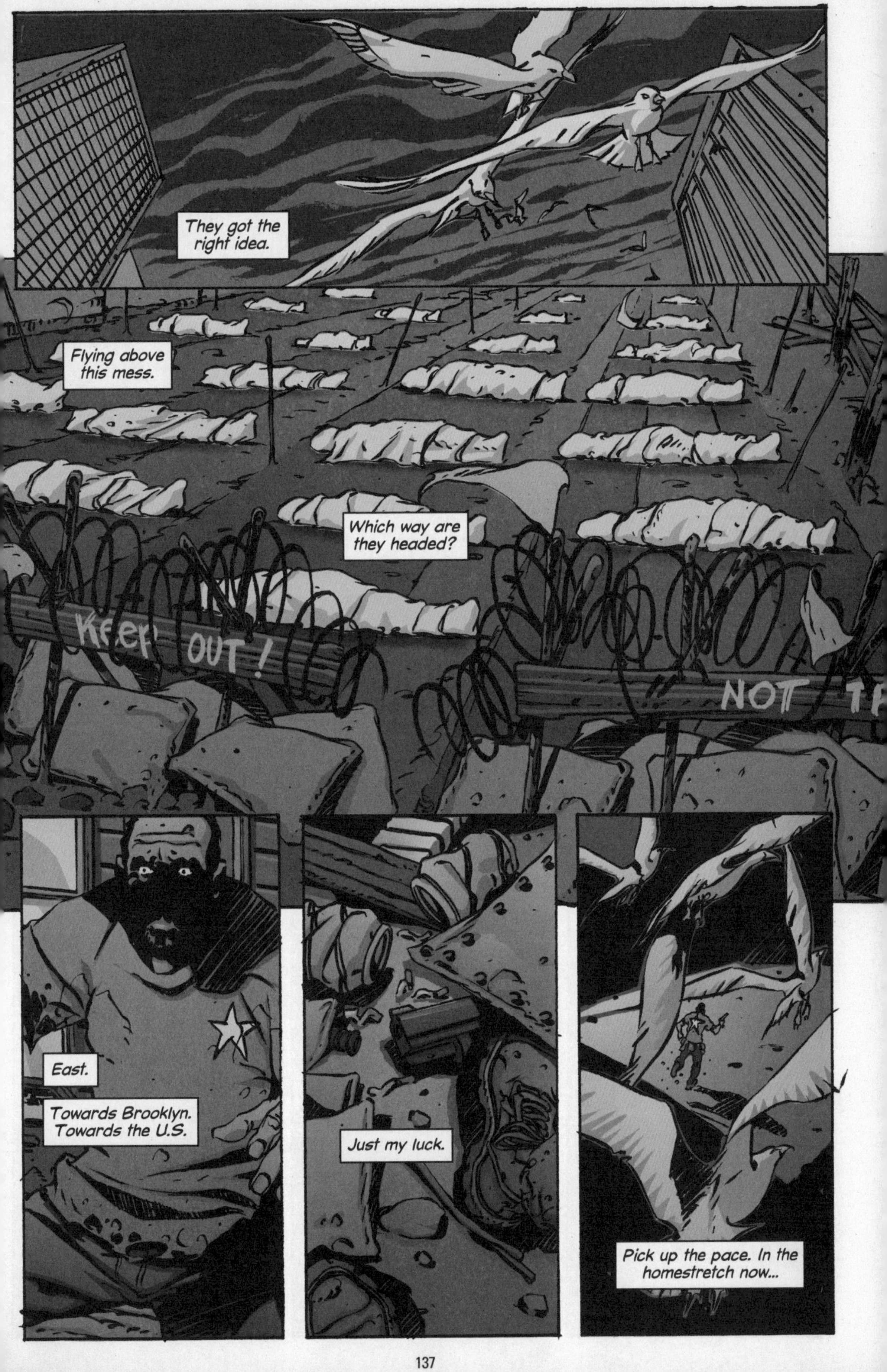
They got the right idea.
Flying above this mess.
Which way are they headed?
KEEP OUT!
NOT
East.
Towards Brooklyn. Towards the U.S.
Just my luck.
Pick up the pace. In the homestretch now...

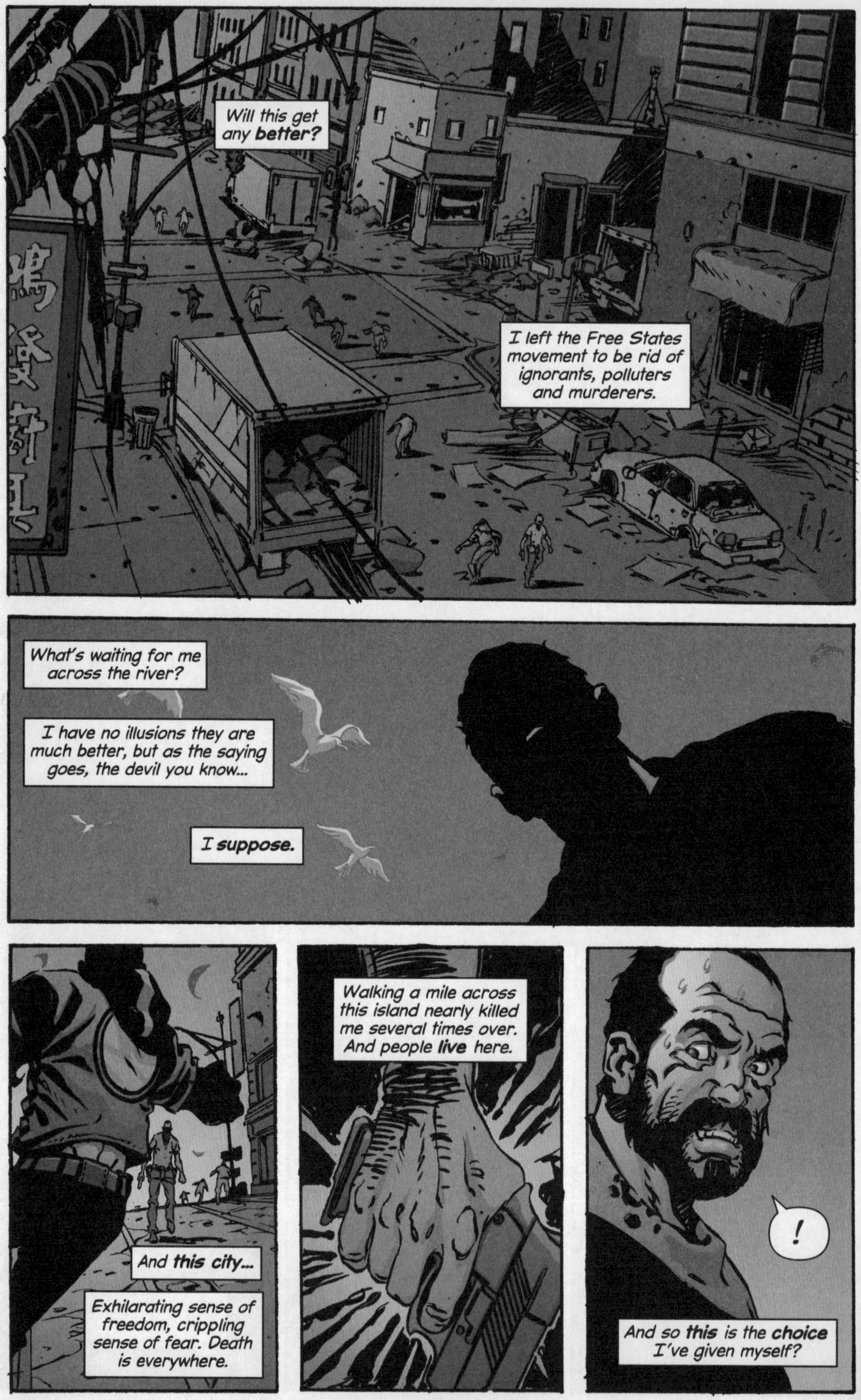
Will this get any **better?**
I left the Free States movement to be rid of ignorants, polluters and murderers.
What's waiting for me across the river?
I have no illusions they are much better, but as the saying goes, the devil you know...
I **suppose.**
And **this city...**
Exhilarating sense of freedom, crippling sense of fear. Death is everywhere.
Walking a mile across this island nearly killed me several times over. And people **live** here.
!
And so **this** is the **choice** I've given myself?

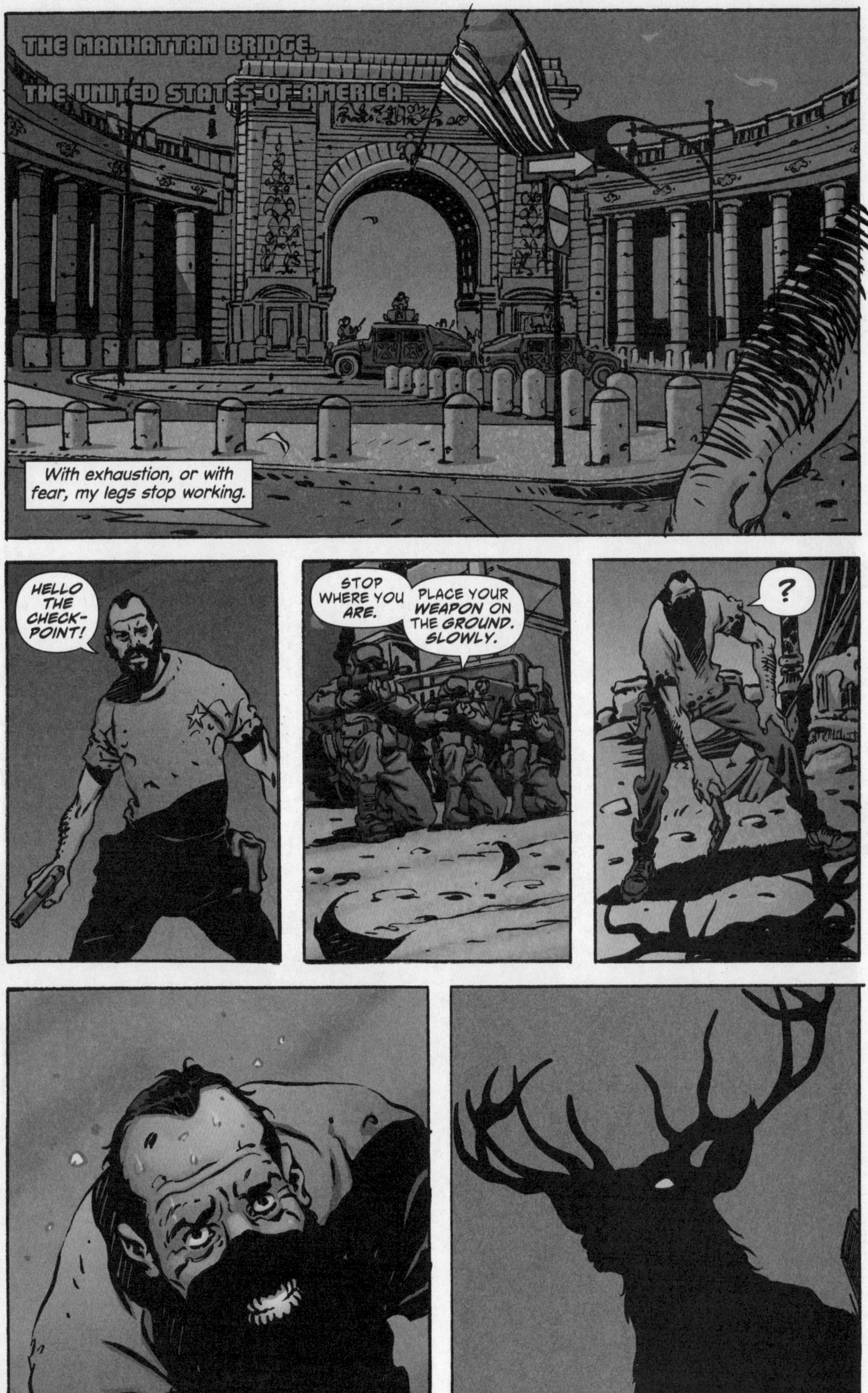
THE MANHATTAN BRIDGE.
THE UNITED STATES OF AMERICA.
With exhaustion, or with fear, my legs stop working.
HELLO THE CHECK-POINT!
STOP WHERE YOU ARE.
PLACE YOUR WEAPON ON THE GROUND. SLOWLY.
?

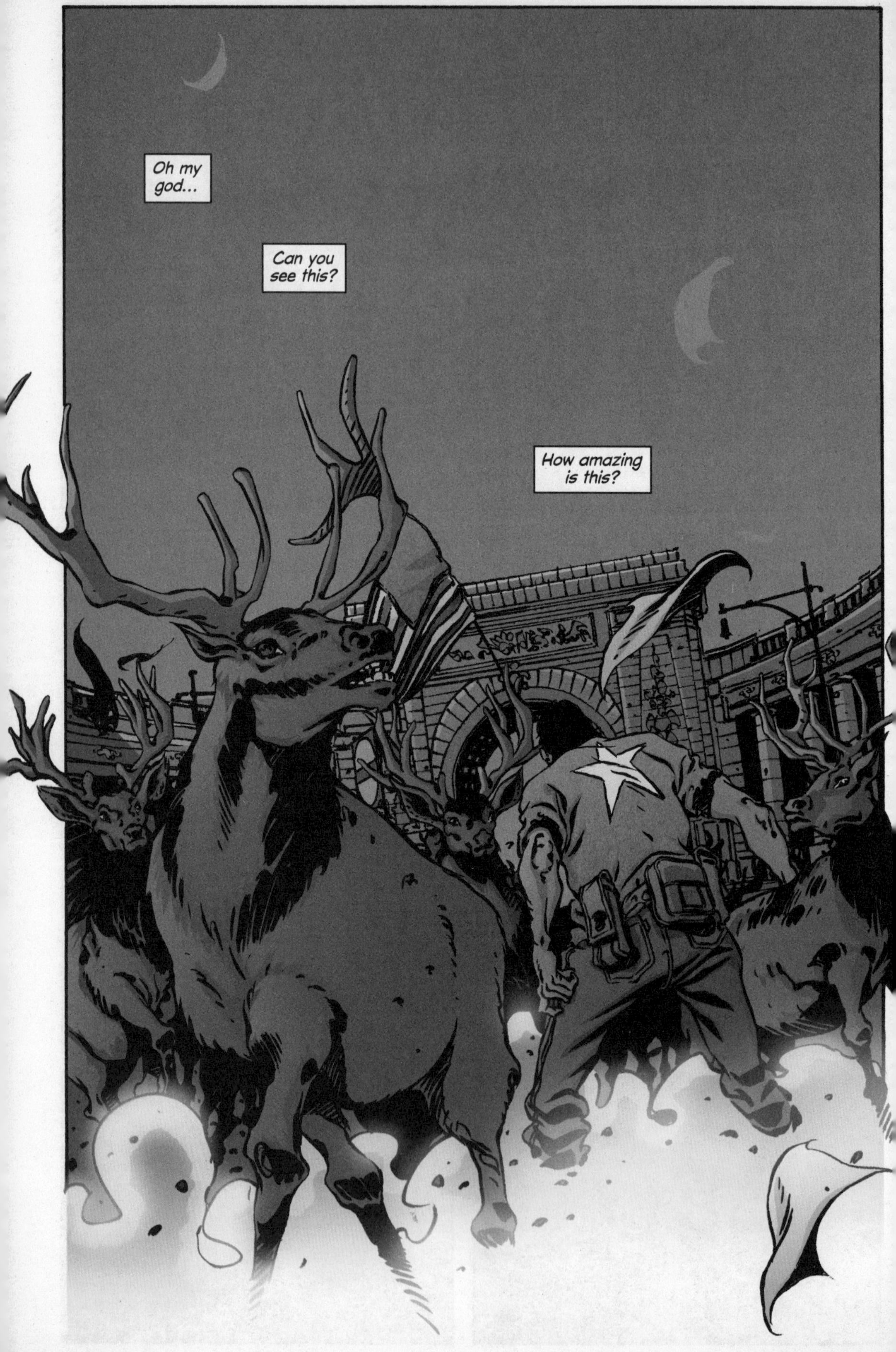
Oh my god...
Can you see this?
How amazing is this?

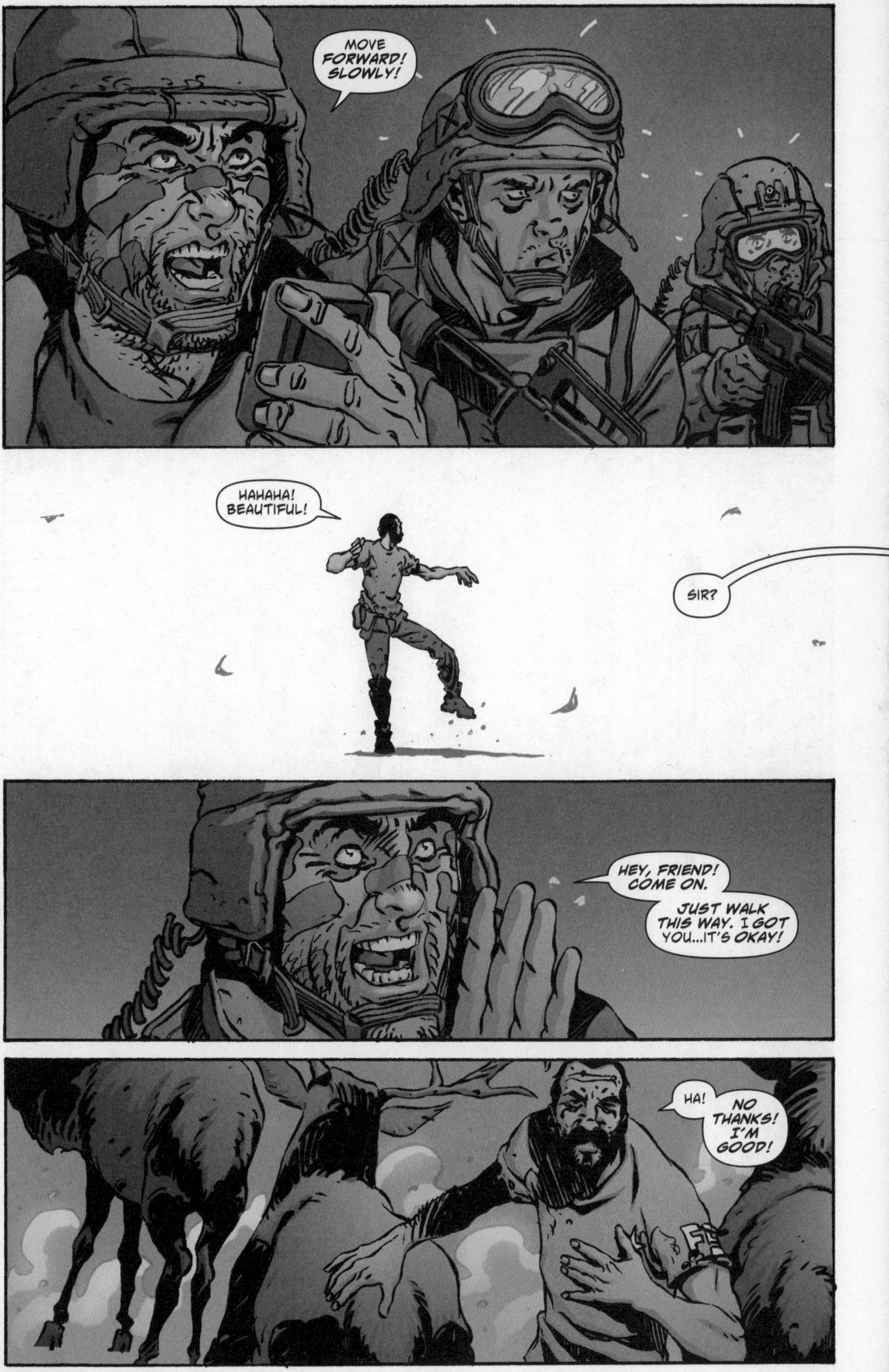
MOVE FORWARD! SLOWLY!
HAHAHA! BEAUTIFUL!
SIR?
HEY, FRIEND! COME ON.
JUST WALK THIS WAY. I GOT YOU...IT'S OKAY!
HA!
NO THANKS! I'M GOOD!

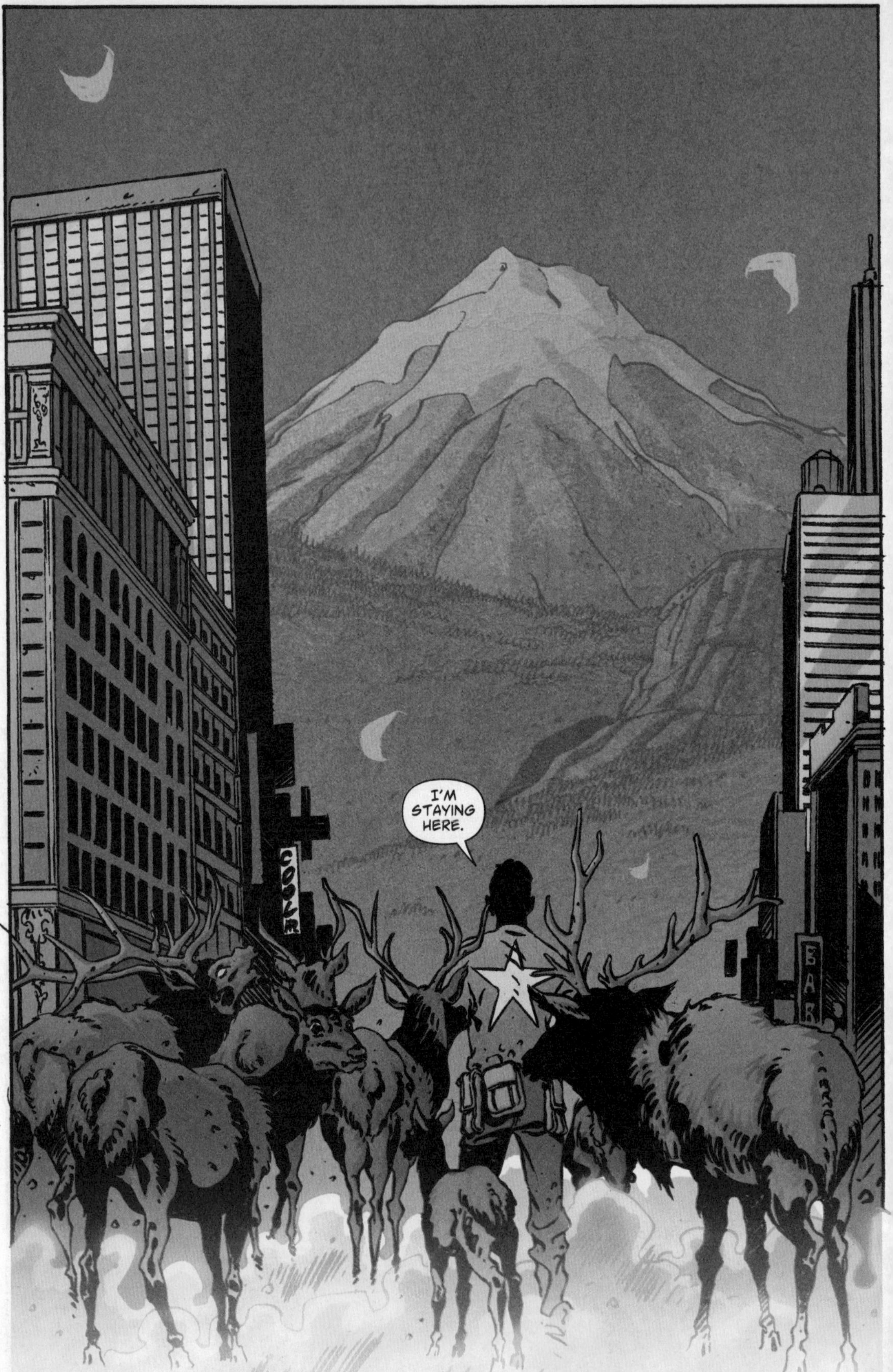
I'M STAYING HERE.
BAR

END

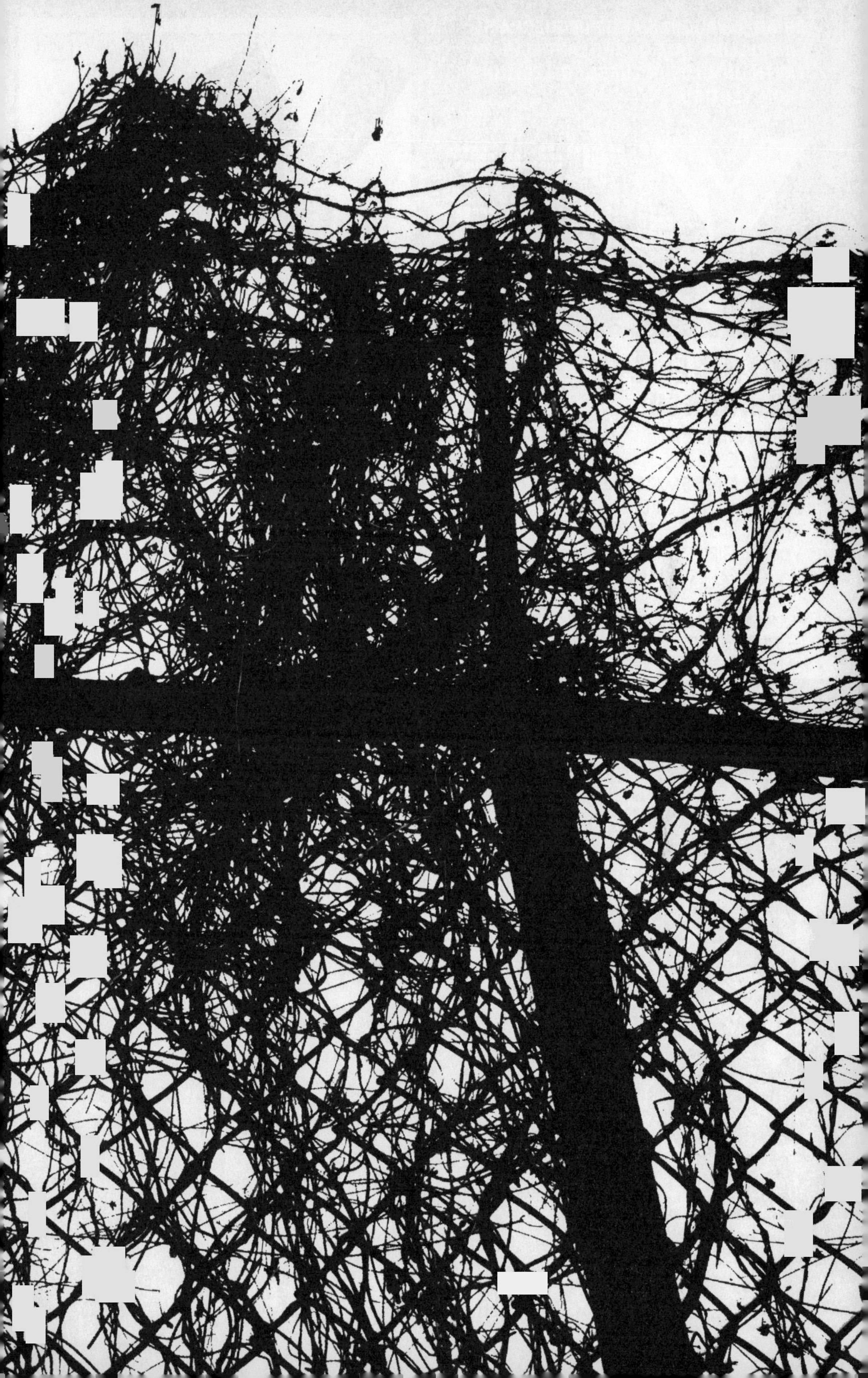

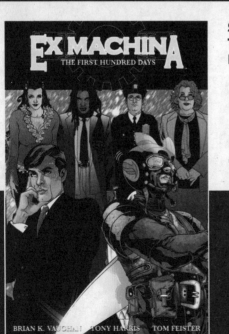